THE PANIC OF
1907

Lessons Learned from the Market's Perfect Storm

ROBERT F. BRUNER
SEAN D. CARR

John Wiley & Sons, Inc.

Published by John Wiley & Sons, Inc., Hoboken, New Jersey.
Published simultaneously in Canada.

Wiley Bicentennial Logo: Richard J. Pacifico

The authors gratefully acknowledge Cambridge University Press, Columbia University Butler Library, Deutsche Bank Group, the Federal Reserve Bank of New York, The Morgan Library & Museum, Ned Lamont, the Southern Economic Journal, and the University of Chicago Press for their research assistance.

For general information on our other products and services or for technical support, please contact our Customer Care Department within the United States at (800) 762-2974, outside the United States at (317) 572-3993 or fax (317) 572-4002.

Wiley also publishes its books in a variety of electronic formats. Some content that appears in print may not be available in electronic formats. For more information about Wiley products, visit our web site at www.wiley.com.

Library of Congress Cataloging-in-Publication Data:

Bruner, Robert F., 1949–
The Panic of 1907: lessons learned from the market's perfect storm
Robert F. Bruner, Sean D. Carr
       p.   cm.
   Includes bibliographical references and index.
   ISBN 978-0-470-15263-8 (cloth)
1. Depressions–1907–United States.   2. Financial crises–United States–
History–20th century.   3. Stock exchanges–United States–History–20th century.
I. Carr, Sean D., 1969– II. Title.
   HB37171907 B78   2007
   333.973'0911–dc22

                                                        2007009236

Printed in the United States of America

10 9 8 7 6 5 4 3 2 1

RFB:

For Bobbie
"Treasure is in knowing that you are loved and that you love because you are loved, and that knowledge of self and relationship and purpose is what treasure is all about."
—Peter J. Gomes

SDC:

For Ladi
"The salvation of this human world lies nowhere else than in the human heart, in the human power to reflect, in human meekness and human responsibility."
—Vaclav Havel

Contents

Acknowledgments

We gratefully acknowledge the thoughtful guidance and generous encouragement offered by Brian Balough (University of Virginia), Charles Calomiris (Columbia University), Dwight Crane (Harvard Business School), Robert Friedel (University of Maryland) and Richard Sylla (New York University). William Harbaugh (University of Virginia), Robert Parrino (University of Texas), Jean Strouse (New York City Public Library), and Richard Tedlow (Harvard Business School) also provided useful insights at various stages of the book's development. Our colleagues at the University of Virginia's Darden Business School, including Peter Debaere, Marc Lipson, Frank Warnock, and the participants in the finance and economics seminar provided especially helpful comments on an earlier draft. Christina A. Ziegler-McPherson gave valuable research assistance underlying the book's early chapters, and we have drawn on her considerable knowledge of the Gilded Age and Progressive Era. Karen Marsh King, at the Darden School Library, rendered excellent bibliographical assistance, and Susan Norrisey, our reference librarian, exhibited an extraordinary degree of diligence, persistence, and patience in collecting archival trading data; she was tireless in her work, and for this we are especially appreciative. Our editors at Wiley brought understanding and perspective to the work, and we are grateful for the insights provided by Pamela von Giessen, Bill Falloon, Emilie Herman, Laura Walsh, and Todd Tedesco. As always, Lewis O'Brien was unflagging is his attention to the correctness of our source materials. Any errors that may remain are ours alone.

RFB and SDC

Charlottesville, Virginia
June 2007

Prologue

These are troublous times.
—Charles T. Barney
Knickerbocker Trust Company
October 21, 1907

A round 10 A.M. on November 14, 1907, Lily Barney and a friend were chatting in the Barneys' second-story bedroom overlooking Park Avenue when they heard the crack of a gunshot echo through the house. The women bolted toward the other bedroom across the hall. Stepping inside, they saw Lily's husband, Charles, lying on the floor near his bed in his pajamas. Beside him was a revolver containing three loaded cartridges and one empty shell. The Barneys had kept pistols on every floor of the house for protection, and this one clearly belonged to Charles.[1]

As Lily Barney came near, her husband raised himself slightly but slumped in pain to the floor. She knelt beside him, cradled his head in her lap, and attempted to ease his discomfort. Ashbel Barney, one of the Barneys' two sons, had been downstairs and had also heard the shot. Running to the bedroom and seeing his mother and her friend bending over his wounded father, he raced to telephone George Dixon, the Barneys' family physician. Then, with the help of his mother and servants the 20-year-old Ashbel lifted his father to his large, brass, canopy-covered bed. Charles T. Barney remained conscious, but silent.

Dixon reached the Barney house in Manhattan's fashionable Murray Hill neighborhood 10 minutes after receiving the call. After administering an anesthetic he began an operation in which he discovered that a .38-caliber bullet had entered the upper left quadrant of Barney's abdomen; it had taken an upward course, torn through the intestines, traveled lengthwise through the left lung, and embedded in the left shoulder just behind the collarbone. Despite their ministrations, around 2:30 in the afternoon Charles Barney was pronounced dead from shock and severe hemorrhaging. Within hours newsboys were bellowing "extras" about the incident all along Park Avenue.

Over the coming days, rumors and innuendoes about Barney's death reverberated throughout the city. Stories appeared about previous suicide attempts (though none could be confirmed)[2] and there were indications, later denied by Lily Barney, that she and her husband had become acutely estranged in recent months and that she had initiated a divorce.[3] One leading newspaper even reported that the letters of "two women, one a Parisian, long a favorite of a French prince," had been found among Charles Barney's papers.[4] Close associates called the man's morals into question. "Mr. Barney was not a God-fearing man," said A. Foster Higgins. "He could not live happily because his life was not moral. He lived a lie to his wife and children."[5]

Whatever his personal faults, though, the death of Charles T. Barney aroused extreme public interest and suspicion for one reason only: Barney had presided over New York's famed Knickerbocker Trust Company when its dramatic failure in October 1907 became the tipping point for a financial crisis of monumental proportions.

■   ■   ■

Charles Tracy Barney was truly a man of the Gilded Age. The son of a prosperous Cleveland merchant, he had married into the prominent Whitney family when he wed Lily Whitney, the sister of the financier and former U.S. Secretary of the Navy, William C. Whitney. Barney pursued a career in banking, and his Whitney connections ensured him lucrative business opportunities in New York real estate development and speculation. By 1907 Barney had become a director of at least 33 corporations, and he was among the founding investors of New York City's new subway system.

Barney's ascent to New York's financial firmament coincided with his association with the Knickerbocker Trust Company. By the 1890s, he had become its vice president, and in 1897 he was elected to the firm's top office. The handsome but high-strung Barney emerged as one of the leading figures in New York's financial community, and he had developed a reputation as "one of the most imperious of Wall Street's bankers, who ruled every undertaking that he had anything to do with."[6]

Such a man, at the height of his wealth and power, could scarcely have foreseen how swiftly and ignominiously his downfall would come. In early October 1907, two unscrupulous (and colorful) speculators, F. Augustus Heinze and Charles W. Morse, had contrived an elaborate scheme to corner the market in the stock of a copper mining company. The attempt failed miserably. Such a scheme would hardly have bothered the members of New York's financial elite, such as Charles Barney, but Heinze and Morse had convinced several New York trust companies, including the Knickerbocker, to fund their venture.[7]

As word spread that the Knickerbocker—and perhaps even Charles Barney himself—was embroiled in the Heinze-Morse scheme, the 18,000 depositors of the trust company panicked. Simply an association with the speculators was more than most depositors could bear. On Friday, October 17, a "run" on the Knickerbocker was under way, and dozens of depositors clamored at the trust company's doors to claim their funds.

Given the close financial relationships among all the banks and trust companies in New York City, panic gripped investors and depositors alike. In an attempt to quell this spiraling hysteria, on October 21 the directors of the Knickerbocker Trust convinced Charles Barney to tender his resignation. In a statement issued later that night, Barney said humbly, "I resigned to give my associates in the company a free hand in the management." But when he was asked about the financial condition of the Knickerbocker, Barney laughed at any suggestion that the institution might be in trouble. "Nothing could be more absurd," he said. "The company was never in a stronger position. It remains the next to the largest in the city and as sound as any. There is not the slightest question of its entire solvency."[8]

A few days after his resignation from the Knickerbocker Trust Company, Barney drafted a statement in which he boasted of his role at the bank. "I built the Knickerbocker up from a company with eleven million dollars in deposits to one with over sixty-five million dollars," he said. "I am willing to take responsibility for anything pertaining to the condition of the company." Nonetheless, he steadfastly refused to accept that he should be culpable for the trust company's failure. "So far as the suspension is concerned," he said, "if there is any institution in New York that could without aid have withstood the run that the Knickerbocker experienced last Tuesday [October 22], I do not know it."[9] Less than a month later Charles Barney would be dead.

■ ■ ■

Many surmised that Charles Barney's death was caused by his fears of personal financial failure, but reports indicate he was nowhere near insolvency. In October 1907, Barney's assets exceeded his liabilities by more than $2.5 million, mostly represented by equities in real estate.[10] Moreover, most of Barney's creditors were bank and trust companies, including the Knickerbocker itself. Just a week before his death Barney's attorneys had worked out an arrangement that would have enabled him to stay afloat. "There was every reason why Mr. Barney should have been feeling encouraged," Barney's physician, Dr. Dixon, said. "Daylight had begun to break ahead financially. He had begun to see his way clear. If he was [sic] going to commit suicide, two weeks ago would have been the most likely time. But now, when things had begun to look up, was a time when he should have been feeling in better spirits than for two weeks."[11]

Friends of Charles T. Barney believed that neither financial crisis nor a professional reversal was his downfall. It was the loss of confidence that hurt him most. "Mr. Barney's heart was broken by the cruel treatment of his associates; that is the cause of his death," said Charles Morse, the man whose association most likely led to Barney's undoing. "It is absurd to talk of financial ruin as a cause of his act, for though he had lost money, he was by no means ruined. Mr. Barney was always an honorable man of business, and it was grief at being abused in the newspapers and suspected by his business associates that caused his death."[12] Another family friend said, "Had there been a little leniency on the part of those who were forcing him to the wall, Charles T. Barney would be alive today and in a position to revive his business standing."[13]

■   ■   ■

The failure of the Knickerbocker Trust Company was but the beginning, not the end, of a panic that would engulf a turbulent and rapidly growing nation as it entered the twentieth century. The run on other banks and trust companies, some of which were associated with the Heinze-and-Morse scheme, continued unabated even after the Knickerbocker closed its doors. Lines in front of banks in New York and elsewhere extended for blocks, and Wall Street was gripped by a paroxysm of fear. In the coming days, money would become scarce, banks would fail, the stock market would plummet, and the city of New York itself would reach the precipice of bankruptcy. Only a small cadre of astute and cool-headed financiers and government officials could steer a course through the oncoming gale. Like Charles Barney, the nation had lost its confidence. It would take leadership and courage to bring it back.

Introduction

History may not repeat itself, but it rhymes.[1]

—Attributed to Mark Twain

W hy do market crashes and banking panics happen?* Conventional wisdom on this question has gathered, like iron filings, at two intellectual poles. At one extreme, we find explanations that are highly detailed and idiosyncratic to a particular event—often comprised of a hodge-podge of period-specific causes.[†]

---

* We use "crash" to suggest a sharp decline in stock prices; "panic" refers to a run on a bank that is inconsistent with economic reality, the ability of a bank to meet withdrawals. These terms are imprecise, though experts then and now use these terms to describe the events of 1907. Their usage among experts varies considerably, as shown in Appendix B.
† In his book, *Fifty Years in Wall Street,* originally published in 1908, the Wall Street observer Henry Clews cited nine causes for the panic of 1907, all specific to that year (p. 799): "The real causes of all the trouble can be summed up as follows: (1) the high finance manipulation in advancing stocks to a 3.5 to 4 percent basis, while the money was loaning at 6 percent and above, on six and twelve months, time on the best of collaterals; (2) capital all over the nation having gone largely into real estate and other fixed forms, thereby losing its liquid quality; (3) the making of injudicious loans by the Knickerbocker Trust Co., hence suspension; (4) the unloading by certain big operators of $800,000,000 of securities, following which were the immense sales of new securities by the railroads; (5) the California earthquake, with losses amounting to $350,000,000; (6) the investigation of the life insurance companies; (7) the Metropolitan Street Railroad investigation; (8) the absurd fine by

1

At the other extreme are conclusions that might be broadly described as "one big idea": a sole cause large enough to cover a multitude of sins. A favorite big idea among some economists, for example, is that financial crises follow a lack of liquidity in the financial system.* Another popular big-idea explanation is simple greed or venality.†

Unfortunately, the one big idea often ignores the considerable richness of detail that the recounting of a single crisis can reveal, and thus produces simplistic conclusions and inappropriate recommendations for decision makers. One wants more, an explanation that is neither too much nor too little; neither too idiosyncratic nor too simplistic. Therefore, by drawing on a detailed history of the crash and panic of 1907 and on an extensive body of research about financial crises, we offer an alternative view that is as applicable to the past as to the future.

From 1814 to 1914, the United States saw 13 banking panics—of these, the panic of 1907 was among the worst.[2] The panic had coincided with a series of major market downturns, culminating in a 37 percent decline in the value of all listed stocks. Triggered by the literal and figurative shock of a massive earthquake and a rash of fires that destroyed the city of San Francisco in 1906, the financial crisis of 1907 had global implications, and it called forth the leadership of a small group of powerful financiers. Though the duration of the crisis was relatively brief, the repercussions proved far-reaching, resulting in the formal establishment of a powerful central bank in the United States through the Federal Reserve System.

To understand fully the crash and panic of 1907, one must consider its context. A Republican moralist was in the White House. War was fresh in mind. Immigration was fueling dramatic changes in society. New technologies were changing people's everyday lives. Business consolidators and their Wall Street advisers were creating large, new combinations through mergers and acquisitions, while the government was investigating and prosecuting prominent executives—led by an aggressive young

---

Judge Landis of $29,400,000 against a corporation with a capital of $1,000,000; (9) the Interstate Commerce Commission's examination into the Chicago & Alton deal and the results thereof." Other contemporary writers offered similar explanations.

* For example, the economist Milton Friedman and the monetarists have blamed the government's failure to manage well the money supply as a leading contributor to such events.

† Writing about the stock market bubble and collapse of 1997 to 2001, Roger Lowenstein (2004, pp. 218–219) boiled the explanation down to the distortion of the credo of shareholder value.

prosecutor from New York. The public's attitude toward business leaders, fueled by a muckraking press, was largely negative. The government itself was becoming increasingly interventionist in society and, in some ways, more intrusive in individual life. Much of this was stimulated by a postwar economic expansion that, with brief interruptions, had lasted about 50 years. Bring, then, a sense of irony informed by the present to an understanding of 1907.

Stock market crashes and banking panics had surfaced periodically in the United States and elsewhere throughout the nineteenth century. Market crashes often sprang from occasional bubbles in asset prices: extreme speculations in land and new securities would "correct" when investors' expectations failed to be realized.[3] Banking panics were often the consequence of these corrections as adjustments in asset valuations sent shock waves through the young country's financial system. The nation's banks, realizing that the value of pledged collateral had impaired the creditworthiness of their loans, would call in their credits. Borrowers, unable to repay their debts, would default and declare bankruptcy. Consequently, nervous bank depositors would fear for the survival of the bank and rush to withdraw their funds. If one institution failed in the process, then a panic would spread—a classic "run on the banks."* Unlike France, Germany, and Britain, the United States lacked a central banking authority that could supply extra liquidity in such times of credit anorexia.

By 1907, economic growth in America had lifted business expectations; a cataclysmic disaster in California would shatter them. How the effects of an external shock to the economy would wend their way into violent price changes a year later tells a story of how complex systems process information. The markets for stocks, debt, currency, gold, copper, and other commodities form such a complex system—they are interrelated in the sense that fundamental changes in one can affect prices in the others. Common factors such as inflation, real economic

---

* For example, the panic of 1857 was triggered by the failure of the Ohio Life Insurance & Trust Company. The failure of the Missouri, Kansas, and Texas Railroad to make timely payments to New York Warehouse & Security Company and the collapse of financial houses Keyon, Cox and Co., and Jay Cooke & Co. sparked the panic of 1873. The panic of 1884 was initiated by the failure of Grant and Ward, a financial house in which President Ulysses Grant was an investor. In 1893, the panic was spawned by the failures of the Philadelphia and Reading Railroad, National Cordage Co., and Lake Erie and Western Railroad and by investor concerns about asset values in the silver mining industry.

growth, liquidity, and external shocks can affect them all. How we make meaning of crashes and panics, then, is fundamentally a question of information: its content, how it is gathered, and how the complex system of the markets distills it into security prices.*

Over the years the occurrence of large and systemic financial crises has been the focus of considerable research—both directly and through varied intellectual streams: macroeconomics, game theory, group psychology, financial economics, complexity theory, the economics of information, and management theory. The following detailed account of the events of 1907 draws upon this rich literature to suggest that financial crises result from a convergence of forces, a "perfect storm"[4] at work in the financial markets. Throughout the dramatic story of the panic of 1907, we explore this metaphor as we highlight seven elements of the market's perfect storm:

1. **System-like architecture.** Complexity makes it difficult to know what is going on and establishes linkages that enable contagion of the crisis to spread.

2. **Buoyant growth.** Economic expansion creates rising demands for capital and liquidity and the excessive mistakes that eventually must be corrected.

3. **Inadequate safety buffers.** In the late stages of an economic expansion, borrowers and creditors overreach in their use of debt, lowering the margin of safety in the financial system.

4. **Adverse leadership.** Prominent people in the public and private spheres implement policies that raise uncertainty, which impairs confidence and elevates risk.

5. **Real economic shock.** Unexpected events hit the economy and financial system, causing a sudden reversal in the outlook of investors and depositors.

---

* The efficiency with which the financial markets incorporate news and events into prices quickly and without bias was then, in 1907, and remains to this day, a bone of contention among business practitioners and academicians. There is the general sense that markets today are more efficient than they were a century ago. Those who would argue that markets are not very efficient point to the periodic occurrence of bubbles and crashes, when violent swings in security prices appear to be unrelated to fundamental changes in economic conditions. Those who find the market relatively efficient strive to link price fluctuations to changes in underlying conditions.

6. **Undue fear, greed, and other behavioral aberrations.** Beyond a change in the rational economic outlook is a shift from optimism to pessimism that creates a self-reinforcing downward spiral. The more bad news, the more behavior that generates bad news.

7. **Failure of collective action.** The best-intended responses by people on the scene prove inadequate to the challenge of the crisis.

This pluralistic approach affords a framework through which the alert observer can make sense of unfolding events; we invite reflection on their application to the crisis of 1907, and we return to them at length in the final chapter.

Interpreting and even anticipating future financial crises requires insights into the forces suggested here—not merely individually, but also collectively—how they *interact* to produce a crisis. This approach may lead us, perhaps, to a more complicated explanation of financial crises than pundits and politicians want to hear, yet the metaphor of the perfect storm reveals a possible outlook for decision makers—one that suggests that the way to forestall a financial crisis is to anticipate the storm's volatile elements and, perhaps, even to fight their potential convergence.

Chapter 1

Wall Street Oligarchs

A man I do not trust could not get money from me on all the bonds in Christendom.

—J. Pierpont Morgan[1]

In 1907, the young American economy was roaring. Between the mid-1890s and the end of 1906, the nation's annual growth rate was a stunning 7.3 percent, which had doubled the absolute size of all U.S. industrial production during a relatively brief period. The volatility of this growth also leaped from just over 6.5 percent to 8.0 percent per year—although, relative to the high rate of growth, this economic volatility was slightly lower than what it had been during much of the nineteenth century. Even so, compared with previous periods of major industrial expansion, the U.S. economy in 1907 was larger and growing faster than ever (see Figure 1.1).[2]

With the dramatic growth and economic development of the United States at the turn of the century came an enormous demand for capital. In 1895 the U.S. economy added $2.5 billion to its fixed plant and inventories, and by 1906 the annual rate of capital formation was running at nearly $5 billion, a blistering pace (see Figure 1.2). Much of this was

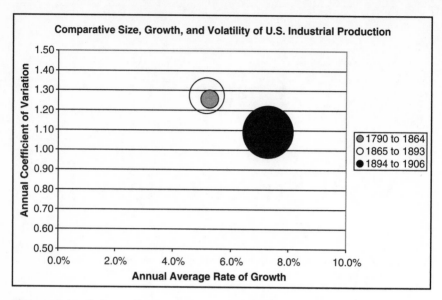

Figure 1.1 Comparative size, growth, and volatility of U.S. industrial production.

NOTE: The size of the circles indicates the relative size of the U.S. industrial production at 1864, 1893, and 1907 respectively. The growth rate is the compound average over each period. The coefficient of variation is a measure of relative volatility of growth (calculated as the standard deviation of growth rates divided by the compound average rate of growth for the period).

SOURCE: Authors' figure based on data from NBER, David Industrial Production Index.

financed by the country's exports, which appeared as a bulging current account surplus after 1895. But even exports were insufficient to finance the very large growth rate in the formation of capital in 1905 (12.7%) and 1906 (21.8%).

Into this prodigious vacuum moved a tightly knit network of financiers in New York and London who possessed the sophistication and credibility to raise the necessary funds for America's factories and infrastructure in the world's capital markets.* Their success in attracting foreign capital to America's "emerging market" was reflected in the immense importations of gold in 1906:† the inflow of gold to the United States spiked sharply upward to $165 million, dwarfing all gold flows after the Civil War, except during the year of a significant economic downturn in 1893.

---

* In part, the financial houses these financiers built served as a certification of quality that the securities of U.S. firms being sold in Europe were attractive investment opportunities
† Gold was typically imported through the sale of bonds or other promises to repay.

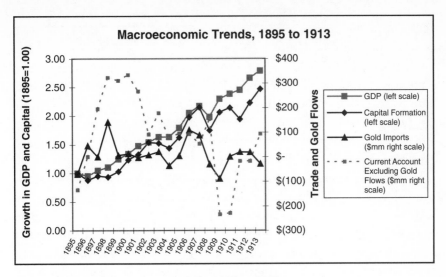

Figure 1.2 Macroeconomic trends, 1895 to 1913.
SOURCE: Authors' figure based on data from NBER Macro History Database.

America's rapid industrialization during this period also hastened the emergence of business entities of unprecedented scale, complexity, and power. Between 1894 and 1904, more than 1,800 companies were consolidated into just 93 corporations.[3] Some of these large firms had grown by buying up smaller competitors during times of economic distress, while others were organized by financiers seeking to control competition and build efficiencies of scale.* Much of the volume of new debt and equity financing for these large corporations again flowed through a relatively small circle of financial institutions in New York, including J. P. Morgan & Company; Kuhn, Loeb & Company; the First National Bank; the National City Bank; Kidder, Peabody & Company; and Lee, Higginson & Company.[4]

In 1907, the informal but undisputed leader of this financial community in the United States was J. Pierpont Morgan, known to his family and friends simply as "Pierpont." A complex man, biographers have found unusual clues to Morgan's personality. Historian Vincent Carosso characterized him as a devoted family man, a "strong-willed,

---

* The companies these financiers organized were popularly called "trusts," which a leading economist of the day defined as "an organization managed by a board of trustees to which all the capital stock of the constituent companies is irrevocably assigned; in other words, the original shareholders accept the trustees' certificates in lieu of former evidences of ownership." [See Ripley (1916), p. xvii.] The first and most famous of these business entities was John D. Rockefeller's Standard Oil Trust, created in 1882.

affectionate, protective, and generous paterfamilias."[5] Biographer Jean Strouse divined that Morgan was estranged (but not divorced) from his wife, that he had amorous relations with other women, and at the same time was a prominent figure in the Episcopal church in New York City. Strouse also determined that Morgan suffered from periods of clinical depression—indeed, business and family letters are replete with open references to his bouts with the "blues." But all biographers are agreed that Morgan was a forceful personality.

Historian William Harbaugh wrote of Morgan, "What a whale of a man! There seemed to radiate something that forced the complex of inferiority...upon all around him, in spite of themselves. The boldest man was likely to become timid under his piercing gaze. The most impudent or recalcitrant were ground to humility as he chewed truculently at his huge black cigar."[6] Morgan's nickname in the street was "Jupiter," suggesting godly power. Once he reputedly dismissed the threat of a government inquiry with a comment to President Theodore Roosevelt that, "If we have done anything wrong, send your man [the attorney general] to my man [one of Morgan's lawyers] and they can fix it up."[7]

J. P. Morgan operated within a circle of talented professionals and influential figures in the New York and European financial communities, and he demonstrated great faith in their collective abilities to "fix things up." Biographer Frederick Lewis Allen described vividly Morgan's attitude about the role of the Wall Street oligarchs, of which he was the most prominent:

> Morgan seemed to feel that the business machinery of America should be honestly and decently managed by a few of the best people, people like his friends and associates. He liked combination, order, the efficiency of big business units; and he liked them to operate in a large, bold, forward-looking way. He disapproved of the speculative gangs who plunged in and out of the market, heedless of the properties they were toying with, as did the Standard Oil crowd. When he put his resources behind a company, he expected to stay with it; this, he felt, was how a gentleman behaved. His integrity was solid as a rock, and he said, "A man I do not trust could not get money from me on all the bonds in Christendom." That Morgan was a mighty force for decent finance is unquestionable. But so also is the fact that he was a mighty force working toward the concentration into a few hands of authority over more and more of American business.[8]

Two of the leading figures in Morgan's circle were George F. Baker, president of First National Bank of New York, and James Stillman, president of New York's National City Bank. Though Stillman and Baker were direct competitors of Morgan for securities underwritings, the three men commanded great mutual respect having worked together in business and on charitable boards. Morgan's son once told a biographer, "Mr. Baker was closer to my father than any other man of affairs. They understood each other perfectly, worked in harmony, and there was never any need of written contracts between them."[9] Baker and Pierpont Morgan were indeed warm friends; they respected each other and shared similar views on business matters. With Stillman, the relationship was perhaps more distant: "[T]hey did not always see eye to eye," wrote a biographer. "Their mutual attitude, however, was one of respect and a certain degree of friendship."[10]

Morgan's preference for the consolidation of power was matched by a record of consistent leadership in times of crisis and advocacy on behalf of investors. In 1893 Morgan stepped into the breach to help President Grover Cleveland raise gold in Europe as a means of resolving the deepening liquidity crisis facing the country. He was instrumental in the consolidation and reorganization of failed companies, most importantly railroads that had overexpanded prior to the depression of the mid-1890s. In the process, Morgan introduced firm discipline and an investor-oriented point of view. In one prominent exchange with a resistant railroad executive, J. P. Morgan, said, "*Your* railroad? Your railroad belongs to my clients."[11]

Morgan also sought actively to avoid what he viewed as "ruinous competition" by merging competitor firms to produce corporations whose names remain memorable a century later: American Telephone and Telegraph, International Harvester, American Tobacco, National Biscuit (Nabisco), to name a few.* In 1901, Morgan played a central role in the formation of U.S. Steel, the largest corporation in America. Capitalized at a value of $1 billion dollars, U.S. Steel was twice the size of the entire budget of the U.S. government in 1907. Carosso thus

---

* Other companies under the influence of Morgan also included Adams Express Co.; Atchison, Topeka, & Santa Fe Railroad; Baldwin Locomotive Co.; Chicago-Great Western Railroad; Erie Railroad; International Agricultural Co.; International Mercantile Marine Co.; Lehigh Valley Railroad; New York, New Haven, and Hartford Railroad; Northern Pacific Railroad; New York Central Railroad; Pere Marquette Railroad; Philadelphia Rapid Transit Co.; Public Service Corporation of New Jersey; Pullman Co.; Reading Railroad; Southern Railroad; United States Steel Co; and Westinghouse Co.

described J. P. Morgan's general approach to business consolidation:

> Conservatism . . . stood at the center of Morgan's general business views. If he had any fundamental, guiding business policy at all, it was to promote stability through responsible, competent, economical management, and to be aware of his obligations to an enterprise's owners and bondholders. There was nothing he disliked more than unrestricted competition and aggressive expansionism, which he considered wasteful and destructive. Morgan believed in orderly industrial progress, and he endorsed policies aimed at promoting cooperation. Large enterprises, he affirmed, should adhere to the principle of community of interest, not the Spencerian doctrine of survival of the fittest.[12]

Morgan was more than just a consolidator of existing businesses; he also played the role of venture capitalist. Not only were several Morgan partners investors in Thomas Edison's company, but Drexel, Morgan (the precursor to J. P. Morgan & Company) also served as the depository for the cash of Edison's firm, arranged loans for the company, facilitated foreign transactions, and helped to manage Thomas Edison's private wealth.* Morgan even helped Edison with mergers and acquisitions and underwrote the initial public offering for the Edison General Electric Company.[13]

By 1906, J. Pierpont Morgan was disengaging slowly from the day-to-day activities of his firm to attend to his passion for collecting art and literature, serving on boards of charitable institutions, and touring Europe. He relied heavily on his son, J. P. "Jack" Morgan Jr., to manage his firm's daily affairs, as well as his "right-hand man," George W. Perkins, a partner in J. P. Morgan & Company. On April 17, 1906, the aging Morgan turned 69 years old. By this time, he was unquestionably, according to one biographer, "the most powerful figure in the American world of business, if not the most powerful citizen of the United States. His authority was vague, but it was immense—and growing."[14] On the morning after his birthday, an historic catastrophe devastated the city of San Francisco, California, setting in motion a chain of events that would eventually call for all the power, wisdom, strength, and influence that Old Jupiter could muster.

---

* In the summer of 1882, Morgan himself patronized Edison's new technology, installing electric lighting in his Madison Avenue house, making it the first private house in New York City to be illuminated by Edison's new incandescent bulbs.

Chapter 2

A Shock to the System

General affairs here are about as bad as they can be.

—J. P. "Jack" Morgan Jr.
August 8, 1907

T he earthquake that destroyed San Francisco in April 1906 was unprecedented in scale and scope. In the wake of the temblor itself, broken gas mains ignited massive fires throughout the city. Disruptions to municipal water lines prevented fire suppression, and San Francisco's mostly wood-framed architecture only fueled the flames. The conflagration eventually engulfed the city, leveling over four square miles, or about half of San Francisco, such that most historical accounts speak of both the earthquake *and* the fire as the source of the city's destruction. San Francisco's damages were reported to range between $350 and $500 million, or 1.2 to 1.7 percent of the U.S. gross national product in 1906.[1]

The strains from the catastrophe in California rippled instantly through the global financial system. At the time, San Francisco was the financial center of the West and home to the western branch of the U.S.

Mint, so anything that disrupted business in San Francisco threatened the entire western region economically.

On the New York and London stock exchanges, news of the quake led to an immediate sell-off in stocks and a significant drop in share prices. Economists Kerry Odell and Marc Weidenmier have estimated that the disaster led directly or indirectly to about a $1 billion (or a nearly 12.5 percent) decline in the total market value of New York Stock Exchange securities. Prices of railway stocks fell more than 15 percent, and those of insurance companies declined between 15 and 30 percent during the two weeks after the cataclysm.[2]

Relief funds were drawn into the city from around the country and the world: England supplied $30 million; Germany, France, and the Netherlands collectively provided another $20 million. Such international effects of the earthquake were further amplified because many foreign insurers had provided San Francisco's underwriting protection. What most severely hurt the insurance industry was that most people were insured against fire but not earthquakes. British insurance firms, for instance, had accounted for about half of the city's fire insurance policies; after the quake, they faced losses of close to $50 million. In fact, several insurers were overwhelmed by the claims and could not meet their insurable obligations; Fireman's Fund Insurance Company, for example, faced liabilities of $11.5 million, exceeding its total assets by $4.5 million.[3] Consequently, some underwriters imposed lengthy delays in paying for damages, while others discounted their claims, insisting that any earthquake-related fire damage was not explicitly covered in their policies. The Hamburg-Bremen Insurance Company demanded a discount of 25 percent for all San Francisco claims. Only six companies fully honored their obligations.[4]

While some British insurers funded their payments by selling their holdings of American securities, others liquidated assets heavily in foreign markets. This liquidation prompted major shipments of gold from London to the United States—$30 million in April and another $35 million in September 1906, amounting to a 14 percent decline in Britain's stock of gold—the largest outflow of gold from Britain between 1900 and 1913. Eventually, these outflows of gold created liquidity fears for the Bank of England.[5] The declining liquidity of the London capital market sparked the spread of rumors in New York that British financial houses were in trouble and required support from the Bank of England.*

At the time of the earthquake in the spring of 1906, the global market for capital was dominated by London. The British Empire was at its zenith, and London was the locus of immense flows of capital. Charged with the responsibility of maintaining liquidity for the Empire, the Bank of England—the "Old Lady of Threadneedle Street"—held reserves of gold with which to meet the liquidity demands of banks and trading partners. Keeping the British mills, factories, and shops supplied with goods from the commonwealth was a fundamental premise of England's economic system.

In an attempt to stanch the depletion of the country's gold supply, the Bank of England raised its benchmark interest rate from 3.5 to 4.0 percent. Fearing further demands for gold with the coming Egyptian cotton crop,[6] the Bank raised its rate again on October 19, 1906, from 4.0 to 6.0 percent—the highest rate posted by the Bank of England since 1899.[7] Central banks in France and Germany followed suit and sharply raised their interest rates as well.[8] Panic had not yet set in, but telegrams flew across the Atlantic between the world's leading financiers, reflecting a growing anxiety within the financial community about liquidity and the likely actions of the Bank of England.[9]

In New York City, capital was becoming scarce, too, as its gold reserves also migrated to San Francisco. The timing of these relief shipments to the West Coast was particularly unfortunate since they coincided with the ordinary demands for funds induced by the U.S. agricultural cycle: The harvesting and shipment of crops required credit until the crops reached the consumer. As a result of the capital shortage, the price of money in New York grew dear, and other sectors of the American economy started to feel the pinch. By the winter of 1906–1907, severe credit shortage had set in.

On December 18, 1906, Jack Morgan, writing to his affiliate partners in London, offered stark language about these stringent credit conditions: "Things here are very uncomfortable owing to the tightness of money . . .

---

* To the queries from J. P. "Jack" Morgan Jr. about these rumors, Edward "Teddy" Grenfell, a partner in J. S. Morgan & Company in London, the British affiliate of J. P. Morgan & Company, denied any basis in fact.

we are likely to have a stiff money market for some time to come."[10] A few days later he wrote with a clarification: "There is plenty of money in the country everywhere except in New York, and the only really alarming thing about the situation appears to be a very undefined feeling that there is something wrong in New York. This feeling extending to the large centres in the West has interfered with the natural flow of money to this centre to take advantage of the high rate."[11] As the year 1907 began, there was a deep sense of foreboding among the nation's money men.

Complicating the capital scarcity problem was a bull market in stocks, which had been spurred by the buoyant economic growth of the American economy through 1905. A "mammoth bull movement," in the words of one observer, was running its course on the New York Stock Exchange. Jack Morgan, under whose direct supervision J. Pierpont Morgan had left J. P. Morgan & Company, noted a speculative sentiment prevailing in the stock market:

> For the first time in three years the public—with stocks at their present high prices—have begun to come in and buy heavily with the result that the so called market-leaders are no longer in charge, and that the stock market is running away in a fashion which I must say suggests to me possible trouble in the future although not in the immediate future.[12]

Meanwhile, enormous new issues of securities, particularly by railway and industrial companies, placed further demands on the resources of the money market. Henry Clews, a contemporary Wall Street authority, said, "Indeed, the year 1906 from beginning to end witnessed a continuation of those inordinately heavy demands for money from Wall Street and corporations, and these led to the disturbed monetary conditions."[13]

While the equity market was attracting popular attention, the debt markets (i.e., bonds and loans) overshadowed stocks in both volume and significance. During 1906, debt market conditions diverged sharply from equities: While stock prices rose, bond prices fell (and thus, interest rates increased). The price movement in the debt markets coincided with the increasing demand for credit driven by the continued real economic growth in the United States, the agricultural cycle that drew financing to bring the bumper crop of 1906 to market, and the shock of the San Francisco earthquake. Alexander Dana Noyes, a leading observer of Wall Street, wrote in 1909, "Beginning about the middle of 1905, a strain on the whole world's capital supply and credit facilities set in, which increased at so portentous a rate during the next two years that long before October, 1907, thoughtful men in many widely separated markets were discussing, with serious apprehension, what was to be the result."[14]

Chapter 3

The "Silent" Crash

The whole situation is most mysterious; undoubtedly many men who were very rich have become much poorer, but as there seems to be no one breaking, perhaps we shall get off with the fright only.[1]

—J. P. "Jack" Morgan Jr.
March 14, 1907

B y early 1907, it seemed that the steady progressive tightening of money, which had been accelerated by the massive capital demands of San Francisco's earthquake, had precipitated a slow and steady decline in equity prices—considered by some contemporaries to be a "silent" crash in the U.S. financial markets.

Between its peak in September 1906 and the end of February 1907, the index of all listed stocks fell 7.7 percent, a five-month change in value unremarkable in view of the long history of the market, but pertinent as the beginning of a trend. Indeed, on March 6, 1907, telegraph correspondence between Jack Morgan and his partner in J. P. Morgan & Company's London affiliate, Teddy Grenfell, reflected the deepening anxiety between the world's financial centers:

Grenfell: Can you give us any information and what is your opinion of the immediate future of your market?[2]

Morgan: Do not get any information showing real trouble our market although of course continued liquidation must hurt some people and may do severe damage in places. From what I can make out do not think stocks are in weak hands. Shall be surprised if immediate future brings much more liquidation, although of course impossible form opinion.[3]

In the coming days, Teddy and Jack exchanged more anxious telegrams about rumors of gold shipments. Grenfell thought that at the "first indication [of] considerable withdrawals of gold," the Bank of England would raise its interest rate. He wondered whether the U.S. Treasury would relieve the situation by releasing gold from its vaults into the financial system. On March 13 Jack wired back that he could discover no intentions to ship gold from London *this* week, though there might be attempts to buy gold next week.[4]

By mid-March the "silent" crash had become audible as equity prices turned decidedly and sharply for the worse. Declining over a series of days (March 9 to 13 and 23 to 26) rather than on a single day, the index of all listed stocks fell 9.8 percent. Especially damaged were shares in shipping (off 16.6 percent), mining (down 14.5 percent), steel and iron (down 14.8 percent), and street railways (off 13.8 percent). The *Commercial and Financial Chronicle*, the principal financial periodical at the time, observed, "The liquidation going on in Wall Street . . . is phenomenal. Stock sales . . . are among the high records in the Stock Exchange history."[5]

J. Pierpont Morgan was absent from New York during these disturbances in the market; he had sailed for Europe at midnight on March 13, the day of the sharp market break. There, Pierpont met old friends, toured the art markets for possible acquisitions for his collection, and relaxed at various spas and villas. Meanwhile, Jack Morgan in New York grappled with the confusion and chaos in the financial system, writing in a letter to his partners in London on March 14:

> Here we are, still alive in spite of the most unpleasant panic which we are going through. The whole trouble lies, in my mind, in the mystery of the conditions; no one seems to be in any trouble, there is money at a price for anyone who wants it, and in our loans, and in those of all the Banks I have talked to, there has been no trouble whatever of keeping the margins perfectly good, except the physical difficulty of

getting the certificates round quickly enough.... I could not yesterday finish this letter owing to the panic and general trouble, there being so much to see to with Father and Perkins both away. Today, things seem to be so much quieter that I am in hopes that most of the trouble is over, certainly for the present.... The whole situation is most mysterious; undoubtedly many men who were very rich have become much poorer, but as there seems to be no one breaking, perhaps we shall get off with the fright only.[6]

As the price declines continued during the next week, rumors of the failure of financial institutions began to circulate. The London partners of J. P. Morgan & Company cabled to Jack: "*London Daily Telegraph* today states that house of international prominence has been helped in New York. Is there any truth in this? Who is it? Do you expect much further liquidation?"[7] Jack replied, "As far as we know there is no truth in rumor international house having been helped. Newspaper reports here is that various stock exchange houses in London are in difficulties. Cable any information you can obtain. Urgent liquidation seems to be pretty well done but as many parties heavily hit look for depressed markets for some time."[8]

Indeed, conditions remained unsettled as the unrest spread to other financial markets. On March 23, 1907, the *Commercial and Financial Chronicle* noted, "Lack of confidence [among investors] is never reflected more unerringly than in the money market; and the seriousness of the situation in that regard is shown in the inability of the railroads for over a year past to finance their new capital needs."[9] Both the municipalities of Philadelphia and St. Louis made bond offerings, and in neither case was the underwriting successful. "Money is commanding such high rates that it is impossible to float even gilt-edged securities at the low figures offered by Philadelphia and St. Louis," the *Chronicle* reported.

Finally, during the week of March 25, cables between Morgan's partners suggested that the worst was past. New York investors took courage from the announcement that the U.S. Treasury would deposit at least $12 million with national banks to ease the money situation. On March 29, 1907, Jack Morgan reflected on the change in mood to his London partners:

The two panics within the last ten days have given people a big scare, and the losses of course are frightful. The fact that no one has failed is more of the nature of a miracle than of ordinary business, but it simply shows, as far as I can see, that practically no one was overtrading. . . . My own belief, however, is that the panic is over, and the fact that the Treasury is putting out money rather fast and that that action has really been the cause of the restoration of confidence makes me feel that it was at bottom a money panic. Not a money panic such as we have heretofore had, but an apprehension that, in view of enormous calls being made upon huge stock issues during the next few months the market might be so far drained of money that those who were obliged to pay the calls would have difficulty in arranging to get the necessary fund. The whole thing has been an interesting experience, although an extremely painful one and I shall be greatly relieved when matters finally drift—as they seem to be doing—into a state of dullness and cheaper money. . . . From all this long screed you may see that I am tired but hopeful, hopeful because of the simple fact that there is a tremendous productive capacity in this country, and that this productive capacity has not been one whit reduced by the colic we have all been having.[10]

Almost as suddenly as it had begun, there was a sense that the mounting crisis had been stopped. The source of optimism in the market was the prospect of Americans buying £4 million in gold in London for shipment to New York; the U.S. Secretary of the Treasury, George B. Cortelyou, also ordered that $15 million be placed on deposit with New York City banks, thus giving much-needed liquidity to the capital markets. The *Commercial and Financial Chronicle* concluded that this "made a material change on Tuesday in the financial sentiment, the panicky tendency being arrested and a general advance in stock values taking place."[11] Within a few weeks, the disturbance in the markets seemed to have subsided.

Reflecting the financial anxieties caused by the March crash in equity prices, call money interest rates had spiked upward during this period, but they subsided when the flush of cash and gold into the New York money markets produced lower interest rates and a modest recovery in equity prices (see Figure 3.1).* On April 13, the *Commercial*

* *Call money* consisted of loans from banks to brokers that had to be repaid upon demand and were secured by bonds or shares of stock. The interest rates on call loans were the leading barometer of money market conditions. The variability of those rates in March and July 1907 reflected the deep-seated anxieties of investors.

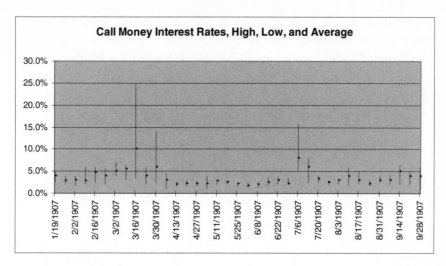

Figure 3.1   Call money interest rates.

and Financial Chronicle observed, "The monetary situation has reversed its character for call money, from abnormally high to abnormally low rates—the relief in New York communicating a like tendency elsewhere. This change has opened the stock market here to more venturesome buying, and consequently speculative operators have again been in evidence."[12]

While an optimistic mood may have returned, robust buying behavior had not. The *Chronicle* noted an eerie slackening of trading and persistently low stock prices, which suggested an absence of investors from the exchange. During April and May, the index of all stocks fell 3 percent, with large declines in shipping (down 12 percent), household goods (off 12 percent), machinery (off 10 percent), and copper (down 10 percent). On April 20, the *Chronicle* remained gloomy, saying, "no refuge from the old instability has been found. . . . A harsher and deeper economic irregularity is what the doctors have to deal with before real recovery will be under way."[13]

Business fundamentals also looked bleak. For the month of April, the value of claims in bankruptcy had grown 38 percent over the same month a year earlier, with the sharpest growth in the manufacturing sector.[14] On May 2, Teddy Grenfell in London queried Jack Morgan in a telegram about the stock market and when the banks in San Francisco might reopen.* Morgan replied, "Think further demand for gold is probable but impossible estimate amount. Stock market—believe decline largely speculative. Do not hear of any serious trouble any where though market vaguely apprehensive of difficulty arising largely from varied activities President USA."[15] For financiers and investors in 1907, the "varied activities President USA" were an overriding concern.

■   ■   ■

Despite his patrician mien and pedigree, President Theodore Roosevelt was masterful at giving voice to the nation's popular will. By 1907, Americans had become increasingly disturbed by the tumultuous changes that had accompanied the country's impressive industrial growth. They were worried about the number and type of immigrants entering the country; the size, noise, and frenzy of the nation's large cities; the effectiveness of their elected representatives; the consequences of old age, illness, and injury on the job; the day-to-day hazards of urban life; and even the quality of their food and water. Yet most of all they reacted with alarm to the rise of big business and the corporate merger movement. Some Americans, calling themselves "progressives," argued vociferously for the right of a community to protect itself against those who pursued their economic self-interest without concern for the common good.[16] President Theodore Roosevelt became their most outspoken proponent.

Progressives especially looked at J. P. Morgan and Wall Street with fear, some of it well founded. Since the Civil War, the history of corporate finance had been punctuated by instances of looting and self-dealing by the financial promoters. It seemed that the very intimate engagement of financiers as both insiders and outside investors opened conflicts of interest against which the public would not be able to guard. Moreover, many of the combinations these investors organized resulted in oligopolies and monopolies that sacrificed the welfare of consumers

---

* The main reason why San Francisco's banks remained closed for several weeks after the earthquake and fire was to allow time for the vaults to cool. The fire was so hot in the financial district that if banks had reopened their vaults immediately after the fire had ended, the residual heat would have caused paper inside the vaults to burst into flame. This need to wait stilted economic recovery and made the city dependent on outside cash to pay for labor needed for the city's intense rebuilding effort.

for the benefit of investors. The sheer scale of the new corporate trusts raised concerns about the possible abuse of economic power to achieve political ends. Standard Oil, for instance, had the power to extract rebates from railroads for shipping their products that were not given to its competitors. Muckraking writers such as Sinclair Lewis famously focused attention on unsanitary conditions in meatpacking. Lincoln Steffens exposed unsafe compounds used in pharmaceuticals. In this context, the rather closed world of high corporation finance seemed highly suspicious.

President Theodore Roosevelt was the personification of this progressive movement, and he applied his executive power to challenge the influence of large corporations and to mediate between labor and capital. He was a pragmatist in a time of great political ferment, and he carefully navigated between opposing attitudes. Most relevant for the events of 1907 were his attitudes and policies toward large corporations. On the one hand, Roosevelt accepted industrialization and the large scale of firms that it brought.[17] He believed that large corporations were here to stay, and that the stance of government should not be to eradicate the large firms, but rather to identify and eliminate the types of combinations that were dangerous.* "I believe in corporations," Roosevelt said early in his presidency. "They are indispensable instruments of our modern civilization; but I believe that they should be so supervised and so regulated that they shall act for the interest of the community as a whole."[18]

However, to deal with the perceived ills of large corporations, Roosevelt also implemented a policy of aggressive enforcement of the antitrust laws, mediation, and regulation. In 1902, for example, Roosevelt initiated a series of important antitrust actions, beginning with a suit against the Northern Securities Company, a railroad trust organized by J. P. Morgan, James J. Hill, John D. Rockefeller, and E. H. Harriman in 1901 just five weeks after Roosevelt took office. Two years later, the Supreme Court ordered the company dissolved. Roosevelt also filed suit

---

* Just weeks after the Panic, Roosevelt said, "It is unfortunate that our present laws should forbid all combinations instead of sharply discriminating between those combinations which do good and those combinations which do evil...The antitrust law should not prohibit combinations that do no injustice to the public, still less those the existence of which is on the whole of benefit to the public." Quoted from a public speech by Theodore Roosevelt, "Sherman Antitrust Law" dated Dec. 3, 1907. Used with permission of Columbia University Rare Book and Manuscript library.

against the unpopular "beef trust," an action that the Court upheld in 1905. When states began filing state antitrust suits against Standard Oil between 1904 and 1907, Roosevelt directed the Justice Department to assume leadership of the campaign against the oil monopoly.[19] By 1907, the Roosevelt administration had sued nearly 40 corporations under the Sherman Antitrust Act.

In that same spirit, Roosevelt revitalized the Interstate Commerce Commission, which had been created in 1887, by signing the Elkins Act of 1903 and the Hepburn Act of 1906, which gave the Commission the power to set maximum shipping rates for railroads. He also reenergized the presidency and asserted executive powers to protect particular social groups and supervise the economy in ways not seen since Reconstruction. In a Memorial Day speech at Indianapolis, President Theodore Roosevelt railed that the "predatory man of wealth" was the primary threat to private property in the United States:

> One great problem that we have before us is to preserve the rights of property, and these can only be preserved if we remember that they are in less jeopardy from the Socialist and the Anarchist than from the predatory man of wealth. There can be no halt in the course we have deliberately elected to pursue, the policy of asserting the right of the nation, so far as it has the power, to supervise and control the business use of wealth, especially in the corporate form.[20]

Progressive activism was reflected at the state level as well; various states passed legislation sharply limiting the prices railroads could charge passengers. Business analysts believed these prices yielded revenues below the costs necessary to provide the services, thus inducing downward pressures on stock prices.[21] The *Chronicle* opined, "What is ailing the railroads and the stock market? . . . The underlying cause is the same as it was at the time of the collapse in March, the same, indeed, as it has been for about a year and a half, during all of which period a shrinkage in values has been in progress. Owing to the assaults of those high in authority and adverse legislation both by Congress and the State legislatures, confidence is almost completely gone. No one is willing to buy at what appear like ridiculously low prices because no one can tell what the future may bring forth."[22]

■   ■   ■

The initial judgment of knowledgeable observers was that the break in stock prices in March 1907 had been sparked by investor fears arising from the Roosevelt administration's aggressive attitude toward railroads and industrial corporations. "For a year we have been foretelling this catastrophe, an assured result of the trials railroad property, railroad men and other large capitalists have been forced to suffer," the *Commercial and Financial Chronicle* said, commenting on a newly launched investigation of E. H. Harriman's Union Pacific railroad. "What has just taken place is not the final scene. Hereafter, if the irritant is continued, as we presume it will be, it will not be so exclusively securities and security-holders that will suffer; all sorts of industrial affairs are sure to get involved."[23] That irritant, of course, was the president of the United States.

Chapter 4

Credit Anorexia

*According to our belief, there is no other man in this country who could
have done what he has done on this occasion.*

—Commercial and Financial Chronicle
September 21, 1907

B y mid-spring 1907, the annual financing cycle for agriculture
had resumed in earnest. While 1906 had yielded a bumper crop
in the western United States, 1907 seemed less promising; a
weak harvest would have a possible negative impact on exports from the
United States and the subsequent ability of U.S. firms to find financing
in Europe. Anxieties about the capital available in London soon surfaced among leading financiers. On May 2, Teddy Grenfell wrote to his
partners at J. P. Morgan & Company in New York: "Can you give me
any information as to further shipments of gold? We are getting short at
Bank of England and may have to raise bank rate sharply. I am hoping
get [J. Pierpont Morgan] lunch at Bank of England tomorrow with the
Governor. What is wrong with your market and is there any fear serious
troubles?"[1]

On May 24, the *Commercial and Financial Chronicle* reported "violent declines" in selected stocks and that "security markets remain very unsettled."[2] By June, Jack Morgan was writing to his partners in London, saying, "All the world is still in the dumps here, and with it we have everything else that comes with the Summer-time, and transactions on the Stock Exchange become smaller and more nominal daily. A rest is just what is needed, however, and I think that the next change ought to be an improvement of business, since it could not be worse. But when the next change will come I cannot as yet see—nor what will start it."[3]

In the summer of 1907, a major economic shock hit the American capital markets. In an effort to harbor gold reserves, the Bank of England imposed a prohibition on U.S. finance bills, which were loans with which U.S. firms could import gold.* The contemporary economist, O. M. W. Sprague, considered this action "the most important financial factor in the panic of 1907."[4] The prohibition slashed the volume of finance bills in the London market from $400 million to $30 million by late in the summer of 1907. This meant that American debtors could not simply refinance their obligations in London. As a result, the flow of gold to America suddenly lurched into reverse as gold was remitted to London to settle the payment on finance bills. This further contracted U.S. gold reserves by nearly 10 percent between May and August of 1907 and contributed to a national liquidity drought.[5]

Despite relatively high U.S. interest rates, the United States *exported* $30 million in gold to London during the summer of 1907, according to the economists Ellis Tallman and Jon Moen. "As a result," they wrote, "the New York money market was left with an uncharacteristically low volume of gold entering the fall season of cash tightness."[6] Meanwhile,

---

* Economists Tallman and Moen (1990, p. 3) described finance bills in these terms: "Contracts to extend credit—essentially bonds issued to borrow overseas in hope of profit from anticipated exchange-rate fluctuations. The dollar's exchange rate varied over the year, strengthening during the harvest season when foreign demand for dollars to purchase crops was high and weakening thereafter. Finance bills were most frequently drawn in the summer, two or three months before crop movement, when the dollar price of sterling was quite high. . . . Banks and trust companies then sold sterling notes for dollars when sterling was stronger and repaid the notes when the dollar value of the sterling was lower, thus making a profit. Increased use of finance bills seems to have reduced the volatility of exchange rates and the volume of gold shipments overseas, enhancing the efficiency of the international exchange market. . . . Finance bills also provided a crude futures or forward market in foreign exchange."

the U.S. Treasury withdrew $30 million of deposits from national banks in order to redeem certain U.S. bonds maturing in July. While from a national funds-flow point of view, the effect on liquidity would be nil, the reality was that the funds would have to come from the major money centers, since national banks in the agricultural regions held relatively low cash reserves owing to agricultural financing.

Financial unrest continued to unfold. On June 28, New York City failed to place a $29 million bond offering, having received bids for only $2.1 million of the issue. Plainly, the 4 percent tax-exempt rate of interest offered on the bonds was inadequate, and a law prevented the city from offering a higher rate. By way of comparison, the *Chronicle* commented that "very good notes of railroads and other corporations can be bought at figures to net 6 and 7 percent."[7]

Jack Morgan bemoaned the worsening conditions, writing on July 19: "The money situation is now controlling everything, and there is not enough money around in this country, or in England, or on the Continent, at the moment, to finance a stock-market speculation if it arrived. As against this, people are saving money all the time and are making few new commitments, and also there seems to be a decrease in the money-hunger of the railroads, so that with care and conservatism we ought to be able to get through the Autumn stringency without any more panic."[8]

"The market keeps unstable," the *Chronicle* reported on July 27. "No sooner does the optimist settle into a half belief that things have passed the dangers that threatened the industrial situation, and a few stocks, encouraged by that belief, have begun in a half-scared, timid way to creep up on a comparison with last year's smaller earnings and fresh promises of higher dividends—no sooner are these signs of new life in evidence than something like a suggestion of a new outflow of gold to Paris sends a tremble all through the list, and the gain in values and hope is gone."[9] Reflecting the deteriorating economic fundamentals, U.S. Steel Corporation reported on August 1 a 25 percent decline in its book of business compared to the same period a year earlier. This news coincided with reports of unsatisfactory conditions in the market for copper, despite recent price cuts, and a slackening demand for iron and steel.[10]

From June through September 1907, amid an atmosphere of capital stringency, the stock market dropped another 8.1 percent, accumulating to a decline of 24.4 percent for the first three quarters of the year. The downturn over the long summer nearly did as much investment damage as had occurred in March alone. Many of the descriptions for the mood of the market over these four months resembled those from the early spring. The *Chronicle*, for instance, reported that the stock market was "extremely variable," and that it seemed to have "very little recuperative force."[11] The French economist, M. Leroy-Beaulieu, characterized the malaise in August 1907 as follows:

> The civilized world, so far as it can be reckoned upon, provides $2,400,000,000 in available capital annually for investment in securities; it is asked in 1906 to provide $3,250,000,000; there was a demand, in America at any rate, for even more than its part of the above estimate to be provided during 1907. But the world has not got it; therefore it cannot provide it. Add to this the effect of catastrophes such as the San Francisco and Valparaiso [August 17, 1906] earthquakes, which cost something like $200,000,000, and you will have a perfectly clear explanation of the existing crisis, rise in the interest rate and the fall of investment securities. The truth is, nations, quite as well as individuals, have reached the point where they must limit their undertakings to the possibilities of the case; that will be done, if not willingly, then by force of events.[12]

On August 3, 1907, Judge Kenesaw Mountain Landis fined Standard Oil Company of Indiana $29.24 million for violations of laws prohibiting secret rebates from railroads—the decision was remarkable not only for the relatively large size of the penalty (Standard Oil's book value of equity was only $1 million),[13] but also as a signal that the federal government would vigorously enforce new corporate regulations. Again, President Theodore Roosevelt repeated his famous theme on the wealthy, blaming them for having caused the financial distress of the country:

> It may well be that the determination of the Government, in which, gentlemen, it will not waver, to punish certain malefactors of great wealth, has been responsible for something of the troubles, at least to the extent of having caused these men to combine to bring about as much financial stress as they possibly can, in order to discredit the

policy of the Government and thereby to secure a reversal of that policy, that they may enjoy the fruits of their own evil doing.[14]

The editor of the *Chronicle* retorted, "It seems almost incredible that a person of superior intelligence like the President should seriously advance such an argument."[15] Ostensibly, Roosevelt was referring to the men of Standard Oil and other industrialists, but many observers assumed the president was also talking about J. Pierpont Morgan.

In late August 1907, New York City once again attempted to reenter the bond market. New York's municipal government was, the *Chronicle* reported, "face to face with impending disaster." Overdue debts were pressing for payment; existing contracts for municipal improvements in progress added to the debt load; and there was the concern that if the city could not secure the requisite financing, it would be forced to impose layoffs. It would have seemed that the city had nowhere to turn, given the strained conditions in the markets in the summer of 1907.

In financial circles, however, rumors circulated that this time the city had a savior, and the *Chronicle* captured the essence of the insinuations:

> A person commanding large capital in Europe and America, whose name suggests success in such matters, and who has often been sought as especially capable for wisely handling threatened financial dislocation, has been named as being at the head of an important subscription for the [New York City] bonds. The rumor, however, is without authoritative confirmation, though it is quite generally believed. Yet whether true or not, the gods have clearly declared that the loan is to be a pronounced success; that Europe is to have a large share in it, and the public has full faith in that outcome.[16]

In 1907, only one man in the world could wield such financial power and influence. Unable to wait any longer and yet perceiving the strained conditions in the market, the city had approached directly J. Pierpont Morgan for assistance in underwriting an issue of $40 million in tax-exempt bonds priced to yield 4.5 percent.

The rumored news hit Morgan's partners in London quickly; they wrote to Jack: "Is there any truth in the statement that JPM&Co. are going take $40,000,000 New York City 4½ percent bonds? If so, [we] think [we] could place [a] considerable amount here if terms [are] favorable."[17] Jack replied that bids for the issue were due on September 10 and that the company would be unable to fill orders before then. To assist the placement of the New York City bonds, U.S. Treasury Secretary George B. Cortelyou committed to place $40 to $50 million in gold on deposit with banks. In addition, in order to take some of the pressure off the U.S. capital markets, Morgan proposed placing the New York City bonds in Europe.

In the final event, 960 bidders subscribed fully for the issue; the offering was a complete success. Morgan's role in the financing came to light and was reported by the *Chronicle*:

> According to our belief, there is no other man in this country who could have done what he has done on this occasion. He did not want the bonds and only acted as an intermediary. His name, his judgment in financial centres of Europe and his knowledge of the financial markets give him an influence among the capitalists of the world unequaled, probably, by any other individual. Mayor McClellan voices the sentiment of the best circles in this country when he said: "I take this opportunity of thanking you on behalf of the city for the great public spirit you have shown." He saved the city's credit.[18]

The concern of the financial community next turned to deteriorating conditions in the natural resources sector, particularly copper mining. The volume of transactions in raw copper had declined precipitously, as had the price: from 24 cents per pound in January to 18 cents per pound at the end of August. The effect on stock prices of copper mining companies was significant: An index of share prices of these companies fell 41 percent over the first three quarters of 1907.

By October 1, 1907, financial markets in the United States were battered and straining to afford the liquid capital for growth and the ordinary flow of business. The stock market had again declined significantly, and virtually all sectors of business showed deep losses in share values. Interest rates had gyrated upward, reflecting the growing illiquidity of currency and gold in the financial markets. Economists Odell and Weidenmier have noted that, "The New York money market entered the fall of 1907 low on gold reserves and vulnerable to shocks that might otherwise have been temporary in nature."[19] The liquidity strain in the United States was felt elsewhere in the world as well. Financial institutions in

Amsterdam and Hamburg were on the verge of collapse, triggering the sales of U.S. securities. Investigations, litigation, and the rising regulation of an activist president impaired investor confidence in the corporations that had driven the extraordinary economic expansion since 1893. In short, the volatile and falling asset prices in the first three quarters of 1907 manifested deeper problems in the American economy—the dark clouds of the perfect storm were gathering on the near horizon.

Chapter 5

Copper King

There is little doubt that this week's episode in United Copper shares on the New York curb will go into Stock Exchange history as one of the most absurd pieces of speculative jugglery ever attempted.

—*Wall Street Journal*
October 19, 1907

I t is entirely possible that capital market conditions alone in the fall of 1907 would have been sufficient to precipitate a banking panic. Volatile and falling asset prices, battered financial markets, interest rate gyrations, illiquidity, investigations, litigation, and the regulations and pronouncements of an activist U.S. president were certainly enough to strain investor confidence and vex the intestinal fortitude of owners and managers. Yet, even though there had been a "silent crash" of the stock market in March and the Bank of England had imposed restrictions on finance bills over the summer, there were no subsequent shocks to prompt any sudden public response.

But somewhere at the confluence of weak and decentralized bank regulations, deepening liquidity constraints, brazen financial manipulations by bank managers and directors, rampant speculation, and pyramid-like interdependence among banks, there appeared an individual whose actions would inadvertently expose the failures and weaknesses of the entire system. A Brooklyn-born copper mining magnate with the audacity to challenge the most powerful financial interests in the world would provide the spark for an economic conflagration that would consume the American banking system. This man's "speculative jugglery" in the fall of 1907 provided the impetus for events to come, and that story begins amid the wild, untamed western slopes of central Montana.

Fritz Augustus Heinze, adventurous and sociable, stood 5 feet 10 inches tall and weighed some 200 pounds. Described as having "the torso of a Yale halfback, muscles of steel, and a face of ivory whiteness, lighted up with a pair of large blue eyes," Heinze was "a fine musician, a brilliant linguist, and, when necessary, could box like a professional."[1] Widely considered a buccaneer, who sought fortune and fame in the copper mines of Montana, Heinze earned grudging respect on account of his tenacity and cleverness. "Heinze was shrewd and unscrupulous," a contemporary said. "He was considered to be tough in the days when a man to be considered tough had to earn the reputation."[2]

Educated in Germany and at the Columbia School of Mines in New York City, the 20-year-old Heinze moved to Butte, Montana, in 1889 to make his fortune on the "richest hill on earth."[3] With the widespread applications for electric illumination, the ores of the highly conductive copper mineral held the promise of vast riches. In Butte, Heinze lived alone in a small log cabin, and for two years he worked for five dollars a day as a mining engineer for the Boston & Montana Consolidated Copper and Silver Mining Company. In 1891, Heinze conceived the idea for a custom smelting operation to treat the ores of small, independent mining concerns. Around that time, after raising about $300,000 in capital in New York, Heinze established the Montana Ore Purchasing Company (MOPC).[4]

Drawing upon his scientific training, Heinze successfully pioneered advanced methods of mining and smelting, but he ultimately found a more clever way to make money in Butte.[5] After establishing MOPC, Heinze bought mines adjacent to rich copper properties owned by other companies. Once he discovered that their veins of ore surfaced on his property, he threatened litigation under the state's controversial "apex" law. Under this law, a mine's owner was entitled to follow any vein that surfaced ("apexed") on his property, even if it reached beneath neighboring properties. The mine owner could then seek an injunction to prevent his neighbors from continuing to mine any veins that apexed on his land, and he could file suit if they failed to comply. Thus, Heinze, employing as many as 37 lawyers, tied up other mining companies with injunctions and lawsuits; at one point, there were 133 suits pending between Heinze and his opponents.[6]

Heinze's chief opponent during these years was John D. Rockefeller's Standard Oil Company, one of the largest business enterprises in the world. Henry H. Rogers and other principals of Standard Oil saw the promise of consolidating copper mining interests in the West, and they had formed Amalgamated Copper Company in 1898 with a capitalization of $75 million.[7] As it happened, many of the properties Amalgamated purchased were those against which Heinze had already been litigating heavily under the apex theory. Thus, not only did Heinze refuse to join the Amalgamated combination, but he also continued to fight quixotically against Standard Oil in the courts.[8] Not to be bowed by an upstart, Amalgamated brought counterclaims against Heinze amounting to $32.5 million,[9] and H. H. Rogers himself vowed to destroy Heinze, saying, "The flag has never been lowered at 26 Broadway [Standard Oil's headquarters], and I'll drive Heinze out of Montana if it takes ten millions [sic] to do it."[10] It did take millions. In February 1906, after years of litigation and nuisance, Amalgamated Copper bought Heinze out, purchasing most of his active copper interests for $12 million.[11]

Flush with cash from Amalgamated and overflowing with bravado for having bested Standard Oil, the 37-year-old Heinze turned his attentions to Wall Street. Upon moving back to his native New York, Heinze's decision to enter banking was heavily influenced by his association with one of New York's most colorful and notorious Wall Street figures. Charles W. Morse, "a small, compact, portly man, of dark gray suit and neat appearance,"[12] controlled the National Bank of North America and the New Amsterdam National Bank, and was a heavy stockholder in the Mercantile National as well.[13] Variously known as the "Ice King" and the "Steamship King," Morse had long been a conspicuous figure in the financial world, first through the promotion of his American

Ice Company and then with his purchase and consolidation of coastal steamship lines.[14]

Morse, who once said, "Banks mean credit, and credit means power,"[15] proposed to accrue power by gaining control of a network of banks. Given the widespread prohibitions against the establishment of branches at the time, Morse pursued a strategy that was followed by many others in the industry, called "chain-banking." Morse's group would buy a controlling interest in one bank and then use that bank's equity as collateral to borrow money for purchasing shares in other financial institutions. Such a technique would be repeated until Morse and his associates had created a pyramid of interlocking banking relationships.[16]

F. Augustus Heinze had had only a few, small banking interests in Montana previously, but Morse's scheme held the promise of great wealth and the opportunity for becoming a major player in New York's financial circles. Through Morse's influence, Heinze used a portion of his buyout money from Amalgamated to purchase the Mercantile National Bank in New York, becoming its president in February 1907.[17] Thereafter, Heinze joined Morse as a director in a chain of other financial institutions that included at least six national banks, 10 or 12 state banks, five or six trust companies, and four insurance concerns.* Heinze, who still had a number of properties in Nevada, California, Mexico, and elsewhere, consolidated his remaining mining interests within a holding company he had previously incorporated in 1902 for tax reasons, called United Copper Company.[18] F. Augustus and his two brothers, Otto and Arthur, were each major stockholders and directors of this firm.

Heinze also established a direct presence on Wall Street by purchasing a $96,000 seat on the New York Stock Exchange for his brothers, Otto and Arthur, creating the brokerage house of Otto C. Heinze & Company.[19] In fact, that firm occupied offices directly across the hall from the United Copper Company at 42 Broadway—both firms used the

---

* Heinze, had interests in the Mercantile National Bank, Consolidated National Bank, Northern National Bank, Mechanics and Traders Bank, State Savings Bank of Montana, Utah National Bank of Salt Lake City, Merchants' Exchange National, Bank of Discount, Riverside Bank, Carnegie Trust Company, Empire Trust Company, Interboro Trust Company, Hudson Trust Company, Aetna Indemnity Company of Hartford, Cosmopolitan Fire Insurance Company, Title & Guarantee Company of Rochester, and Provident Savings Life Assurance Society.

same entrance and even split the cost of the rent.[20] Using Otto C. Heinze & Company as their primary agent on Wall Street, the Heinze brothers then entered into a speculative stock pool with Charles W. Morse, in which 30,000 shares of United Copper Company stock were exchanged for shares of comparable value in Morse's Knickerbocker Ice Company. During the summer and early fall of 1907, as money rates tightened and as equity prices fell broadly, the brothers became concerned about their holdings in United Copper, whose stock had been used to secure their positions in numerous banking concerns. In an attempt to support the price of their United Copper Company shares, the Heinzes began purchasing large quantities of the company's stock and placing them on margin with as many as 20 brokerage houses on Wall Street. A dangerous game was afoot.[21]

Chapter 6

The Corner and the Squeeze

Never has there been such wild scenes on the Curb, so say the oldest veterans of the outside market.

—*Wall Street Journal*
October 17, 1907

On Wednesday, October 9, 1907, Otto Heinze, who was monitoring the activity in the Heinze-Morse stock pool, conducted a precise audit of all United Copper Company shares.[1] To his great surprise, he discovered that some 450,000 shares were trading in the market—*25,000 shares in excess of those in existence!*[2] Otto surmised that this was only possible if certain securities brokers were secretly loaning out their shares of United Copper to traders who wanted to speculate in the stock. Those traders, he believed, were then selling the borrowed shares at prevailing prices in the expectation that the prices of those shares would fall. If United Copper prices did fall, then when the traders were called upon to return the borrowed shares they could repurchase them at lower prices and pocket the difference.*

Otto Heinze believed, however, that he and his brothers owned the majority of United Copper shares, including many of those that had been secretly loaned to the short sellers. If the Heinzes "called in" those loaned shares, then the "shorts" would be squeezed. Basically, the Heinzes could force the short sellers to scramble to find United Copper on the market; finding none available, they would either have to buy at inflated prices or be forced to settle directly with the Heinzes. This technique, sometimes known as a "bear squeeze," could succeed only if the Heinzes truly owned the majority of actively traded shares. In order to execute this move, the Heinzes would first need to purchase aggressively any remaining shares of United Copper. This would result in driving up the stock price further still, thereby attracting even more short sellers to the security. Once the Heinzes had achieved the necessary controlling interest, or "corner," in United Copper, they could then issue the call for all their outstanding stock and initiate the squeeze.[3]

Excited by the prospect of the squeeze, Otto approached his brother, Fritz Augustus, on Thursday, October 10, for help (his other brother, Arthur P. Heinze, was traveling in Europe). Augustus was aware that over the past several months, in an ongoing effort to support United Copper's price, they had been buying the company's shares through brokerage houses in New York, Philadelphia, and Boston. They had paid for most of these purchases by borrowing money from brokers, in a method called buying *on margin*. As such, the securities they purchased served as collateral for the loans and the certificates remained in the brokers' possession. Thus, it was indeed possible for the brokers to have lent those same shares to short sellers. By the fall of 1907, the Heinzes had become indebted to their brokers for $2 million for these margin purchases, and as the market at large had weakened there were increasing calls for more money from the Heinzes. If the Heinzes initiated the squeeze by calling in their shares, these brokers would have to be paid the full amount for the cost of these shares immediately.[4]

---

* Such a trading maneuver, known as a *short sale,* is often used when a security or market is considered to be overpriced.

Otto believed that in order to carry out the scheme he would need at least $1.5 million (he would make up the remaining difference for his margin debts from squeezing the shorts). When he approached his brother on October 10, however, Augustus denied Otto's request, saying that he lacked the money and could not jeopardize his position as president of the Mercantile National Bank. Over the past four months, Augustus revealed, there had been a "silent run"* on his bank and depositors had quietly withdrawn $4 million. Augustus had already called in the Mercantile's outstanding loans and thus could not make any substantial advances to his brother.[5]

Yet, in an apparent effort to facilitate the maneuver, Augustus arranged a meeting for himself and Otto with Charles W. Morse and Charles T. Barney. Barney was the president of the Knickerbocker Trust Company, the third largest in the city, and he had been involved in various Morse schemes. They met at Barney's Fifth Avenue home, where Morse told the Heinzes that they were *wrong*. The squeeze would require far more than $1.5 million—perhaps as much as $3 million.[6] All three men rebuffed Otto. Meanwhile, the margin calls from brokers accelerated, and Otto feared the cash reserves of his own firm would be wiped out.

The stock of United Copper Company was not listed on the New York Stock Exchange. Rather, it was traded among a crowd of brokers literally trading "on the curb" outside the Exchange building on Broad Street in Manhattan. On Saturday morning, October 12, during a short day of trading on the Curb, United Copper shares opened at 45$\frac{1}{2}$. During the day's two hours of trading it sold down to 37$\frac{3}{4}$, and it appeared to the Heinzes that again the shorts were active in the stock.[7] Convinced the time was right, on Sunday night Otto Heinze had determined to engineer the corner and the resultant squeeze by himself. He called a meeting with Philip Kleeberg, a partner in the stock exchange firm of Gross & Kleeberg, and issued two instructions. First, he ordered the

---

* Heinze's choice of words is interesting and unusual. Then and now, sophisticated and well-informed depositors monitor the condition of banks very carefully; they will be the first to withdraw funds from a bank because they gain the insight about deteriorating conditions first. The less-informed depositors will follow, perhaps having observed the actions of the sophisticates. The actions of the sophisticated depositors speaks volumes. To the extent that the departing depositors were the sophisticates, Heinze might more aptly have called it a "screaming run."

broker to purchase 6,000 shares of United Copper stock at ascending prices on Monday, hoping to force the shorts to settle. Second, he would issue a call for all the Heinze-owned United Copper certificates that had been out on loan in order to punish the brokers who had apparently been providing them to short sellers.

On Monday morning, the stock of United Copper opened quietly, with a few sales at 37⅞, and then one at 39. Observers reported that within a few minutes of the opening a broker representing a well-known stock exchange house entered the crowd excitedly and began bidding up the stock and asking for offers on 5,000 shares. Within 15 minutes the price rose in rapid increments: 100 shares at 40, 100 at 41, 100 at 49⅞, 1,000 shares at 51, 100 at 52, 100 at 53, 700 at 57, 1,000 at 59, 1,000 at 60.[8] By 10:50 A.M. the first advance was over, the stock having risen nearly $23 above the previous day's close. Four thousand shares had been traded in.[9]

"Traders noticed that there was very little anxiety on the part of those in the United Copper group to take real stock at the higher prices," the New York Times reported. "The bid and asked quotations were kept 2 or 3 points apart, and those who had stock to sell found that to get it off their hands they had to throw it out at the bid price or find the bidders dropping from the market. These circumstances, together with the fact that United Copper had been almost impossible to borrow, and as therefore avoided by short sellers, were taken by curb traders as indicating deliberate bidding up of the stock rather than a squeeze of shorts."[10] After the initial flurry on Monday morning, "which occurred so rapidly that the brokers were not able to get in touch with their clients," the stock dropped almost immediately and remained between 50 and 53 for the balance of the day's session, closing at 52⅞. The total shares traded for the day was 18,200, and the highest bid quoted was $62½.[11]

Meanwhile, thousands of stock certificates were arriving at the offices of Otto Heinze & Company for which payment of $630,000 was due. By the rules of the Exchange, the Heinzes were obliged to pay for these shares in cash by 2:15 P.M. that day.[12] Otto applied once again to his brother, Augustus, for a loan to cover the cost of the incoming securities. The Heinzes calculated that since United Copper was trading around $60, to secure the loan they would need only about one third the value of the securities, which would serve as collateral, in order to repay the brokers that day. This time Augustus consented, and he arranged for a loan from his Mercantile National Bank to cover any of the checks written against the Otto Heinze & Company's account.[13] With the market primed, the shorts scurrying to cover, and cash available, Otto believed the time for the squeeze had finally arrived.

On Tuesday, October 15, Otto Heinze put in motion the final phase of his plan, which the *Chicago Daily Tribune* captured, as follows:

> Twenty stock exchange houses were carrying United Copper stock at the direction of the managers of the corner. It was decided to serve notices on these to deliver their stock at the earliest possible time, which was 2 o'clock Tuesday afternoon, and, it was said, it was undoubtedly the belief of the managers of the corner that they would find many of these houses bare of stock, and expected the brokers to default, in part, in their deliveries. In this event the Heinze brokers could buy in the stock under the rules and force the delinquents to pay the difference between the purchase price and the price at which the stock was carried for the Heinze brokers on the particular firms' books.[14]

United Copper opened Tuesday morning at 50, and trading in the stock remained mostly subdued during the morning session with only a few hundred shares traded in.[15] Responding to the call issued by Heinze, however, and much to his surprise, every one of the 20 brokers produced the stock that had been called.[16] There were no defaults, and United Copper stock was plentiful on the market. *Heinze had been wrong.* In fact, the brokers were producing so much stock that Heinze was eventually forced to refuse delivery. On this news, the stock briefly rose to 59 in heavy trading. Then came the final break. "Thousands of shares began to appear as fast as the mails could carry them from points where news of Monday's rise had penetrated," the *New York Times* reported. "Gross & Kleeberg were unable to stem the flood and the market went to pieces."[17] The brokers, unable to transfer their shares to the Heinzes, had thrown all their shares on the market, and the corner attempt was crushed. Without any warning, the stock broke amid wild scenes. In a few minutes the price crumpled to 50, then to 45, and still to 36, which was the last sale of the day. At the market close the stock was offered at

38 with no bid, and one man rushed into the crowd to make a nominal bid of 25.[18]

The late-day slide in United Copper was stunning. "It is a long time since the Curb has seen anything of the like," the *Wall Street Journal* reported. "In fact, old-timers on the Curb say that they have never seen anything quite like it before."[19] The slide, however, was far from over. After closing at 36 on Tuesday, United Copper opened Wednesday morning with a sale at 30. Scarcely had this sale been recorded on the reporters' books when the stock was offered down to 20 within three minutes of the opening gong. On the way down, a block of 500 shares was traded in, and for a while there was a lull and the stock hovered around 25. This calm lasted about an hour when it started down again. Then came a sale at 18. During the last hour came the grand finale, "with the crowd of brokers rushing up and down the Street shouting and fighting," as the common stock of United Copper Company crashed down to $10 a share.[20] At one point, there were as many as five different simultaneous quotations. The arbitrage business in the stock was practically at a standstill. "Never has there been such wild

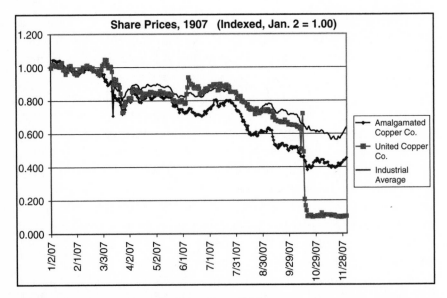

Figure 6.1 United Copper share prices, 1907.
SOURCE: Authors' figure based on price quotations in the *Wall Street Journal*, 1907.

scenes on the Curb, so say the oldest veterans of the outside market," the *Journal* reported.[21]

"Rumors of all kinds were flying round the Curb," the *New York Times* said. "Brokers demanded Stock Exchange names of their best friends and the houses had to be of the best. Traders took a hand, but after one or two had taken quick, but huge, losses they eschewed the United crowd, seeing that it was not the place for even a moderately big trader."[22] With apparently unlimited supplies of the stock at hand and no shorts in sight, the common stock price had declined 50 points in three days; the price of United Copper's preferred had also declined 50 points over two days. The last sale for the common on Wednesday was recorded at 15 (see Figure 6.1). Dealings on the day for the common amounted to 6,800 shares.[23] After the market closed, bankers held conferences across Wall Street and throughout the city trying to assess the fallout.[24]

Chapter 7

Falling Dominoes

... the ramifications of the failure and the possible consequences of the utter collapse of United Copper had a disastrous effect on Stock Exchange sentiment ...

—New York Times
October 17, 1907

The first casualty of the failed corner attempt was Gross & Kleeberg, the brokerage house Otto Heinze had asked to initiate the corner. On Wednesday afternoon, October 16, Gross & Kleeberg closed its doors and suspended all trading after executing a major sell-off of all its United Copper shares. Having been instructed by Otto C. Heinze & Company to purchase 6,000 shares of United Copper, Gross & Kleeberg later found the Heinzes unwilling to pay for them. The brokerage had, in fact, been the most active buyer in United Copper on the rise that began on Monday when the stock went from 39 to 60. When the Heinzes refused to pay for the shares, Gross & Kleeberg was forced to sell off its United Copper holdings at a major loss on Wednesday, driving the price momentarily to $10 a share.[1]

Gross & Kleeberg explained their situation in a letter to the Governors of the Stock Exchange:

> Dear Sir: On Monday, the 14th, by direction of the firm of Otto Heinze & Co., members of the Exchange, we purchased and received for the account of said firm 3,202 shares of United Copper common and preferred, which we tendered them on Tuesday, Oct. 15, 1907, and demanded payment therefore, which payment was refused by them. Inasmuch, therefore, as they failed to comply with their contract, we were obliged to announce our suspension to the Exchange yesterday.[2]

"While the failed firm [Gross & Kleeberg] has not been for many months active on the Stock Exchange," the New York Times later reported, "the ramifications of the failure and the possible consequences of the utter collapse of United Copper had a disastrous effect on Stock Exchange sentiment, which had begun the day with a hopeful attitude toward the market generally."[3] It was estimated that the United Copper purchases had cost Gross & Kleeberg alone some $300,000. "Our principals laid down on us," said Philip Gross in explaining the failure, "that is all there is to it. Everybody knows who those principals are."[4] Another representative of the brokerage, putting it more bluntly, said that Gross & Kleeberg failed because "the firm bought United Copper for the Heinze people, who refused to receive it."[5] The brokerage house, established in December 1904, was immediately placed in the hands of an assignee, and a claim was filed against Otto Heinze & Company.[6] These actions quelled some fears in financial circles, but there was a sense of foreboding that the commitments in United Copper that had brought disaster to one house might extend elsewhere.[7]

As news of the failed corner spread, attention on Wall Street turned to Otto Heinze's more famous brother, Augustus. Not only was Augustus well known and flamboyant, but he also held a controlling interest in United Copper Company and thus stood to gain personally from any attempted squeeze. Moreover, although it was not widely known at the time, Augustus had personally guaranteed the loans for Otto Heinze & Company through the Mercantile National Bank, of which he was both president and a director. Nonetheless, Augustus Heinze and his associates publicly maintained that he had had nothing to do with the ill-fated corner in United Copper stock. They further insisted that Otto

Heinze had managed the attempted corner without consultation with his brother Augustus.[8] "F. Augustus Heinze," the *Wall Street Journal* reported, "is in the dark regarding the affairs of his brother's firm, and in order to ascertain the exact condition he has retained special counsel and auditors."[9]

Throughout the day on Wednesday, October 16, as United Copper came crashing down, Augustus Heinze was seen going about the financial district in consultation with various banking interests. "Mr. Heinze was in conference with Mr. Morse at the latter's office in the National Bank of North America early in the afternoon. Talk of a breach between Morse and Heinze was freely heard yesterday," the *New York Times* said "Friends of Mr. Morse, however, made it plain yesterday, as they have in the past, that Mr. Morse had not been interested in the Heinze ventures."[10] Augustus convened a conference on Wednesday with his brother and several associates in the offices of Otto Heinze & Company that lasted until late in the day.[11]

At 1 P.M. on Thursday, October 17, the next domino fell. The Exchange announced the official suspension of Otto Heinze & Company for failure to meet its financial obligations. Until Wednesday afternoon the firm had given assurances that they would pay their debts, especially those with Gross & Kleeberg.[12] Heinze offered to pay Gross & Kleeberg $100,000, representing a third of its total indebtedness, but such an offer had come too late.[13] For other creditors, the firm made a tentative offer of a 10 percent cash settlement, and the balance in three-, six-, and nine-month notes. However, when Gross & Kleeberg announced its suspension, all settlement attempts were abandoned, and several brokers sold off their Heinze accounts.[14] Announcing the news, a lawyer for the Heinze firm issued the following statement:

> The firm of Otto C. Heinze & Co. feels itself perfectly solvent and will meet and pay all its just and legal obligations in full. It, however, refuses to pay obligations that it does not consider legal or just until a proper adjudication of the matter has been made. Rather than submit to such unjust demands it prefers to permit itself to temporarily be suspended from the privileges of the Stock Exchange.[15]

Upon hearing news of the latest suspension, brokers literally lined up outside the firm's offices waiting impatiently for their checks. "Some of the brokers," the *Wall Street Journal* reported, "after waiting several hours shoved their accounts with certificates over the transom of the Heinze offices, while others kicked at the doors and sought for recognition which was not forthcoming."[16] That same day, the firm announced that Arthur P. Heinze, the youngest of the three Heinze brothers, had been dismissed from the firm because he had incurred individual liabilities of nearly $1 million.[17] Though Arthur Heinze had been in France during the wild gyrations in United Copper of the preceding days, it was reported there were cable messages from him ordering purchases of the stock.[18]

The third domino fell far from the canyons of Wall Street. On the very day the Governors of the Exchange shuttered Otto Heinze & Company, the State Savings Bank of Butte, Montana, announced its insolvency.[19] The incident would hardly have attracted notice, but Augustus Heinze owned this small savings institution and it served as a correspondent bank for the Mercantile National in New York. The bank, which had 6,000 depositors and was the largest savings bank in the state of Montana, had funds on deposit with the Mercantile and loans outstanding to Heinze interests amounting to nearly $1 million; the bank was also holding United Copper Company stock as collateral for some of its loans.[20] Most of the bank's depositors were small wage earners and, according to the bank's officers, its closure had been prompted by fears of a major run. The bank, which had been purchased by Augustus Heinze in 1905, issued a notice on Thursday, October 17:

> Because of unsolid conditions and rumors that cannot be verified, that may cause unusual demands by depositors, and owing to the shortage of currency and inability to secure additional currency immediately to pay demands which may be made, the management has deemed it advisable in the interest of all depositors to suspend for the time being. The bank is insolvent.[21]

Apparently, the failed corner on United Copper, the suspensions of Gross & Kleeberg and Otto Heinze & Co., and the insolvency of the Butte State Savings Bank—all of which were connected with Augustus Heinze—were too much for the directors of the Mercantile National Bank to bear. "It was generally understood that, owing to the close connections between President Heinze and the failed brokerage house," the

Times said, "the situation would be extremely unpleasant for the Mercantile Bank."[22] After a meeting of the bank's directors on Wednesday that lasted until after midnight, the controlling interests of the Mercantile assembled at 11 A.M. on Thursday, October 17, to announce the resignation of Augustus Heinze as president of the bank.[23] In a further attempt to allay concerns about the bank's management, an offer for the presidency of the Mercantile was extended to William Ridgely, the Controller of the Currency of the U.S. Treasury.[24] On Thursday afternoon, Augustus made the following statement regarding his "voluntary" resignation:

> In view of the difficulties in which my brother's firm finds itself, I have determined that it is proper that I should give liberally of my time in assisting them to straighten out their affairs. In aid of this I have, after consulting with my fellow-Directors of the bank and my personal friends, and consulting as well my own personal interests as a large stockholder of the bank, this day resigned as its President, remaining, however, as a Director, and have joined with my fellow-Directors in a request that Mr. Ridgely accept the place made vacant by my resignation.[25]

Friends of Heinze continued to support the Copper King, saying, "He did not pretend to have knowledge of the banking business," and he "meant rather to learn the business as president of the Mercantile than personally to direct its operations."[26] According to the bank's quarterly report in April, the bank showed gross deposits of $19,884,000; by Saturday, October 12, *prior to* the failed corner in United Copper, the bank's deposits had declined 42 percent to $11,569,000.[27] In the next few days the situation would grow much worse, and the interconnected nature of the relationships among the nation's financial institutions would only enable the contagion to spread.

Chapter 8

Clearing House

*. . . the action of the Clearing House on Saturday and Sunday had
eliminated practically all elements of danger from the banking situation.*

—*Wall Street Journal*
October 22, 1907

U nlike most European countries, the United States did not have
a central bank to manage its national money supply. Ever since
President Andrew Jackson had withdrawn the charter for the
Bank of the United States in 1837, the prevailing political sentiment
had reflected a distrust of the economic and political power of banking
institutions and sought to promote a financial system consisting of small,
widely dispersed banks. In 1907 three types of banks were in operation:
national banks, which were authorized to receive federal deposits and
issue government-licensed currency; state banks, which were chartered
by state legislatures; and private banks, which ranged from international
houses, such as J. P. Morgan & Company and Kuhn, Loeb, to immigrant
bankers who ran their businesses out of grocery stores and saloons.

State-chartered banks had proliferated widely in the United States,
and by 1890 they held 57 percent of all commercial bank deposits.[1] At

the end of the nineteenth century, savings bank deposits averaged about a third of all bank deposits. Trust companies, a type of savings bank for the wealthy, invested in long-term assets and paid higher interest rates than commercial or savings banks; in 1906 the United States had approximately 1,000 trust companies.[2] Private banks, especially immigrant banks, provided a wide range of services to their customers; besides financial services such as savings, loans, credit, and exchanging money, immigrant bankers also transferred money abroad, sold steamship and train tickets, read and wrote letters for illiterate or non-English-speaking customers, and helped people find jobs.

As a means of enhancing returns many banks regularly placed a percentage of their reserves on deposit with other financial institutions. Regulations, however, required rural banks to hold reserves equal to 15 percent of their deposits; 40 percent of these reserves had to be held in cash, but the balance could be placed on deposit at "reserve city" banks, where the reserves could earn interest. These reserve city banks had to hold 25 percent of their deposits in reserve and half of those reserves in cash; these banks, in turn, could place their noncash reserves on deposit with banks at major money centers, such as New York. However, many of the banks in New York and other major financial cities were heavily involved in the securities markets, particularly in railroad underwritings. Therefore, instability in securities prices could potentially prompt anxiety among depositors. If that anxiety precipitated a "run on the bank," an abrupt systemwide contraction could result. Interior banks were thus tightly coupled to financial institutions and securities markets in the nation's money centers, making them (and the system) vulnerable to a crisis.

Since the Depression of the 1890s, in which thousands of banks had failed, the American banking industry had begun to stabilize, but it still suffered from volatility. In 1903 there had been 52 bank failures or suspensions, but that number jumped to 125 failures in 1904, most of them by state or private banks. In 1905, 80 banks experienced suspensions, while in 1906 there were only 53 bank failures, again most of them state banks (34 state banks, 13 private banks, and 6 national banks).[3] When a bank failed, its depositors were out of luck; there was no state or federal deposit insurance. While there was no central bank to give liquidity to the financial system in periods of strain, the U.S. Treasury, through a network of subtreasuries, would often shift gold and currency to different regions and deposit the funds in banks that would then relend the funds to debtors. Occasionally, the Treasury would make advance payments of principal and interest on government bonds as an alternative means of injecting liquidity into the financial system.

By the early 1900s, the deficiencies of this system were manifest. First, many contemporary critics charged that the currency of the United States was "inelastic," meaning that the volume outstanding could not adjust easily to meet variations in economic cycles, bumper crops, or shocks. Second, no single regulatory agency monitored monetary conditions or the overall stability of the financial system as a basis for promoting disciplined lending. Third, the mechanism by which banks paid cash against checks (called "clearing") was accomplished only through voluntary associations among banks in certain cities called "clearing houses."

In New York City and other major financial centers, many traditional banks had formed associations through which its members would pay cash, or "clear," in exchange for any checks submitted by other member banks. The association, or clearing house, was usually managed by one of the leading member banks and it would serve as a lender of last resort in the event of any financial emergencies. In effect, the clearing houses would essentially pool the risk that any individual member would not be able to honor individual checks. In such cases, the clearing house would issue "clearing house certificates," a kind of currency backed by all members of the clearing house. There was no uniformity to clearing house organizations and practices; in some geographic areas, no clearing houses existed at all.

Those closest to the financial system saw these difficulties and their attendant risks most clearly. On January 4, 1906, with unusual clairvoyance, Jacob Schiff, senior partner of the house of Kuhn, Loeb & Company (J. P. Morgan's archrival), gave a speech to the New York Chamber of Commerce in which he declared presciently, "the money market conditions which had prevailed the previous sixty days are a disgrace to the country, and that unless our currency system was reformed a panic would sooner or later result compared with which all previous panics would seem as child's play."[4]

In the context of this system, then, anxieties about the solvency of the Mercantile National Bank gripped uneasy depositors and investors alike, prompting a run on the bank. With nowhere else to turn, Augustus

Heinze sought the assistance of the New York Clearing House (NYCH). The NYCH, a consortium of banks in New York City, of which the Mercantile National was a member, convened on Thursday, October 17, 1907, to discuss the events of the past few days, specifically the Mercantile's affairs and the activities related to United Copper. The NYCH announced it would stand by the Mercantile and see it through any troubles in the coming days—as long as the books were sound. The committee then went directly to the Mercantile's offices in the Western Union Building to review its books. The detailed review went late into the night while practically all the Mercantile's staff remained on hand.[5] As one of the bankers present expressed it, "We went through it like a dose of salts."[6] At midnight, the NYCH committee reported that the Mercantile's capital was intact and that the bank would be open for business on Friday morning.[7] In a statement the NYCH said, ". . . the bank was perfectly solvent and able to meet all its indebtedness. The capital of $3,000,000 is intact and with a large surplus."[8] This assessment assumed, of course, that the run would cease.

The bank consortium's decision to aid the Mercantile, however, did not come without strings. A group of nine member banks each agreed to extend $200,000 to meet the Mercantile's debit obligations at the NYCH. But, as a condition for assistance, the NYCH demanded the resignation of all directors of the Mercantile. This move was intended to calm depositors and to give a new bank president a free hand in reorganizing the bank's management. The offer to Controller Ridgely was still outstanding, though he had visited the Mercantile at midday.[9] "The clearing house committee minimized consequent fears," the *Chicago Daily Tribune* reported, "by declaring that the condition of the banks generally was satisfactory, though the qualification was made that in some instances changes in the directorates of other banks might be necessitated. It was insisted that there was nothing alarming in the local banking situation."[10] A representative of the NYCH said reassuringly, "The situation is now under control, and no untoward developments are looked for."[11]

Despite the actions and assurances of the NYCH, the intensity of the run on the Mercantile continued unabated, and fears of unforeseen runs on other banks were growing. On Saturday, October 19, the Mercantile showed another big debit balance in its account at the NYCH. The debit amounted to a stunning $1,137,000, indicating that depositors' with-drawals were running far in excess of the bank's reserves. The Mercantile also reportedly had only $1,745,000 in cash balances, 15.4 percent of its deposits, far less than the 25 percent required by banking law and NYCH rules. More alarmingly, the Mercantile's total debit balances at the NYCH over the previous three days had been $2,400,000, 20 per-cent of its total deposits. It was estimated that at this rate the bank's debit balances would exhaust its deposits in 10 days. Other banks with con-nections to the Mercantile were showing even poorer reserve positions, between 4 percent and 5 percent. Notably, a few of the larger banks un-affiliated with Heinze interests showed heavy increases in their reserves, ranging between 29 percent and 40 percent, indicating that depositors were shifting their accounts to more well-established institutions.[12]

At the opening of the business day on Saturday, October 19, the NYCH met again to consider the banking situation and the exigencies of the Mercantile. It was again agreed to make up the balance of any debits that the Mercantile was unable to pay, although the NYCH made no commitments to address further debit balances in the future. Frankly, the NYCH's member banks did not intend to extend aid to Heinze's Mercantile indefinitely. But as the day wore on, news for the Mercantile only worsened. First, the officers of the Mercantile informed several banks for which it previously provided clearing services that it could no longer do so.[13] Then, in the early afternoon, William Ridgely, Controller of the Currency, announced that he had refused the presidency of the Mercantile National. Finally, the NYCH learned that the Heinzes' loans from the Mercantile had reached a very large, but undisclosed, total.[14]

Meanwhile, Augustus Heinze continued a public defense of his situ-ation, issuing statements from his residence at the Waldorf Hotel, across the street from the offices of Otto Heinze & Company and United Copper Company. He made repeated denials that the clearing house was even assisting his bank, cynically accusing its members of trying to profit from his difficulties, and he asserted his continued control of the Mercantile:

I have not sold a share of my stock and am still in control of the Mercantile Bank. The whole miserable situation is the result of the action of the Clearing House committee. Instead of coming out with a statement saying that the bank was entirely solvent, they made a lot of remarks about the impairment of surplus and started a run on the bank in the hope of attracting deposits to their institutions.[15]

The NYCH, however, had by this time begun to turn its attentions to other banking institutions. It had become clear that over the next two days the situation would extend beyond the Mercantile. Depositors were already beginning to withdraw funds from the banks owned by a man with close Heinze associations: Charles W. Morse.

On Saturday, the NYCH arranged for inspections of two banks controlled by Morse: the National Bank of North America and the New Amsterdam National. The National Bank of North America showed $15,011,600 in loans and $13,063,200 in deposits; its directors included such leading figures as William T. Havemeyer of the American Sugar Refining Company and Charles M. Schwab of U.S. Steel, as well as Charles W. Morse, and Charles T. Barney. The New Amsterdam Bank had $4,447,400 in deposits and $4,495,600 in loans, and it was considered one of the most important of New York's uptown banks. The NYCH committee conducted the inspections all day and worked until late in the night.[16]

By Sunday, the NYCH had decided to take its most drastic measure to date. It ordered the immediate elimination of Augustus Heinze and Charles W. Morse from all banking interests in New York City. The action was both swift and sweeping. Morse resigned from the National Bank of North America, of which he was a vice president and director; the New Amsterdam National Bank; the Garfield National Bank; the Fourteenth Street Bank; the New York Produce Exchange Bank; and two other financial institutions in his hometown of Bath, Maine.[17] Heinze, who had already stepped down from the Mercantile, was likewise removed from at least eight banks and two trust companies. The committee also insisted that Morse and Heinze had to repay their loans to their respective banks and further ruled that any evidence of "chain-banking" would disqualify such banks or bankers from the NYCH. Thereupon, the NYCH announced its willingness to lend aid to any banks that had been under suspicion, having found them to be solvent. It was reported, however, that the Mercantile would undergo a process of slow liquidation.[18]

On Monday, October 21, massive debit balances appeared at the NYCH for several Heinze and Morse banks. On that morning, the debits for Heinze's Mercantile National Bank and Mechanics and Traders

Bank were, respectively, $1,903,000 and $430,000; debits for Morse's National Bank of North America and New Amsterdam National Bank were, respectively, $850,000 and $200,000. Altogether, the NYCH had disbursed $2.5 million in aid since the Mercantile's troubles began; the balance for the ongoing deficits had been covered by the bank's deposits or by calls on the banks' outstanding loans.[19] The National Bank of North America, for instance, started the day with $1,400,000 in cash to meet the demands of its depositors. According to one report, "Large heaps of gold were piled up on the counter in full view of any depositors who entered the bank." This bank repaid its debt at the NYCH from its own reserves and by collecting $1,750,000 from called loans.[20]

Heinze's personal troubles had, of course, only begun. Claims against his brother's brokerage house were estimated to be $2 million,[21] and lawyers for Gross & Kleeberg and other Wall Street firms had filed a petition to declare involuntary bankruptcy for Otto Heinze & Company. At noon on Monday, the Heinze firm called a meeting of its creditors and issued a statement:

> We regret to say that we find our affairs so much more than we had anticipated at first that we have been unable, with the greatest effort, to get them into shape to present them at the meeting called this day, and we are therefore obliged to ask you to meet us at a day later in the week, of which you will be duly notified.[22]

The claims against Otto Heinze & Company alleged that the Heinzes made preferential payments to the Mercantile National Bank of $2 million in order to cover the personal debts of Arthur P. Heinze and F. Augustus Heinze. The filing further sought an injunction restraining the disposition of any further assets by the firm.[23]

The rapid intervention of the NYCH during the preceding days seemed to mitigate the likelihood of a full-blown banking panic. Sounding an optimistic tone on Monday morning, October 21, the *Wall Street Journal* said that "the action of the Clearing House on Saturday and Sunday had eliminated practically all elements of danger from the banking situation."[24] The interventions of the NYCH and the immediate consequences for Heinze and Morse should have been sufficient to restore public confidence. Now, scarcely a year after his triumph over Amalgamated Copper and Standard Oil, Augustus Heinze was ruined, and both he and Charles W. Morse had been ejected from the financial system.

Had Heinze and Morse been merely aggressive speculators, their personal reversals would have prompted no more than the passing interest of traders on the Curb. But investors and depositors understood the tight linkages among Heinze, Morse, and banking concerns throughout the nation's financial capital. Their individual failures had already toppled two brokerages and had infected at least three national banks—all in the span of a week! But on Monday, October 21, the public would also learn that Charles T. Barney, the respectable president of the Knickerbocker Trust Company, was an associate of Charles Morse and Augustus Heinze, and that he may have been involved in their schemes. Should the Knickerbocker fall, its failure would signal to the public that something more endemic was threatening the financial system. By day's end, widespread fear and uncertainty would spread like a brush fire.

Chapter 9

Knickerbocker

Outwardly and according to its balance sheet, the [Knickerbocker] Trust Company was flourishing.

—Herbert L. Satterlee
J. P. Morgan's cousin and biographer[1]

The Knickerbocker Trust Company once stood at the northwest corner of Fifth Avenue and Thirty-fourth Street, the line of demarcation between New York's downtown business district and its uptown residential grandeur.[2,3] On the opposite corner from the Knickerbocker towered the red sandstone palace of the Waldorf-Astoria, New York's most fashionable and grand hotel, placing the Knickerbocker literally in the shadow of the city's social, business, and political hub. As such, the Knickerbocker's designers hoped the building itself would be commensurate with its genteel surroundings. Covered in Vermont marble and fronted by four 17-ton Corinthian columns, the Knickerbocker presented, according to a contemporary reviewer, "a beautiful example of Grecian architecture, treated in the most refined way with every provision known to modern building construction for meeting the demands of the company and the service of its patrons. The structure must be considered a distinct addition to the architectural features of that part of the city."[4]

The Knickerbocker's architects, McKim, Mead & White, had designed an elegant and functional four-story structure that was intended to convey the institution's strength and sobriety. Inside its main gates, white Norwegian marble contrasted brilliantly with interior bronze detailing and mahogany woodwork. The central banking room reached nearly three stories high and had eight adjoining rooms for ancillary banking activities. An alternate entrance on Thirty-fourth Street led to second, third, and fourth floors, each with 5,000 square feet of floor space and four executive offices. In the basement, the massive safety deposit vault contained 2,000 boxes, and its outer vault door weighed nearly nine tons—its hinges alone were 3,700 pounds! Elsewhere in the building was a 6,000-square-foot employee dining hall with a full kitchen.[5]

The Knickerbocker building thus captured the prevailing ethos of early twentieth-century bank construction, as described in *Banker*, a contemporary industry periodical:

> [T]he public expects a bank or trust company to occupy well-furnished quarters, such that the cost of good equipment is more than repaid in advertising value. The lobby should be provided with all possible conveniences for customers, including writing desks supplied with good ink, clean pens and blotters, comfortable chairs, etc. The larger companies often provide separate reading and lounging rooms for customers, with current newspapers and magazines, writing desks and other conveniences, and other committee-rooms for the use of customers who wish to meet or arrange details of business. In many cases there are special quarters for women, equipped with numerous conveniences, and in charge of a matron who looks after the comfort of patrons.[6]

As a trust company, the Knickerbocker represented a relatively new form of financial intermediary. Originally organized in the late nineteenth century to handle various financial tasks for private estates and corporations, the sphere of activity for trust companies gradually expanded to offer services little different from those of traditional banks. As historian Vincent Carosso has explained:

> Beginning in the 1890s, trust companies took on most of the functions of both commercial and private banks. They accepted deposits;

made loans; participated extensively in reorganizing railroads and consolidating industrial corporations; acted as trustees, underwriters, and distributors of new securities; and served as the depositories of stocks, bonds, and titles. Corporations regularly appointed them as registrars or fiscal and transfer agents. Very often they also owned and managed real estate.[7]

Despite their functional similarities to national and state banks, trust companies were generally less well regulated. They were permitted, for instance, to hold a wider variety of assets; unlike national banks, trust companies could own stock equity directly. Also, unique among large financial institutions, trusts were not required to hold reserves against deposits before 1906; in that year, New York State required that trusts hold 15 percent of deposits as reserves, though only a third of the reserves had to be held in cash. This meant that trust companies could earn a higher return on their assets compared to banks, and thus, could pay higher interest rates. Accordingly, the higher interest rates attracted deposits, and the trust companies grew rapidly. In 1906, the assets of all trust companies in New York City, approximated the assets of all national banks, and exceeded the assets of all state banks. According to economists Moen and Tallman, "In the ten years ending in 1907, trust company assets in New York State had grown 244 percent (from $396.7 million to $1.364 billion) in comparison to 97 percent (from $915.2 million to $1.8 billion) for those of national banks, and 82 percent (from $297 million to $541 million) for state banks in New York."[8]

Given the unregulated and somewhat speculative nature of trust companies, they did not enjoy the direct protections of the clearing house system, which was dominated by large, established banking institutions which frowned upon this form of financial innovation. In order to facilitate the integration of trust companies into the broader financial system, however, certain trust companies in larger markets often forged relationships with individual clearing house member banks; those partner banks then agreed to clear for certain favored trust companies, thereby giving the trust companies indirect access to clearing-house protections.[9] The Knickerbocker, given its size and stature, enjoyed the privileges of the clearing-house system in this way; the National Bank of Commerce, one of New York's leading banks, cleared checks for the Knickerbocker and served as its sole clearing-house agent.

By 1907, the Knickerbocker Trust Company had become one of the largest and most successful trust companies in the country. Originally organized in 1884 by Fred Eldridge, who happened to be an old friend and classmate of J. Pierpont Morgan,[10] the Knickerbocker had grown its deposits in recent years by nearly 40 percent. By 1907, the Knickerbocker reported nearly $65 million in deposits, making it the third largest trust company in New York City, with nearly 18,000 depositors. The firm acted chiefly in the traditional roles of trust companies as an executor, administrator, guardian, receiver, registrar, transfer, and financial agent for states, cities, railroads, corporations, trusts, and estates. But, like other trust companies, the firm also offered interest on time deposits and received deposits subject to demand checks.

The architecture of the Knickerbocker's new building on Fifth Avenue, completed in 1906, justly reflected its prominence. The company also maintained a large office downtown near Wall Street and two remote branches in the Bronx and Harlem—at this time branches were an innovation among the trust companies.[11] Adding to the luster of the Knickerbocker was its president, Charles T. Barney, a leading figure in New York's financial and social circles. Not nearly of the same standing as J. P. Morgan or the other heads of national banks, Barney was still well known and well respected. Thanks to his social connections (he was the son-in-law of the financier William C. Whitney) and his general popularity, Barney was able to draw large accounts to the Knickerbocker from railroads, banks, and brokerage houses. During the decade of his leadership, the Knickerbocker had multiplied its deposits 6 times, its surplus 5 times, and its dividends by a factor of 10. "Outwardly and according to its balance sheet, the Trust Company was flourishing," wrote Herbert Satterlee, J. P. Morgan's son-in-law and biographer.[12]

So, as the events of the previous week on Wall Street unfolded in mid-October 1907, few would have suspected that the esteemed Knickerbocker Trust Company could ever be drawn into the morass. The firm's size, the apparent strength of its deposits, the social standing of its president, and even its new building in midtown gave the outward appearance of solidity and security. Of course, in hindsight, some found clues to what would unfold in the following days. "Mr. Barney had a very fine board of directors [at the Knickerbocker]," remarked Satterlee, "but they knew very little of a large part of the business of the Trust Company which Mr. Barney kept 'under his hat.' He ran his company with but few board meetings and with scant reports of his operations to his subordinates or executive committee."[13] Barney even once told a newspaper reporter that he did not "propose to waste his time answering questions asked by Directors who might try to keep in touch with the daily details of the company's business."[14] Moreover, Satterlee added, the company's "list of depositors contained a very large proportion of people of small means and those whose knowledge of banking was so slight that they would be apt to be frightened at the first sign of trouble."[15] Even so, the public at first remained ignorant of the degree of Barney's connections to the turmoil.

On Monday morning, October 21, New York City's bankers were still unsettled from the financial tremors triggered by the activities of F. Augustus Heinze and Charles W. Morse the week before. True panic had not yet set in, but the sudden collapse of the brokerage firm, Gross & Kleeberg, and the ensuing crises at the National Bank of North America, the New Amsterdam National Bank, and the Mercantile National Bank had created an atmosphere of high tension. The quick-witted intervention of the members of the New York Clearing House (NYCH) had nonetheless led many to believe that the problems had been contained. O. M. W. Sprague, a contemporary economist, noted that "there had been nothing in the nature of a crisis during the week the clearing house was putting its affairs in order."[16] The apparent containment of the crisis occurred because as depositors pulled their funds from institutions controlled by Morse and Heinze, they redeposited them in other New York City banks, thereby mitigating the possibility of massive runs on other national banks. Some later scholars, such as Calomiris and Gorton, found that "the Panic of 1907 is practically a non-event from the standpoint of national bank failures."[17] The system had received a shock, but a major banking panic had not been unleashed.

At 1 A.M. on Monday, the NYCH committee concluded a meeting at which they agreed yet again to make further provisions for the payment of debit balances for the Mercantile, North America, and New Amsterdam banks. Whereas initially only 9 of the association's 53 member banks were asked to support the protection fund for these Heinze-Morse institutions, the number of subscribers to the fund was increased to 25. Each agreed to pledge $400,000, bringing the total amount of support to $10 million.[18] Meanwhile, the new president of the Bank of North America, William F. Havemeyer, who had replaced Charles Morse, attempted to calm depositors' fears, claiming the bank's board had made headway in repaying $1.3 million in loans previously made to its own directors. "We are busy trying to get out of debt and have little time to talk," Havemeyer said. "We are raising money and will keep on doing so. Affairs look brighter all the time."[19]

Chapter 10

A Vote of No Confidence

He said that the thing to do was to save the other trust companies and prevent general disaster.

—Herbert L. Satterlee
J. P. Morgan's cousin and biographer[1]

I f the failed corner on United Copper and the troubles of a few national banks a week ago had been but early tremors, then the financial volcano itself would erupt on Monday afternoon, October 21. Twin shocks came in rapid succession. After a meeting of the board members of the Knickerbocker Trust Company, the public learned that Charles T. Barney had been asked to tender his resignation. Shortly thereafter, the National Bank of Commerce, the clearing house agent for the Knickerbocker, announced it would no longer clear for the trust company.

According to a contemporary account, the action of the Bank of Commerce "came as a complete surprise."[2] The *Wall Street Journal* reported that before the National Bank of Commerce had severed its relations with the Knickerbocker Trust Company as its clearing house agent, the bank had requested a loan from the clearing house committee on behalf of the Knickerbocker, which request was denied.[3] Thereafter, the bank issued its notification in an unusual way. Typically, a clearing house agent would send a card over to the clearing house, which would then deliver such news to all other member banks. In this case, the Bank of Commerce sent its notice directly to each bank via messenger. Upon this notification, the bank was compelled to continue clearing for 24 hours.[4] Upon the news, the Knickerbocker's officers released a statement, saying: "Following the practice of other trust companies the Knickerbocker Trust Company has this day arranged to clear over its own counter."[5]

The explicit connections between Barney and the events of the preceding week remained unknown, but the implications were made clear in another statement released by the Knickerbocker's board:

> In view of the fact that Mr. Barney's *outside interests* had become greatly extended, and in view of his personal position in the directorate of certain institutions recently under criticism, in particular because of his connection with Mr. Morse and some of Mr. Morse's companies, he has decided that the best interests of the company would be served by his resignation, although he had no loans with the Knickerbocker Trust Company.[6] *(italics added)*

In addition to resigning from his position as president and director, Barney also submitted his resignation from the National Bank of Commerce, the clearing house agent for the Knickerbocker. At a meeting held at the Knickerbocker's main offices at 66 Broadway, another board member, A. Foster Higgins, was elected to replace Barney immediately.[7]

Despite the evidence to the contrary, Charles Barney continued to defend both himself and the Knickerbocker. "There is not the slightest truth in any report that I was forced out of the company by the clearing house commission or by the action of the Bank of Commerce."[8] Regarding the presumed ailing condition of the Knickerbocker, Barney said, "Nothing could be more absurd. The company was never in a stronger condition. It remains next to the largest in the city and as sound as any. There is not the slightest question of its entire solvency."[9] It was reported that the accounts of the Knickerbocker had been reviewed by state banking examiners as recently as two weeks ago, and that they were then reported to be sound.[10] Moreover, the firm had announced plans in August to spend an estimated $3.5 million for the construction of a new, lavish, 22-story office building at the corner of Broadway and Exchange Place.[11] Nonetheless, the Bank of Commerce's announcement compelled the Knickerbocker not only to dismiss Barney but also to obtain emergency cash guarantees elsewhere. "The Knickerbocker has in its own vaults tonight $8,000,000 in cash," the Knickerbocker's officers declared. "If more cash is needed it will be immediately forthcoming under the guarantees."[12]

The resignation of Barney was merely an effect, of course, and not the cause of the dismay over the condition of the Knickerbocker. The announcement by the Bank of Commerce was far more debilitating. According to historian Jean Strouse, the National Bank of Commerce was often referred to as J. P. Morgan's bank; Morgan had been a director of that bank since 1875, and by the time he stepped down as its vice president in 1904, the Bank of Commerce had become the second largest in the country and one of the most stable.[13] By 1907, Morgan remained a director of the bank and a member of its executive board. Given J. P. Morgan's long association with the Bank of Commerce, the bank's announcement regarding the Knickerbocker telegraphed serious concerns about the trust company among the highest levels of American finance that the crisis was deeper than had been imagined heretofore.

As the previous week's events surrounding the failed attempt to corner the market in United Copper Company stock and the subsequent failures of the Mercantile and other banks unfolded, the 70-year-old J. Pierpont Morgan was in Richmond, Virginia, attending the Triennial Episcopal Convention. Though he was generally focused on the quotidian concerns of the church his partners in New York had kept him informed daily of market conditions and the anxiety that was brewing among the banks. Despite persistent calls for his presence, Morgan resisted any inclination to return to New York in haste, lest his departure before the end of the convention arouse suspicions that a crisis was imminent. By Thursday, October 17, however, two of Morgan's closest partners, Charles Steele and George W. Perkins, felt that the situation had become acute, and they sent a messenger to stress the matter with Pierpont directly. Finally, Morgan relented and without fanfare took a private train back to New York on Saturday evening, October 19. On Sunday morning, October 20, J. P. Morgan was once again ensconced in his "library" at Thirty-sixth Street and Madison Avenue, a grand repository of the art and priceless manuscripts that were his passion to collect. In the days ahead, this place would become the central headquarters for the coming rescue mission.[14]

By Sunday afternoon, the news that Morgan had returned from Richmond had already spread, and a line of newspaper reporters formed outside Morgan's library. Numerous bank and trust company officials came to see him throughout the day, and Morgan spent much of his time trying to get a complete picture of the situation. He assembled two teams, one that consisted of senior bankers, including himself, George Baker, president of the First National Bank, and James Stillman, president of the National City Bank; the other group included three younger, yet highly capable men: Morgan partner George Perkins, Henry P. Davison, vice president of the First National Bank, and Benjamin Strong, vice president of the Bankers Trust Company. Morgan carefully reviewed the financial statements of the clearing-house banks, which showed they were all in good condition, but the status of the trust companies was questionable. Morgan finally asked his council to assess the trust companies and to determine which should be supported and which should be allowed to fail. During the day, Charles Barney, the president of the Knickerbocker, also visited the library; Morgan refused to see him.

Around 10 A.M. on Monday, October 21, Morgan drove downtown with Charles Steele to his offices at 23 Wall Street—a building known simply as "the Corner"—where a committee of the Knickerbocker directors personally informed him of their request for Barney's resignation. As news that the Bank of Commerce would no longer clear for the Knickerbocker rattled over the ticker, Morgan advised the Knickerbocker's directors to assemble a meeting of their full board that night, review the their company's books, and assess if they could carry the company through. Morgan's conferences with other bankers continued throughout Monday afternoon. On Monday, Morgan privately told his son-in-law, Herbert Satterlee, that he was chiefly interested in the Knickerbocker because of its connections to his old friend, Fred

Eldridge, but he suspected it was already too late to save it.* Satterlee wrote, "He said that the thing to do was to save the other trust companies and prevent general disaster."[15]

The nagging question that afternoon was why Charles T. Barney, the respectable president of the Knickerbocker, should have been toppled in the aftermath of the Heinzes' attempted corner of United Copper; Barney was not directly implicated in any of their schemes. During the previous week, however, Charles W. Morse *was* involved in these schemes, and he was under investigation by the New York Clearing House committee; his two banks, the Bank of North America and the New Amsterdam, had been severely compromised in the fallout from the Heinze copper corner. "[W]hen Mr. Morse was explaining his affairs to the Clearing House Committee," the *New York Times* reported, "he told them that they ought to look around in other places too if they were going to push their investigations to the end, and that set the committee thinking. Soon after, stories of the development of the situation in the Knickerbocker got afloat in the financial district."[16] These rumors regarding apparent connections between the Knickerbocker and Morse's activities gained credence on Monday with the statement from the Knickerbocker board that Barney's dismissal was caused, in part, by "his connection with Mr. [Charles W.] Morse and some of Mr. Morse's companies."

According to Satterlee, Charles W. Morse "was regarded as a dangerous man in banking circles."[17] Nonetheless, the respectable Charles Barney had been associated with the unsavory Morse both personally and professionally for many years. For example, Barney was a director in several of Morse's biggest ventures, including the National Bank of North America and the New Amsterdam National Bank; he also served on the board of the American Ice Company, sometimes called the "Ice Trust" because of its nearly absolute monopoly of the ice business in New York City.[18] Barney was also a major shareholder in the Consolidated Steamship Lines, into which Charles W. Morse had merged six coastal steamship companies, thereby dominating all freight and passenger steamship traffic along the eastern seaboard.[19] Furthermore,

---

* The precise reasons that Morgan did not intervene directly on behalf of the Knickerbocker are unknown. There has been speculation that the national banking interests, with which Morgan was aligned, were disposed toward undermining the trust companies, which represented a potentially threatening form of financial innovation.

the connections between Barney and Morse extended directly to the Knickerbocker itself. By the fall of 1907, the Knickerbocker Trust Company had major holdings in numerous Morse-controlled interests, including the Bank of North America, the American Ice Company, the American Ice Securities Company, the Butterick Company, and the Clyde Steamship Company.[20]

Morse himself never revealed why he may have encouraged the New York Clearing House committee to investigate Charles T. Barney, but no less than three weeks previously Morse had been denied a seat on the board of the Knickerbocker Trust Company. After acquiring a signifi-cant block of Knickerbocker stock, Morse had demanded representation on the board, but the majority of its directors threatened to resign in protest should he be elected. Whatever the motivations may have been, by Monday afternoon the implications of Barney's and the Knicker-bocker's connections to Morse (and possibly Heinze) were understood to exist. Barney was out and "J. P. Morgan's bank," the National Bank of Commerce, had turned its back on the Knickerbocker Trust Company.

At 9 P.M. on Monday, the meeting Morgan had proposed for the Knickerbocker directors was assembled at Sherry's, a popular and famous restaurant at Fifth Avenue and Forty-fourth Street. Morgan, Perkins, and Steele retired to a private room for dinner, while the directors and their friends met separately to consider the condition of the trust company. "At the meeting it became evident that the Knickerbocker situation was pretty desperate and, unless promptly in hand, would certainly cause a run on that company which might spread to others," Perkins recalled.[21] By 11 P.M., nothing had been accomplished; Perkins called for other leading bankers and trust company presidents to join them, while Morgan, who was suffering from a severe cold, returned to his library at Thirty-sixth Street.

The conferences at Sherry's lasted until 1 A.M., when the Knicker-bocker board decided to open the trust company the next day; if there were another run by depositors, they would keep the Knickerbocker open as long as it would take them to secure additional assistance from other financial institutions.[22] It was hoped that there would be enough time for other banks to investigate the condition of the Knickerbocker for themselves and to provide relief. Morgan assigned Davison and Strong to examine the Knickerbocker's books; if they determined that it was sound, Morgan would find money to keep it afloat.[23]

Chapter 11

A Classic Run

The worst and most dangerous feature in the view of Wall Street was the alarm among the public.

—*Wall Street Journal*
October 23, 1907

O n Tuesday morning, October 22, the mid-autumn weather in New York City was fair and mild.[1] That was fortunate since there was already an eddying crowd outside the Knickerbocker Trust Company's great bronze doors at Fifth Avenue and Thirty-fourth Street by 9 A.M. Altogether about 100 people, mostly small shopkeepers, mechanics, and clerks, waited patiently on the sidewalk to reclaim their deposits. Even when the firm opened at its regular time an hour later, everything remained orderly and there were no violent scenes, tears, or frantic hand-wringing. Men stood in one primary line and women stepped into a separate room to the left of the bank's main entrance. Within 15 minutes, the line extended out the doors and down the steps to the sidewalk, as company officers and policemen marshaled the growing crowd into formation.[2]

Inside the building, clerks behind the Knickerbocker's ornate bronze gratings were paying off depositors as fast as they could compute interest and stamp vouchers. "Stacks of green currency, bound into thousand dollar lots, were piled on the counters beside the tellers," the *Washington Post* reported. "One by one these stacks were broached and they dwindled rapidly. Clerks went to the vaults from time to time with arms full of notes, piled up like bundles of kindling wood."[3] As the morning wore on, many more depositors arrived carrying satchels, showing they were ready to carry off large amounts. One young man, "with his hands trembling," the *Times* reported, "stacked his trousers pockets full of one-hundred-dollar and twenty-dollar bills."[4] Meanwhile, messengers from the downtown banks were bringing in bags of money, and even one of them came laden with three big wooden boxes of silver.[5]

The line of depositors inside the green-marbled banking room turned in circles, such that every inch of the big lobby of the bank was covered. They crowded the center desk so closely that as they inched along, men and women could make out their checks without leaving the line, resting their blanks on their forearms, handbags, or bankbooks.[6] As word of the run began to spread, a line of broughams, automobiles, and finely appointed carriages formed in front of the Knickerbocker, and women in silks and men in frock coats and ties took their places in the queue. "Around the stock tickers in the offices of the officials women again and again gathered and read the tape, quoting aloud the prices and showing their interest in the values of stocks and bonds as well as in their cash holdings."[7] Meanwhile, the Knickerbocker's vice president, William Trumbull, told depositors that the trust company would keep paying out until the end of official hours at 3 P.M., adding, "It will be a physical impossibility for them to count out and turn over the money they have during the time remaining."[8] For the most part, the depositors took their long wait stoically, but as the hours wore on some showed their impatience. One man complained bitterly at the slowness of those ahead of him counting their money. "Every half hour, he said, "is costing me five dollars. I have got to get cash for the Clearing House, and I am fined for each half hour's delay."[9]

At the Knickerbocker's downtown office in the Metropolitan Life Building at 66 Broadway, the scenes were largely the same. At first, the line there extended only from the banking room out to Broadway, but as the day progressed it doubled upon itself in a great "S."[10] While the morning crowd was comprised of only about 50 people, "as fast as a depositor went out of the place ten people and more came asking for their money," the *Times* reported, "and the police of the West 30th Street Station were asked to send some men to keep order."[11] Despite the apparent orderliness of the proceedings, the *Wall Street Journal* opined on the underlying dread felt by many:

> The worst and most dangerous feature in the view of Wall Street was the alarm among the public. The frightened depositor is a proposition New York has not had to handle in recent times and assurance which would satisfy the Street and its experienced leaders might be meaningless to the sort of crowd which gathered outside 66 Broadway at the opening of business in the morning.[12]

At 12:35 P.M., Joseph T. Brown, an officer of the Knickerbocker Trust Company, stepped on a chair in the middle of the lines of depositors and read a statement from the state superintendent of banks, saying that the New York State banking department had examined the Knickerbocker on September 17, and had found it had assets of $68,884,523 and liabilities of $63,701,531. When he finished, there was a weak-hearted cheer, but nobody dropped out of line and payments continued.[13] The *New York Times* described the scene that ensued:

> About this time the crowd of depositors and messengers from brokerage houses, sent to report on the situation, filled the lobby to the doors. A small overflow on Broadway promised to draw an increasing crowd, and half a dozen policemen from the John Street Station were sent down to keep order. The sidewalks in front of the American Express offices across the street were crowded with a small mob.[14]

The bank officer then announced that no more payments would be made. "Payments of checks will be, probably, resumed in the morning," Brown added weakly. "Louder," came the calls from a number of men in the banking room who could not hear. "The company is solvent," Brown shouted back as he sought refuge in his office. The tellers closed their windows as the remaining depositors and bank messengers within harried the other officials with questions.[15] Meanwhile, uptown, at the Knickerbocker's stately and reassuring building on Fifth Avenue, a telephone message arrived from 66 Broadway. It instructed the cessation of all payments there as well. William Trumbull, a Knickerbocker vice president, said, "Something must have happened downtown. It means that we have the assets, but that we can't realize on them just now to pay off our liabilities." Someone in the crowd shouted, "Will payment be resumed in the morning?" Trumbull said, "I can't tell."[16]

For an hour after the doors were closed most of the waiting depositors stayed in formation, while others clamored at the locked doors for more news about the situation. "Up to that time the crowd had been calm, and, in fact, somewhat sheepish," the New York Times reported. "The words from the doorway had been imperfectly understood, and when the banking office was shut against them those waiting in the lobby gathered in excited groups, demanding of each other what it meant."[17] Many of them simply persevered and waited outside until the close of banking hours.[18] "Idlers stood and stared at the windows in which the shades had been pulled down," Satterlee remarked, "and the police had to be summoned to clear the streets."[19]

Within two and a half hours on Tuesday, October 22, the Knickerbocker Trust Company had returned more than $8 million to depositors at its offices on Fifth Avenue, Broadway, and its two smaller branches in Harlem and the Bronx.[20] Around noon, the new president of the Knickerbocker, A. Foster Higgins, entered the building at Thirty-fourth Street, where he held a series of consultations in the officers' rooms.[21] Despite the assurances of the financiers at Sherry's the day before, the officers of Knickerbocker said that no money was forthcoming when needed.[22] Of the total paid to depositors, $4 million was paid directly in cash, and another $4 million was paid through the clearing house.[23]

The proximate cause for the suspension of the Knickerbocker on Tuesday was the flood of very large checks presented for payment by other banking institutions. Just before the order to suspend, a messenger, reportedly from the Hanover National Bank, appeared at the Knickerbocker's window downtown with a check for $1.5 million, which the Knickerbocker cashed; shortly thereafter, another messenger from a different bank arrived with a check for $1 million, which was also cashed. "The paying teller handed out this money," the Times reported, "and immediately closed down his window. There was still some cash left in the paying teller's cage, but the officers had realized by that time that needed help was not forthcoming, and suspension was the only recourse."[24] Large numbers of messengers from brokerages and banks remained in line, holding large batches of several hundred checks, but these messengers were turned away as the tellers closed their windows.

Chapter 12

Such Assistance as May Be Necessary

If we get help overnight we shall reopen in the morning. If we don't, we won't. That's all there is to it at present. We can't tell now whether we are going to get help or not.

—G. L. Boissevain
Knickerbocker Trust Company[1]

After the Bank of Commerce had announced on Monday, October 21, that it would no longer clear for the Knickerbocker Trust Company, all the other national banks also refused to cash the Knickerbocker's checks, reflecting their growing unease about the Knickerbocker's ability to honor the checks for payment. The banks would, however, accept checks for collection on behalf of the Knickerbocker's depositors, even though those depositors would not be paid until the banks received payment directly from the Knickerbocker. It was in this way that large numbers of checks started arriving at the Knickerbocker late on Tuesday morning. Throughout the day many other banks were also sending messengers to the Knickerbocker on behalf of clients or customers who had deposits with the Knickerbocker and who sought to collect through other institutions. Ultimately, such exchanges accounted for nearly $5 million of the total disbursed that day, and they quickly overwhelmed the Knickerbocker's ability to honor them.[2]

As depositors of the Knickerbocker clamored for their money, J. Pierpont Morgan's young deputy, Benjamin Strong, had been undertaking a hurried review of the trust company's accounts. Working at the Knickerbocker's downtown office, Strong reported to Henry Davison, vice president of George Baker's First National Bank, by midday that the trust company was not solvent.* Based on this report, Morgan and his lieutenants determined it would be useless to help the company at all, confirming Morgan's own suspicions about the Knickerbocker from the day before.[3] When the Knickerbocker's tellers finally closed their windows, Strong, who was still inside the company's offices, remembered, "The consternation on the faces of the people on that line, many of them men whom I knew, I shall never forget."[4] One of the clearing-house bankers also confirmed that any attempts to uphold the Knickerbocker had, in fact, been abandoned early in the day:

> The character of much of the Knickerbocker's collateral is not readily marketable, and now that it has suspended payments temporarily, it is altogether likely that its credit has been so heavily impaired that a resumption would bring about another run. That might mean that support to the amount perhaps of $25,000,000 or more would be needed to carry the institution through. Under the circumstances it is better that the trust company be liquidated than that the reserves of other institutions be so heavily depleted.[5]

The directors of the Knickerbocker had remained in their boardroom all through the harrowing day on Tuesday. "Without exception they wore the looks of men who thought the world had used them hard," the *Wall Street Journal* reported.[6] One of the Knickerbocker's board

---

* As noted earlier, the state banking examiner had reviewed the Knickerbocker's accounts as recently as two weeks prior to the crisis and had determined that the institution had sufficient funds to pay its depositors. The contradictory findings of Benjamin Strong indicate at the very least that the crisis had created an unforeseen strain on the trust company's reserves. This apparent inconsistency raises an interesting speculation about whether Morgan and his associates generally had more access to critical information than banking regulators.

members, G. L. Boissevain, said, "If we get help overnight we shall reopen in the morning. If we don't, we won't. That's all there is to it at present. We can't tell now whether we are going to get help or not."[7] The superintendent of the state's banking department confirmed this assessment of the situation.[8]

In an attempt to reassure all depositors, the New York Clearing House (NYCH) announced that all association member banks were strong and that they would be protected; however, the NYCH refused to provide any relief for the Knickerbocker.[9] One of the chief conferees, an NYCH committee member, tried to sound a note of optimism, saying, "I think it is safe to say that no other financial institution of the least importance will have to undergo the experiences of the Knickerbocker Trust Company. I feel optimistic for the first time since these troubles began."[10] A. Barton Hepburn, president of Chase National Bank, added, "I believe the general banking conditions will continue to improve from now on. The trouble at its origin was due to peculiar methods of certain parties [Heinze and Morse] who have now been forced out of the situation and the clearing house will continue to render such assistance as may be necessary."[11]

Despite the reassurances from the NYCH, news of the run on the Knickerbocker and its subsequent suspension was wreaking havoc on the markets. All loanable funds became tightly held as almost all the banks and trust companies hoarded their funds to an extraordinary degree throughout the day. At the market's opening on Tuesday, the call money rate was quoted at a nominal 10 percent, but by noon there were no offers for money at all on the floor of the exchange. During the afternoon the money rates then advanced to 60 percent, declined to 40 percent, and surged up again to 70 percent a half hour before the market closed.[12] As the call money dried up, stock prices slumped to their lowest level since December 1900. There were also reports of the failure of another prominent stock exchange house, Marcus & Mayer, and vague rumors surfaced about the condition of other institutions, "which shook Wall Street to its foundations."[13]

Back at 23 Wall Street, J. P. Morgan and his associates conferred with an oncoming flood of bankers and trust company presidents. It appeared that the runs on the trust companies were not limited to the Knicker-bocker. In particular, the president of the Trust Company of America told them he was "desperately anxious" because the withdrawals from his company on Tuesday had been exceptionally heavy.[14] The Trust Company of America, also located on Wall Street, was presided over by Oakleigh Thorne, a popular member of a prominent New York family. Like Charles Barney at the Knickerbocker, Thorne had also opened several branch offices for his trust company and had grown its deposit base very rapidly[15]; the Trust Company had about $50 million in deposits and about $100 million in assets.[16] The precise cause for the run there was unknown, but one of the Trust Company's board members was none other than Charles T. Barney.[17]

On Tuesday afternoon, J. P. Morgan decided that the Secretary of the U.S. Treasury, George B. Cortelyou, should be summoned to New York immediately for a conference. As the Secretary took the afternoon train from Washington, D.C., to Manhattan, banks around the country were rapidly pulling their reserves out of New York, resulting in further pressures on available liquidity.[18] Upon leaving the conference at his offices at 6 P.M., Morgan, still suffering from his cold, said to a reporter, "We are doing everything we can as fast as we can, but nothing has yet crystallized."[19]

After Treasury Secretary Cortelyou arrived in New York at 9 P.M., Morgan, Stillman (president of the National City Bank), Baker (president of the First National Bank), and Perkins (partner at J. P. Morgan & Company) went to see him at the Manhattan Hotel. At the meeting the Secretary said he was ready to deposit government money in the banks to help support the situation. "We adjourned at two o'clock [A.M.] feeling that, without much of any doubt, there would be runs on other institutions," George Perkins said.[20] Among the issues discussed that night was the situation concerning Oakleigh Thorne's Trust Company of America, and the group of bankers was considering how to aid that firm. In a statement to the New York Times, George Perkins said:

> The chief sore point is the Trust Company of America. The conferees feel that the situation there is such that the company is sound. Provision has been made to supply all the cash needed this morning. The conferees feel sure the company will be able to pull through. The company has twelve million dollars cash and as much more as needed has been pledged for the purpose. It is safe to assume that J. P. Morgan & Co. will be leaders in this movement to furnish funds.[21]

Around 2 A.M. on Wednesday, October 23, Benjamin Strong was contacted at his home in Greenwich, Connecticut, and was told to assemble a team at once to begin an examination of the Trust Company of America. Morgan wanted a full report on the Trust Company in his office by noon that day.[22] Strong headed directly for Manhattan, and he and his colleagues worked through the night to ascertain the strength of the Trust Company of America.

As the day began, Morgan's health had worsened and his family could scarcely rouse him from bed. "He seemed to be in a stupor," remembered Herbert Satterlee.[23] After his personal physician was summoned, giving Pierpont sprays and gargles, the financier finally came down to breakfast, where he conferred at the library with George Perkins and reviewed the estimates of the cash that would be needed for the day's withdrawals from the banks and trusts. After a few meetings, he drove downtown to the Corner, where E. H. Harriman of the Union Pacific Railroad and Henry Clay Frick of U.S. Steel Corporation, among others, were waiting to see him about the prevailing conditions.

Morgan was acutely concerned about the situations at the trusts. "The Knickerbocker had gone over the dam and the Trust Company of America was nearing the brink," Satterlee observed.[24] By 1 P.M. on Wednesday when he arrived at the Corner, Benjamin Strong had a reached a verdict about the Trust Company. Many of the trust company presidents were already meeting in one room, while Davison, Perkins, Baker, Stillman, and Morgan were in another. When Strong entered, Morgan remarked at once, "Have you anyone with you who can make a report to the gentlemen in the next room? They are the presidents of the trust companies, and when they came into the office they had to be introduced to each other, and I don't think much can be expected of them. Sit down with Mr. Baker, Mr. Stillman and me, and tell us about it."[25]

While an associate of Strong's met in the next room with the trust company presidents, Strong himself offered Morgan, Stillman, and Baker a picture of the situation at the Trust Company of America. Strong described the next few moments as follows:

I remember Mr. Morgan repeatedly saying, "Are they solvent?" He wanted no details, but the general facts and results, and seemed satisfied with the opinions I expressed. There were two or three large loans in the Trust Company which I had to ask Mr. Morgan, Mr. Baker, and Mr. Stillman for their own opinion, and with what I remember telling Mr. Morgan that I was satisfied that the company was solvent; that I thought their surplus had been pretty much wiped out; but that the capital was not greatly impaired, if at all, although were the company to be liquidated there were many assets which it would take some years to convert into cash.[26]

The entire meeting with Strong lasted about 45 minutes, during which J. Pierpont Morgan spoke no more than five or six times. Morgan asked Strong if he though the bankers would be justified in seeing the company through its troubles. Strong answered in the affirmative.

Morgan turned to Baker and Stillman: "This is the place to stop the trouble, then."[27]

Chapter 13

Trust Company of America

*The look of relief on his face when I handed him the first earnest
money I shall never forget.*

—Benjamin Strong, Jr.
Bankers Trust Company[1]

he Trust Company of America was in imminent peril. Around
the time that Morgan was hearing the report from Strong,
Oakleigh Thorne, president of the Trust Company, called the
Corner and told J. Pierpont Morgan that his company's meager cash
supply had dwindled to $1.2 million.

The run on the Trust Company had become formidable indeed,
and Thorne was doubtful he could keep its doors open until the end
of business at 3 P.M. Nearly 1,200 depositors were assembled outside
the Trust Company's main offices in lower Manhattan, grouped in a
line snaking east to William Street and down to Exchange Place. In
an attempt to stem the flow from his vaults, Thorne kept only two
teller windows open all morning; he also arranged to have large piles of

cash on view to reassure anxious depositors that the institution had ample reserves. But in a replay of the previous day's scenes at the Knickerbocker, worried customers, clerks, and office boys took up a desultory vigil to reclaim their (or their employer's) cash. Investors and depositors had lost faith in yet another prominent New York financial institution.

Twenty minutes later, Thorne called on Morgan again in a greater state of panic. His coffers were now down to $800,000, and unless he could raise $3 million, he would have to close the Trust Company instantly. Morgan turned to the 10 trust company presidents in the room with him, whom he had called together earlier to address the widening panic. He suggested that each of them agree to loan $300,000 to the Trust Company of America. The president of the Farmers Loan & Trust Company took up the offer right away, but the meeting fell apart and devolved into a confused debate for another 20 minutes.

At about 1:45 P.M., Thorne again pleaded for aid. Now he had only $500,000 remaining. The trust officials continued to argue. In their view it was not their place to intervene, and they were prepared to abandon one of their own.

At 2:15 P.M., a committee from the Trust Company of America entered the room and reported they had only $180,000 left and they had decided to cease operations. "Well," Morgan exclaimed, "I don't see anything else to do."[2] Exasperated by the temporizing of the trust companies, he abruptly dismissed the meeting. At the suggestion of his partner and close associate, George W. Perkins, Morgan summoned the presidents of the city's two largest banks: James Stillman of the National City Bank and George F. Baker of the First National Bank of New York. After opening a direct phone line to the offices of the Trust Company of America, Morgan told Oakleigh Thorne to come see him at once, bringing with him the most valuable securities held in his company's vaults.

Within minutes, the doors of Morgan's office were thrown open and in walked a long line of men with bags and boxes filled with securities owned by the Trust Company of America. Stillman sat in an adjoining room where he maintained an open telephone line with the National City Bank. Morgan commanded a large table as Thorne and his clerks laid out the Trust Company's securities for the purpose of valuing them in exchange for a loan. Making notes on a pad as they went along, Morgan assessed the securities, and as he determined that enough collateral was available for an advance, he asked Stillman to have National City Bank send that amount in cash over to the Trust Company. Every few minutes, at Morgan's direction, money was carried in sacks and taken directly to the Trust Company's vaults. Morgan and his men proceeded in this way until $3 million had been delivered. The doors stayed open until 3 P.M. and the Trust Company of America had been saved for a day.

At 3:15 P.M., Morgan convened the trust company presidents again, making urgent appeals for them to take action. Now they agreed to form a committee to monitor the trust company situation over the coming days, which would have the power to call for information from any of the other trust companies. In this way, the committee would function like the banks' clearing house, to which any assistance for the trust companies could be referred. The new trust company committee would have five members and its chair would be Edward King, president of the Union Trust Company. Once these arrangements had been made, Morgan instructed the trust company presidents to report that night at 9 o'clock at the uptown offices of the Union Trust on Fifth Avenue. Meanwhile, Morgan dispatched Benjamin Strong Jr., the 35-year-old secretary of the Bankers Trust Company, to proceed with another thorough examination of the Trust Company of America's books.

As these emergency measures were undertaken on behalf of the Trust Company of America, there were signs that economic and financial conditions were deteriorating elsewhere. The Westinghouse Electric & Manufacturing Company had been placed in the hands of a receiver, the Pittsburgh Stock Exchange had suspended trading, and a run had begun at another leading New York trust institution, the Lincoln Trust Company. At the same time, the mayor of New York City, George B. McClellan (the son of the Civil War general), called for a conference with all his department heads when he learned that the city would be unable to pay its salaries and contractors. The *New York Times* reported that the mayor proposed cutting the city's budget to an "irreducible minimum" because the municipal government was running up against a $12 million year-end shortfall, and the flotation of another successful bond issue seemed unlikely given the stringency in the capital markets.[3]

Even as Morgan was imploring the trust company presidents to act, others were entreating *him* to solve other problems throughout the city. At one point, he received a call on Wednesday about falling prices on the New York Stock Exchange, to which he said that if any member of the Exchange sold "short" in an attempt to promote the panic and profit from falling prices, he would be "properly attended to" after the crisis was over. Morgan's admonition was widely broadcast and apparently gave pause to the bears.[4] At another time that afternoon, one of the bank presidents was greatly disturbed about the negative turn of events, and he said to Morgan, "Mr. Morgan, my reserve is down to 20 percent and I don't know what to do." Morgan replied sharply, "You ought to be ashamed of yourself. Your reserve *ought* to be down to 18 percent or 20 percent. What is a reserve for if not to be used in times like these?"[5] (italics added)

Exhausted by the day's events at his downtown offices, Pierpont returned to his library late in the afternoon, by which time he was suffering mightily from his cold. His voice was hoarse and his eyes were watery, but he was still alert and energetic. After taking his dinner at the library, he left by the back door and walked the one block to the offices of the Union Trust Company on the northeast corner of Thirty-sixth Street and Fifth Avenue. Before seeing the trust company presidents, though, Morgan met first with his partners George W. Perkins and Henry P. Davison. The trio sat in a small coupon room in the Union Trust basement where Benjamin Strong offered his personal assessment of the condition of the Trust Company of America. After spending a day poring through its books, Strong reported that the Trust Company had about $2 million in equity, and that its ability to pay its creditors would depend on its continued survival. Morgan had little to say, but he nodded his head in assent vigorously from time to time.

Armed with Strong's appraisal, Morgan and his men marched upstairs to a small meeting room in the Union Trust building. One after another the trust company presidents arrived. Morgan demanded a bold and decisive move on their part that would not only stop the run but also restore the public's wavering confidence. He recounted Strong's report for the trust officials and said it was distinctly the responsibility of the trust companies to save the Trust Company of America. He also assured them that both the clearing house member banks and the firm of J. P. Morgan & Company would do what they could to assist the trust companies in doing so. Astonishingly, they again demurred. "Tension was obvious on every hand, and there was general reluctance to make any commitments," Strong later recalled.[6] Finally, Morgan challenged them. He said $10 million was required and that it must be ready by the next morning.

The first to come forward was the president of Bankers Trust Company, who agreed to provide $500,000, and as much as $1 million, if necessary. Morgan reassured them that the Secretary of the Treasury, George B. Cortelyou, who had just traveled from Washington, D.C., to New York, would make deposits in select New York banks so the trust companies would have access to new sources of cash. *Still*, the trust presidents balked. They shared enthusiasm neither for saving the Trust Company of America nor for weakening their own cash positions. Their aimless discussions continued.

Morgan was clearly exhausted. At first, he sat quietly smoking, until his cigar went out. Then his head dropped forward and he fell asleep in his chair. Another 30 minutes passed. Morgan then abruptly awoke, and he immediately asked Benjamin Strong for a pencil and a sheet of paper. "Well, gentlemen," Morgan continued. "The Bankers Trust Company has agreed to take its share and more of a loan. Mr. Marsten [president of the Farmers Loan & Trust Company], how much will the Farmers Loan & Trust Company subscribe?" Marsten answered that his firm would offer just as much as Bankers Trust had.[7] In just this fashion, Morgan continued around the room, one by one, until he had secured $8.25 million. He then rose from his chair and said that the First National Bank, the National City Bank, and the Hanover National Bank would temporarily be responsible for the balance of the $10 million requested, but that they would expect the trust companies to relieve them of their contribution as soon as the loan could be organized. It was nearly midnight.

During these discussions, Oakleigh Thorne was waiting outside. After the meeting Morgan asked Strong to go with Thorne to Thorne's house on Park Avenue, where the two would pull together the securities necessary to secure the next day's loan for the Trust Company of America; as chair of the trust company committee, Edward King was responsible for providing the cash on Thursday morning from the Union Trust Company's downtown office. Meanwhile, George Perkins left for the Manhattan Hotel to see the Treasury Secretary and to provide a statement to the newspaper reporters gathered there. Morgan took a cab home to Thirty-sixth Street, played a game of solitaire, spoke briefly with George Perkins again, and then went to bed.

Through the night and into the early hours of the next day, Benjamin Strong labored with Oakleigh Thorne to prepare a complete schedule of the collateral the Trust Company of America would need to deliver on Thursday morning. After finishing their work, Strong made his way downtown to see Edward King at the Union Trust Company by 8:30 A.M. When Strong arrived at the Union Trust, however, he was astonished when King demanded further verification of the Trust Company of America's assets; in fact, King flatly refused to deliver the promised loan to Strong. It was now 9:45 A.M., and the Trust Company was scheduled to reopen in 15 minutes. Without the fresh infusion of cash, the ongoing run at the Trust Company would jeopardize everything Morgan and the others had planned the night before.

Immediately, Strong rushed uptown again to see Morgan and Perkins, who were by then having a breakfast meeting at Morgan's library. Having been apprised of the situation, Morgan instructed Strong to bring forth immediately all of the Trust Company's securities remaining in the vaults of J. P. Morgan & Company; Pierpont himself had valued these securities with Thorne the very day before. Morgan then told Strong to exchange these securities for cash and thus secure a temporary loan from Stillman's National City Bank. Leaving Morgan and Perkins, Strong raced frenetically back downtown to provide life support to the Trust Company of America:

> We ran down Wall Street to the National City Bank with some millions of securities, the street being thronged with sightseers and a long line of waiting depositors also extending down William Street from the Trust Company of America office and into Exchange Place. A very hasty examination of the collateral was made at the National City Bank, and I remember giving Mr. Whitson a pencil receipt for a bundle of gold certificates—I cannot now recall whether it was $600,000 or $1,000,000—but I put them in my pocket, ran down Wall Street, and at almost exactly ten o'clock found Mr. Thorne walking up and down the gallery overlooking the banking room in the utmost anxiety lest he was to be disappointed in the loan. The minute he saw me he said that the trust companies had failed him, the money was not forthcoming,

and that he expected to close the institution promptly at ten. The look of relief on his face when I handed him the first earnest money I shall never forget.[8]

The Trust Company of America was saved a second time in as many days. Though Morgan had doused the first fire, the conflagration of panic was just beginning to take hold.

Chapter 14

Crisis on the Exchange

Why don't you tell them what to do, Mr. Morgan?

—Belle da Costa Greene
J. P. Morgan's personal librarian

I don't know what to do myself, but sometime, someone will come in with a plan that I know will work; and then I will tell them what to do.

—J. Pierpont Morgan[1]

As Oakleigh Thorne was opening the doors to the Trust Company of America on Thursday morning, October 24, J. Pierpont Morgan was boarding a Union Club brougham drawn by a white horse, which would take him to his offices at 23 Wall Street.[2] By this time people throughout the city had already seen Morgan's picture on the front pages of many newspapers, which had proclaimed him the city's savior. Herbert Satterlee, Morgan's son-in-law, was traveling in the brougham with Pierpont, and he provided a vivid description of the atmosphere surrounding the titan that morning:

All the way downtown people who got a glimpse of him in the cab called the attention of passersby. Policemen and cabbies who knew him well by sight shouted, "There goes the Old Man!" or "There goes the Big Chief!" and the people who heard them understood to whom they referred and ran beside the cab to get a peep at him. Near Trinity Church a way through the crowd opened as soon as it was realized who was in the cab. The crowd moved with us. He might have been a general at the head of a column going to the relief of a beleaguered city such was the enthusiasm he created. All this time he looked straight ahead and gave no sign of noticing the excitement, but it was evident that he was pleased.[3]

People literally filled the streets at the corner of Wall Street and Broad in lower Manhattan. As Morgan descended from the carriage and hurried up the steps of J. P. Morgan & Company, the mob first became quiet, and then they fought their way forward to peer at the man through the windows. When he arrived inside, his office was thronged with men desperate to borrow money. Morgan went directly to his private office where he began a conference with George Baker, James Stillman, and several other bank and trust company officials.

While Morgan conferred with his lieutenants, dozens of vehicles were parking outside the Federal Subtreasury building not far away on Wall Street. After a late-night meeting with Morgan's partner, George Perkins, Treasury Secretary George B. Cortelyou announced his formal support for Morgan, offering to provide $25 million dollars in additional liquidity during the crisis. "Not only has the stability of the business institutions impressed me deeply," Cortelyou said, "but also the highest courage and the splendid devotion to the public interest of many men prominent in the business life of this city."[4]

Throughout the morning on Thursday men carried bags and boxes of gold and satchels of greenbacks from the federal vaults at the Subtreasury to the various banks approved by Cortelyou. Meanwhile, John D. Rockefeller Sr. also called on Morgan to assure him of his willingness to help. Rockefeller deposited $10 million with the Union Trust Company, and promised additional deposits of $40 million, if needed.*

The panic, however, had already spread further. An acute shortage of money had occurred on the New York Stock Exchange, and brokers were intensely anxious. At 10 A.M. the interest rate on call money at

---

* An audit in 1902 showed that John D. Rockefeller Sr. was worth about $200 million; by comparison, at the time of his death in 1913, J. P. Morgan's estate was valued at approximately $80 million.

the Exchange was fairly normal—around 6 percent. Yet sometime later in the morning a bid was made for 60 percent and still no money was offered. By 1 P.M., call money was being loaned at the extreme rate of 100 percent. "It was evident that difficulty was being caused by the calling of loans by a good many trust companies which, alarmed by the run that already had taken place on three companies [Knickerbocker Trust Company, Trust Company of America, and Lincoln Trust Company] were hurrying to strengthen their own cash position," George Perkins observed.[5] An already tight money market was now further strained by the trust companies pulling their cash out of the market. With money so scarce, prices on the Exchange were headed into a tailspin.

Around 1:30 P.M., Ransom H. Thomas, the president of New York's Stock Exchange, and one of his assistants came over to the Corner in a state of great excitement. When he arrived, the offices of J. P. Morgan & Company were full of other agitated men, but Thomas rushed up to the financier and said, "Mr. Morgan, we will have to close the Stock Exchange." Morgan turned to him and asked sharply, "What?" Thomas repeated, "We will have to close the Stock Exchange." Morgan asked, "At what time do you usually close it?" Thomas answered, "Why, at three o'clock." Morgan thundered, "It must not close one minute before that hour today!" emphasizing each word by keeping time with his right hand, middle finger pointing directly at the president of the Exchange.[6]

Thomas then explained that unless a significant amount of money was offered on the stock exchange in a very short time, a large number of failures would result. Morgan said he would take immediate steps to arrange a loan, and he sent Thomas back to the Exchange. The situation only seemed to get more desperate with each passing moment. "One broker after another came into our office, begging us to do something—many with tears in their eyes and others almost weak with the shock of being suddenly faced with failure," George Perkins recalled. "They had the securities on which to raise money but there was no money to be had."[7] Finally, at about 1:45, Morgan asked that all of the presidents of the banks (not the trust companies, this time) be called to his office immediately. The city's bankers started to arrive around 2 P.M.; the moment that the brokers on the Exchange feared most would be in 20 minutes when the Exchange customarily compared all the day's sales and adjusted brokers' accounts. This would be literally a moment of reckoning.

When the bank presidents had finally gathered at the Corner, Morgan explained the situation to them. He said simply that unless they raised $25 million within the next 10 to 12 minutes, at least 50 Stock Exchange houses would fail. James Stillman, president of the National City Bank, promptly offered $5 million; the other bankers quickly fell in line. By 2:16 P.M., Morgan had secured $23.6 million from 14 banks. Within minutes, word of the new "money pool" buoyed the Street, as Perkins later observed:

> Our outer office at this moment was filled with brokers awaiting the result of the conference. The bank presidents hurried out of our private offices into these outer offices and someone must have exclaimed that a $25 million fund had been raised because, as I hurried from the office to start the machinery of loaning in motion, I saw some man's hat sail towards the ceiling as he shouted, "We are saved, we are saved!"[8]

When the money hit the market at 2:30 P.M., men clambered over one another to get to the Exchange's "money post" seeking a loan; in the mayhem, even one of Morgan's associates had his coat and waistcoat torn off. The *New York Times* reported that money brokers scrambled wildly for the funds as fast as borrowers names could be written down, adding that for the first time in 10 days the mood on the trading floor was cheerful. At 3 P.M., when the Stock Exchange closed, there was "a mighty roar of voices" that could be heard from the floor of the Exchange. The members had joined in yelling, "What's the matter with Morgan? He's all right!" followed by three cheers.[9] Of the total raised for the money pool by Morgan on Thursday afternoon, nearly $19 million was loaned out in 30 minutes at interest rates ranging from 10 percent to 60 percent. After the market close, scores of men crowded in front of J. P. Morgan & Company carrying boxes of collateral to secure their share of the pool.

Around 7 P.M. Morgan and Perkins finally left their offices to head uptown. As they started to leave the building, the normally reticent Morgan approached a throng of reporters. Straightening up and squaring his shoulders, he said slowly and earnestly, "If people will keep their money in the banks, everything will be all right."[10] Then he quickly turned, went out the door, and drove uptown.

J. P. Morgan's efforts had kept the Stock Exchange open on Thursday, October 24, but his victory there had not been decisive. The Twelfth Ward Bank and Empire City Savings Bank suspended in the afternoon. The Hamilton Bank of New York ceased operations, and many more institutions closed in rapid succession: First National Bank of Brooklyn, International Trust Company of New York, Williamsburg Trust Company of Brooklyn, Borough Bank of Brooklyn, and Jenkins Trust Company of Brooklyn. By Friday morning, the Union Trust Company of Providence, Rhode Island, failed to open as well. Most worrisome of all, severe runs continued unabated at the beleaguered Trust Company of America and the Lincoln Trust.

Early in the morning on Friday, October 25, George Perkins made successive visits to Cortelyou, Stillman, Baker, and Morgan, securing their agreement once again to save the Trust Company and the Lincoln Trust. At Morgan's library after breakfast they finally decided to place more funds at the disposal of the two firms, and, if necessary, to consider taking up another money pool in the afternoon. In the meantime, Perkins met hurriedly with Lincoln Trust and Trust Company of America officials. He strongly urged them to open for business on time, even suggesting that they resort to paying depositors as slowly as possible, and by artifice if necessary. "It was not because we were particularly in love with these two trust companies that we wanted to keep them open," Perkins later explained. "Indeed, we hadn't any use for their management and knew that they ought to be closed, but we fought to keep them open in order not to have runs on other concerns and have another outburst of panic and alarm."[11]

At 10 A.M. on Friday, trading on the stock exchange began as usual, but "with the air charged in every direction with panic."[12] Prices quickly began to collapse, and rumors abounded that one brokerage or another was in peril. "At all times during the day there were frantic men and women in our offices," Perkins recollected, "in every way giving evidence of the tremendous strain they were under."[13] Again the panic-stricken trust companies were calling in their loans, which caused an acute shortage of money. By noon, interest rates on the money market reached 150 percent. Morgan and his associates pleaded with the trusts to extend their loans and implored the president of the Exchange to cease all buying or selling on margin. However, their efforts could not outpace the speed with which the trust companies were pulling their cash out of the market. By 1:30 P.M., the market was in exactly the position it had been in the day before with no money available and numerous firms on the brink of failure.

Finally, Ransom Thomas, president of the Exchange, went to see J. P. Morgan personally, asking him to call another meeting of the 14 major bank presidents. Morgan agreed, but he decided he should go in person to meet with them at the offices of the New York Clearing House (NYCH) itself, where he would ask them to raise another pool of $15 million. When he did so this time, the banks were less willing to be so generous, and they agreed only to provide $9.7 million. That would have to do. Morgan insisted that these funds carry restrictions: No margin sales were allowed (only cash could be used for investments), and the full amount of the pool would not be released until the afternoon.

Following the meeting at the NYCH, J. P. Morgan, clearly at the height of his power, marched on foot to his own offices at the Corner. Herbert Satterlee, Morgan's son-in-law, provided a description of him at that very moment, which has become among the most vivid and enduring images of the man:

> Anyone who saw Mr. Morgan going from the Clearing House back to his office that day will never forget the picture. With his coat unbuttoned and flying open, a piece of white paper clutched tightly in his right hand, he walked fast down Nassau Street. His flat-topped black derby hat was set firmly down on his head. Between his teeth he held a cigar holder in which was one of his long cigars, half smoked. His eyes were fixed straight ahead. He swung his arms as he walked and took no notice of anyone. He did not seem to see the throngs in the street, so intent was his mind on the thing that he was doing. Everyone knew him, and people made way for him, except some who were equally intent on their own affairs; and these he brushed aside. The thing that made his progress different from that of all the other people on the street was that he did not dodge, or walk in and out, or halt or slacken his pace. He simply barged along, as if he had been the only man going down the Nassau Street hill past the Subtreasury.

He was the embodiment of power and purpose. Not more than two minutes after he disappeared into his office, the cheering on the floor of the Stock Exchange could be heard out in Broad Street.[14]

The second money pool was loaned out at once on the Exchange, at rates ranging from 25 percent to 50 percent, and it proved sufficient to meet all demands: No brokerage failures were reported, and again the Exchange stayed open until 3 P.M. By the time of the market's close, $6 million of the new pool had been loaned out on the Exchange; the rest was offered after hours in an attempt to discourage speculation. Overall trading volume was down to 637,000 shares from one million the day before. By the end of this day, however, seven more banks still had failed; in an attempt to protect themselves further, the presidents of the savings banks imposed a rarely invoked requirement that depositors must give a 60-day notice for any withdrawals.

At the library on Friday evening, Morgan and his associates acknowledged they could not continue bailing out the banks and forming money pools to assist the Exchange. They turned their attention toward reassuring the public. They formed a committee responsible for disseminating all information about the financial rescue efforts to the press; all inquires would be directed here, and any attempts at evasion or secrecy were to be avoided. They also appointed a second committee to reach out directly to the clergy, encouraging them to make reassuring statements to their congregations over the weekend. "We arranged so far as we could that sermons should be preached in the various churches on Sunday," Perkins said, "cautioning people to act calmly and not to withdraw the money and lock it up."[15] According to Satterlee, a member of this committee then visited every possible clergyman, priest, or rabbi in New York on Friday or Saturday. Having won the day's battles, Morgan finished his day with a game of solitaire in the library and then went to bed around 2 A.M.

Chapter 15

A City in Trouble

A millionaire is wicked, quite;
  His doom should quick be knelled;
He should not be allowed to grow,
  If grown he should be felled,
But when a city's bonds fall flat
And no one cares for them,
Who is the man who saves the day?
  It's J.P.M.

When banks and trusts go crashing down
  From credit's sullied name,
While speechifying Greatness adds
  More fuel to the flame,
When Titan strength is needed sore,
  Black ruin's tide to stem,
Who is the man who does the job?
  It's J.P.M.

—McLandburgh Wilson
New York Times
October 27, 1907

Wtrading on Saturday morning, October 26, the atmosphere
hen the Stock Exchange opened for its regular, short day of
remained tense. However, since the markets would close at
noon and money could be neither called nor loaned on Saturdays, there
was an incipient sense of calm. In part, the morning papers had provided
the palliative that Morgan's public relations campaign had been intended
to achieve. The *New York Times* quoted financier Jacob H. Schiff, head
of the banking firm, Kuhn, Loeb & Company, who praised the actions
of both Morgan and Cortelyou. "We are doing everything we can to
support the heroic efforts of Mr. J. P. Morgan to strengthen the banking
situation generally," Schiff said. "The prompt, decisive, and effective
course of the Secretary of the Treasury deserves unstinted praise, and all
must seek in every way to aid in allaying needless alarm which has sprung
up and which, I believe, is already subsiding."[1] Industrialist Andrew
Carnegie also heralded Morgan's work and admonished depositors to
have courage. "Above all, let no man or woman selfishly lock their
hoardings in private security," Carnegie said, "but let them bring forth
their surplus and add it to the public exchequer, so as to relieve the
present famine in the money market."[2]

Across the Atlantic, further encouragement was heard as well. The
papers printed a tribute to Morgan from Britain's Lord Rothschild, who
remarked on his "admiration and respect" for the American financier.[3]
A French manufacturer said, "So great is the confidence of the great
French bankers in Mr. Morgan and Mr. Stillman personally, that were
they to come to France tomorrow they could find $100,000,000 gold
without the slightest difficulty."[4] A banker from Germany added, "We
are telling our customers that it is our duty to uphold the sound American industrial situation, and heavy buying orders are resulting."[5] While
the international financial community was genuinely supportive of the
situation in the United States, clearly they also saw opportunity for
profiting from the severely depressed prices of American securities.

Besides the gift of rhetorical support, Morgan and his associates also
received word by cable on Saturday morning that $3 million of gold was
en route to New York from London. The news could not have come at a
more propitious moment. In their weekly report on Saturday, the banks
reported a loss of $12.9 million in cash, which was accounted for partly
by the shipments of currency to the interior and the increase in loans

to other institutions needing ready money. Given the nation's dwindling supply, the news of the gold shipments, which was reported immediately by Morgan's committee to the ticker agencies, heartened both investors and depositors throughout the city. On Saturday, another $1.8 million in gold and $185,000 in silver dollars were removed from the Subtreasury's vaults and taken to various banks in the city. Meanwhile, several tons of silver and gold and bales of paper money arrived on Saturday from Washington, mostly of small currency, with another shipment expected by Sunday.

Despite the generally good news of the day, Morgan, Stillman, and Baker remained concerned that the financial system was presently incapable of meeting all the borrowing demands in the week to come. Chicago, St. Louis, and other cities continued to draw heavily on New York for two or three days' worth of currency. Moreover, Perkins reported that a large part of the money that Secretary Cortelyou had disbursed to the banks and which, in turn, had been handed over to depositors, had since been locked up in safe deposit vaults. He learned that nearly 2,000 new safe deposit boxes had been rented since Monday morning, and stories circulated about depositors locking up their cash or taking it home. As it was, however, the national banking system did not have an efficient mechanism for increasing the supply of currency quickly.

During previous financial crises, such as in 1873, 1884, 1890, and 1893, the New York Clearing House (NYCH) had resorted to issuing temporary, emergency loans to its member banks in the form of clearing house certificates. The banks had substituted these certificates for currency when clearing accounts with one another at the clearing house each day. Since the certificates circulated among member banks as a substitute for cash, they effectively freed up actual cash for the public, thereby artificially expanding the nation's money supply. Without a central bank to provide this function, the certificates proved to be extremely effective at restoring liquidity to the financial system during critical periods of stringency. However, the issuances of these certificates were *ad hoc*, and they often indicated a desperate, last-resort attempt to address a deepening, systemic crisis.

At various times during the preceding week, the use of clearing-house certificates had been suggested in New York, especially during the conferences of the clearing house member banks. Morgan, however, had steadfastly opposed the idea of using them, convinced that their issuance would only signal deeper trouble. He was adamant about avoiding any measures that could further frighten the public. In addition, one can imagine the complex dynamic within the clearing house membership—some bankers might resist suspending convertibility on moral grounds believing that as long as they have the resources, they should give depositors their cash. More darkly, delay might serve the interests of strong banks that want to discipline the weaker banks—as historian Elmus Wicker has argued, such behavior represented a conflict of private interest over the public interest.

Having already weathered the raging storm for two weeks, the financiers were left with few other options than to issue clearing-house certificates. Major cities, such as Chicago, Pittsburgh, and Philadelphia, in fact, had already announced plans to use certificates. Finally, Morgan, Stillman, and Baker conceded the necessity of the measure and authorized the 53 member banks of the NYCH to issue $100 million of certificates to be available on Monday, October 28, providing much-needed liquidity for the system.

At a later meeting of the NYCH banks, it was determined that each of banks would provide securities to the clearing house as collateral for the certificates, which would be issued for up to 75 percent of the value of these securities. Interest charged on the certificates would be a standard 6 percent. As an additional means of freeing up currency, the bankers also agreed that the trust companies should hereafter use certified checks (i.e., checks certified by clearing-house member banks) in lieu of cash to pay any depositor submitting personal checks for payment to the trust companies. Furthermore, the clearing house also discussed the possibility of admitting the trust companies as members, with a possible 15 percent reserve requirement. The bankers were reported to be generally in favor of this measure, particularly if it would include a system of inspection and examination for the trusts.

To promote the atmosphere of calm engendered by the announcement of the certificates, Morgan and his men encouraged Treasury Secretary Cortelyou to return to Washington. They hoped news of his departure would be perceived as an indication of his confidence in the situation in New York. Likewise, Morgan himself left the city on

Saturday afternoon to spend the rest of the weekend at Cragston, his country home in Highland Falls on the Hudson River. He slept soundly on the train, not having had more than five hours of sleep on any night that week.

On Sunday morning, October 27, as planned, religious leaders urged calm, offering advice for nervous depositors and investors throughout the city. At the NYCH on Cedar Street, clerks worked busily through the day attending to the mass of details in preparation for the issuance of the certificates on Monday. Encouraged by the certificates plan, the Chase National Bank announced the importation of an additional $2 million in gold from Europe. "We have seen the worst of the 'panic' phase," the *Standard of London* opined sanguinely, "and it has to be remembered that the crisis, at any rate, so far as it is connected with extraordinary trade activity, constitutes only a striking example of a complaint common in almost every financial centre, namely, a growth in the demands upon capital out of proportion to the supply."[6]

The most startling announcement of the day was the publication of a glowing, congratulatory letter by President Theodore Roosevelt to Treasury Secretary Cortelyou. During much of the financial crisis, Roosevelt had been absent, having been on a hunting expedition in the canebrakes of Louisiana. (Upon his return, the *New York Times* quipped that, "he had added several deeper shades to the bronze acquired during the Summer months at Oyster Bay."[7]) The president's first utterance about the panic was on Tuesday, October 22, en route to Washington. He stopped in Nashville, Tennessee, where in an impromptu speech he insisted that his policies had not caused the panic. In his remarks, he made the stock speculator the focus of his ire, saying, "That man is doing all that he can to bring down in ruin the fabric of our institutions, and it is our business to set our faces like flint against his wrongdoing, to war to undo that wrongdoing in the interest of the people as a whole, and primarily in the interests of the honest man of means."[8]

Within two days of making that statement, however, Secretary Cortelyou had advised Roosevelt to offer a less belligerent message to the public. In a letter written on Thursday, October 24, and published widely in the newspapers on Sunday, Roosevelt praised not only the work of the Treasury Secretary but also "those conservative and sub-stantial business men who in the crisis have acted with such wisdom and public spirit." The crusading U.S. president who had only recently impugned Morgan and other industrialists and financiers as "malefactors of great wealth," continued in his praise:

> By their action they did invaluable service in checking the panic which, beginning as a matter of speculation, was threatening to destroy the confidence and credit necessary to the conduct of legitimate business. No one who considers calmly can question that the underlying condition which make up our financial and industrial well-being are essentially sound and honest. Dishonest dealing and speculative enterprise are merely the occasional incidents of our real prosperity. The action taken by you and by the business men in question has been of the utmost consequence and has secured the opportunity for the calm consideration which must inevitably produce entire confidence in our business conditions.[9]

Surely, J. P. Morgan must have taken some degree of satisfaction in this apparent vindication by the president. Around 4 P.M. on Sunday, Morgan boarded a train back to New York City. Despite the rainy weather, it appeared that the skies were finally clearing.

On Monday morning, October 28, the wave of good news continued. The first issue of clearing-house certificates was made, thereby expanding the supply of currency by $100,925,000 by the day's end. Gold shipments arrived from all over the world, including England, Argentina, Paris, and Australia, and the total was expected to reach $20 million. Though numerous depositors were still waiting at the Trust Company of America and the Lincoln Trust, no new runs were reported. The state superintendent of banks, Clark Williams, even announced that several banks that had closed during the past week had submitted applications to reopen.

On the stock exchange, call money rates reached as high as 75 percent, but the day's final loan was made at 6 percent, and all brokerages were able to obtain the money they needed. Around 11 A.M., several brokers had approached Perkins asking if more money would be available through the banking pools, but he and the others were opposed to resorting to this measure again. The bankers were convinced that sufficient liquidity was available, and money pools were all but abandoned. "The various pools which were formed last week to render assistance to the call money market have by reason of the action taken by the New York Clearing House Association been dissolved," A. B. Hepburn, president of Chase National Bank announced. "Brokers should now make their arrangements for loans with their own banks."[10] To show his confidence in the situation, J. P. Morgan remained uptown at his library all day long.

The apparent calm, however, belied a new crisis that was brewing. "Outwardly, in the newspapers and as far as the public knew, everything was serene," Perkins said, "but four or five of us were possessed of information that made us fear that all the work we had done in the preceding week might come to naught at any moment."[11] Perkins, Morgan, and the other leading bankers had learned that the City of New York itself was on the verge of financial collapse.

On Sunday evening, an official from the City of New York came to George Perkins privately to explain that unless the municipal government could raise $20 or $30 million by November 1, the city would be insolvent. It was already unable to meet its payroll obligations and could not pay its contractors. The city had tried, and failed, to float bonds over the previous summer, and succeeded in doing so in September only with Morgan's intervention. During the fall, the city had been financing its expenditures with the $40 million in short-term loans that had been previously underwritten by J. P. Morgan & Company. In September, the city felt confident of its ability to repay these debts quickly, but the intervening financial crisis and resultant market conditions now made that impossible. The city official said they had tried to access the public markets for three or four days, but they had succeeded in raising only a few million dollars. "To raise even one million dollars seemed about as possible at that moment as to move a mountain," Perkins said.[12]

Around 4 p.m. on Monday, October 28, Mayor McClellan, his deputy, the city controller, and the chamberlain, came to see Morgan personally at the library. They explained that after last summer's financing they discovered that they needed to use the entire $40 million almost immediately, and now they needed additional funding to carry them through the rest of the year. After a few hours spent discussing the city's finances, they adjourned and agreed to meet again the next day at 3:30 p.m. Neither Morgan nor his associates believed they could place the city's short-term obligations on the market in Europe, and there would certainly be little appetite for them in America; given the current rates on money, a 6 percent return was hardly attractive. But the consequences of the city's financial failure would be severe. "We all realized the gravity of the situation," Perkins said. "How much fuel would be added to the flame if the credit of the City of New York should be questioned at such a moment?"[13]

The next day at the appointed time, Morgan and the others renewed their discussion with the mayor and his delegation. Then, without saying a word, Morgan sat at his desk in the library and took up a pen and began to write. "With scarcely a hesitation, without even stopping to select a word," Perkins recalled, "he covered three long sheets of paper and then after reading it over, he handed it to me and said, 'See what Messrs. Baker and Stillman think of that.'"[14]

With astonishing speed and clarity, Morgan had crafted a proposal that J. P. Morgan & Company would take $30 million of the city's revenue bonds, with optional terms of one, two, or three years, bearing an interest rate of 6 percent. There was an option on $20 million more, and the city was required to appoint a commission to examine its finances. Morgan planned to exchange these bonds for clearing-house certificates by handing them over to the First National and National City Banks. This measure would thereby result in an additional $30 million in liquidity for the City of New York as well as provide $30 million in credit for the city through the banks.

After a discussion lasting about 20 minutes, the bankers and a lawyer concluded that Morgan's extemporaneous term sheet "was practically perfect both from the standpoint of an offer and the concise manner in which it had been put."[15] The meeting adjourned just before 7 P.M., and the representatives of the City of New York departed with a contract to receive $30 million from J. P. Morgan & Company, the First National Bank, and National City Bank the very next day. With the flourish of his pen, J. P. Morgan had thus vanquished the financial threat to the City of New York.

The remainder of the week was very encouraging. On Wednesday, October 30, the Trust Company of America accepted over $100,000 in deposits *more* than it had paid out; it also reported seeing the fewest number of depositors than on any previous day, with fewer than 20 remaining at the close of business. By Thursday, the Trust Company had refunded $1 million that had been loaned to it over the past week.

Money rates were still relatively high and stress was apparent on the Exchange, but the average interest rate on call money had declined to 20 percent, and at one point had even reached a low of 8 percent. During the week, the Bank of England raised its discount rate from 4.5 to 5.5 percent, indicating that the Bank was trying to stanch the flow of gold to the United States. By November 4, the Bank of England's rate would rise to seven percent, the highest since 1873. Central banks in France and Germany followed suit. Secretary Cortelyou noted "severe pressure" on the money markets in those countries, and observed that the grave conditions were not "localized in the United States."[16]

These global conditions reflected the fact that gold continued to arrive in the United States at a volume not seen since 1893. Still, very few firms on the Exchange were accepting margin business and the demand for cash remained strong because of numerous end-of-month payroll and debt obligations. The one alarming event during the week was the failure of a stock exchange house, Kessler & Company. That failure might have passed unremarkably, but it foreshadowed a new and unexpected turn in the crisis for which J. P. Morgan's own motivations would ultimately be called into question.

SAN FRANCISCO DOOMED

EXTRA **Oakland Tribune.** EXTRA

VOL. LXV   OAKLAND, CALIFORNIA, WEDNESDAY EVENING APRIL 18, 1906   NO. 49

GREAT EARTHQUAKE!

DEATH AND DESTRUCTION SWEEP THE BAY CITIES!

HUNDREDS DIE IN RUINS!

THIS MORNING AT 5:44:48 O'CLOCK AN EARTHQUAKE SHOCK WAS EXPERIENCED IN OAKLAND AND A NUMBER OF OTHER CALIFORNIA CITIES. THE TEMBLOR LASTED FOR 8 SECONDS. MANY CHIMNEYS IN PRIVATE HOUSES, MERCANTILE ESTABLISHMENTS AND MANUFACTURING INSTITUTIONS WERE KNOCKED DOWN. IN SOME CASES HOLES WERE TORN IN THE WALLS OF BUSINESS PLACES, BUT NO STRUCTURES WERE ENTIRELY DEMOLISHED. WATER FOR A TIME WAS CUT OFF FROM CONSUMERS, AND TELEGRAPH AND TELEPHONE COMMUNICATION WAS INTERRUPTED. THE LOSS WILL AGGREGATE SEVERAL HUNDRED THOUSAND DOLLARS. FIVE LIVES WERE LOST. THESE VICTIMS WERE CRUSHED TO DEATH IN A ROOMING HOUSE. IN SAN JOSE AND SAN FRANCISCO THE LOSS OF PROPERTY AND LIFE WAS EXCESSIVE, ESPECIALLY IN THE LATTER PLACE, WHERE THE EASTERN PART OF THE CITY, INCLUDING THE PALACE HOTEL, THE CALL BUILDING, THE CHRONICLE BUILDING AND THE CITY HALL AND A NUMBER OF OTHER STRUCTURES WERE REDUCED TO ASHES BY FIRE WHICH BROKE OUT IN THE DISMANTLED STRUCTURES. THE LOSS THERE WILL RUN INTO MANY MILLIONS.

TO THE PEOPLE:

Keep cool. Keep your heads. Keep your courage. Don't exaggerate. Don't get panic stricken.

An earthquake shock of great violence and long duration is an appalling calamity, but a panic is infinitely worse.

Reason, courage, and calmness dissolve in times of panic like snow in a spring thaw, and confusion, irresolution prevail at a time when judgment and action are the supreme necessity of the hour. Beware of crediting and circulating wild rumors, and avoid idle lamentation.

A great disaster has befallen San Francisco, Oakland and several other California cities, due to mysterious elemental disturbance. There has been widespread damage to property and considerable loss of life. Careless and imperfect in construction responsible for nine tenths of the damage and a great majority of the casualties.

It may be a thousand years before there is such another disturbance in this locality, but the consequences of this one is an admonition not to repeat the errors of the past.

The damage is so far from being irreparable that it should dishearten no one. Therefore it is wise to take counsel of reason and courage, and shun the fearful infection of timid, the superstitious and weak-minded.

Now is the time for the citizen of Oakland and San

(Continued on Page 11)

FIVE ARE KILLED

Five people were killed in the Empire Building on Twelfth Street, near Broadway.

The dead are:

OTTO WISHER, forty-five years of age.
AMELIA WISHER, thirteen years of age.
EDWARD WISHER, about twenty-five years of age.
MRS. EDWARD MARNEY, twenty-five years old
Unknown man, about twenty-five years of age.
JOHN JUDD dropped dead of heart disease.

BUNKERS IN BAY

The docks near the Southern Pacific Wharf here completely collapsed. Many of the bunkers fell into the bay carrying thousands of tons of coal.

The Long Wharf is one of the most important shipping points about the bay.

REMOVING THE DEBRIS

The Board of Police and Fire Commissioners this morning set all the street employes cleaning up debris left by the earthquake. Gangs of men with wagons, picks and shovels, have been put to work and natural disaster of this city had few deaths or were working as fast as possible. Scores of the earthquake.

STANFORD BUILDINGS DOWN

PALO ALTO, April 18.—All the university buildings here but one are a total wreck.

KILLS HEAD OF ASYLUM

Superintendent Fred Hatter, who returned from San Jose in his auto this afternoon, states that the Agnew asylum is a total wreck, that many of the inmates were killed and that the remainder are milling around loose, terrorizing the community.

The superintendent of the institution at San Francisco said all the inmates had been killed.

THE CALL IS BURNING

SAN FRANCISCO, APRIL 18.—THE SAN FRANCISCO CALL BUILDING IS ON FIRE, AND AT THIS WRITING IT SEEMS CERTAIN THAT IT WILL BE TOTALLY DESTROYED.

FLAMES ARE RAPIDLY EATING AWAY THE STRUCTURE DESPITE THE EFFORTS MADE TO SAVE THIS MAGNIFICENT BUILDING. STREAMS OF WATER ARE BEING TURNED INTO THE BLAZING PILE, BUT SO INTENSE IS THE HEAT THAT THE WATER BECOMES STEAM, AS SOON AS IT REACHES THE FIERY FURNACE.

GREAT DAMAGE HAS ALSO BEEN DONE TO THE EXAMINER AND CHRONICLE BUILDING.

MINISTER IN DANGER

The Brooklyn Presbyterian church on East Fifteenth street and Twelfth are.

SHEDS ARE DESTROYED

MAYOR MOTT APPEALS TO THE PEOPLE

TO THE PEOPLE OF OAKLAND: THE EARTHQUAKE THIS MORNING VISITED UPON OUR CITY A GREAT CALAMITY. YET IT IS A SOURCE OF MUCH SATISFACTION THAT WE WERE SPARED FROM A CONFLAGRATION AND SERIOUS LOSS OF LIFE. THE OFFICIALS OF THE CITY HAVE THE SITUATION WELL IN HAND, BUT I DESIRE TO APPEAL TO THE PEOPLE TO CO-OPERATE WITH THE AUTHORITIES IN MAINTAINING PEACE AND ORDER.

AS MANY BUILDINGS ARE IN AN UNSAFE CONDITION THE PUBLIC ARE ADMONISHED TO KEEP OFF THE STREETS, AND PARTICULARLY WARNED AGAINST CONGREGATING IN GROUPS. IT IS ALSO VERY ESSENTIAL THAT PRECAUTION BE USED IN THE BUILDING OF FIRES UNTIL THE CHIMNEYS HAVE BEEN INSPECTED AND REPAIRED. THOSE WHO HAVE NOT EITHER GAS OR OIL STOVES ARE ADVISED THAT DANGER MAY BE AVOIDED BY MOVING THEIR STOVES OUT OF DOORS. FRANK K. MOTT, MAYOR.

Front page headlines from the *Oakland Tribune* (Calif.) reporting the devastation in San Francisco, April 18, 1906.

Source: Reprinted by permission of NewspaperARCHIVE.com.

Charles T. Barney, president of the Knickerbocker Trust Company.

Source: Reprinted by permission of Brown Brothers, Sterling, PA 18463. www.brownbrothersusa.com.

F. Augustus Heinze, president of the Mercantile National Bank.

Source: Reprinted by permission of Brown Brothers, Sterling, PA 18463. www.brownbrothersusa.com.

J. Pierpont Morgan.

Source: Reprinted by permission of Brown Brothers, Sterling, PA 18463. www.brownbrothersusa.com.

Theodore Roosevelt, President of the United States (1901–1909).

Source: Courtesy of Picture History.

George B. Cortelyou, United States
Secretary of the Treasury.

Source: Courtesy of Picture History.

George F. Baker, president of the First
National Bank.

Source: Reprinted by permission of Brown
Brothers, Sterling, PA 18463.
www.brownbrothersusa.com.

James Stillman, president of the National
City Bank.

Source: Reprinted by permission of Brown
Brothers, Sterling, PA 18463.
www.brownbrothersusa.com.

George W. Perkins, partner, J.P. Morgan &
Co.

Source: Reprinted by permission of Brown
Brothers, Sterling, PA 18463.
www.brownbrothersusa.com.

Lines of depositors form at the midtown offices of the Knickerbocker Trust Company, October 17, 1907, 9:00 AM.

Source: Reprinted by permission of Brown Brothers, Sterling, PA 18463. www.brownbrothersusa.com.

Depositors and messengers at the Lincoln Trust Company, October 1907.

Source: Reprinted by permission of Brown Brothers, Sterling, PA 18463. www.brownbrothersusa.com.

Panic erupts outside the United States Subtreasury Building in New York, October 1907.

Source: Reprinted by permission of Brown Brothers, Sterling, PA 18463. www.brownbrothersusa.com.

J.P. Morgan appearing at the Pujo Committee hearings in Washington, D.C., December 1912.

Source: Reprinted by permission of Brown Brothers, Sterling, PA 18463. www.brownbrothersusa.com.

Chapter 16

A Delirium of Excitement

What can be accomplished by one man and associates has been abundantly demonstrated in this city during the last week.[1]

—Elbert H. Gary
United States Steel Corporation
October 30, 1907

Early on Saturday morning, November 2, J. P. Morgan called an emergency conference at the library. There was a new problem on Wall Street. One of the largest brokerage houses was teetering on the verge of collapse, and its failure threatened to spark another massive wave of panic. The brokerage firm, Moore & Schley, had borrowed more than $30 million from numerous banks, trust companies, and other financial institutions in New York and elsewhere. To secure its many loans, the firm had used the stock of the Tennessee Coal, Iron & Railroad Company (commonly known at the time as Tennessee Coal and Iron, or simply TC&I) as collateral. However, the strained market conditions had raised questions about the value of the TC&I shares, and on Monday many of the banks would likely call in Moore & Schley's loans. If the loans were called and creditors liquidated the TC&I shares *en masse*, then the market would be flooded with TC&I stock. TC&I's price would plummet, devastating Moore & Schley and causing a sudden catastrophe on the stock market.

Under ordinary circumstances, Moore & Schley's loans would not have constituted a heavy burden for the major banks and trust companies. However, the unusually heavy demands for cash by depositors now required that lenders hold securities or other assets that could be quickly converted into liquid assets. TC&I's stock, it seemed, was not so easily convertible. In fact, the market for TC&I's shares was thin; only a few investors, including Grant B. Schley, the senior partner of Moore & Schley, owned the securities; for months, Schley and his small pool of investors had been artificially supporting TC&I's stock price. So, even though the stock had been trading steadily at $130 per share for some time, if the banks disposed of the stock, then its price would likely fall by at least $50 or $60 before any other buyers would emerge for it. By then, both Moore & Schley and the many other institutions holding TC&I securities as collateral for Moore & Schley's loans would be in serious trouble.

J. P. Morgan was gravely concerned about this turn of events. "It is very serious," he said. "If Moore and Schley go, there is no telling what the effect on Wall Street will be and on financial institutions of New York, and how many other houses will drop with it, and how many banks might be included in the consequences."[2] Morgan quickly dispatched two of his most reliable aides, Thomas "Tommy" Joyce from J. P. Morgan & Company and Richard "Dick" Trimble from U.S. Steel, to examine the books of Moore & Schley. He also told Grant B. Schley, the Moore & Schley partner *and* the brother-in-law of his friend George F. Baker, president of the First National Bank, to join them.

Morgan continued the meeting at the library, discussing the general condition of TC&I and the magnitude of Moore & Schley's loans held by his friends and associates, especially the senior bankers. The simplest method for saving the brokerage house would have been to raise a loan for about $25 million, but it was unlikely such an amount could be found, particularly for an institution that was already so highly leveraged. Moreover, margin trading was down, and it was felt that the immediate outlook for the bond market was poor. However, Lewis Cass Ledyard, a lawyer representing the syndicate controlling TC&I and a personal friend of Morgan's, had a bold idea. Upon hearing his daring and ultimately controversial proposal, Morgan adjourned the morning's discussion and called for an immediate meeting of the finance committee of the United States Steel Corporation. He told them to come to the library by 2:30 that afternoon.

J. P. Morgan had been intimately connected with the United States Steel Corporation for years. In 1901 Morgan, Elbert H. Gary, and Henry Clay Frick had created U.S. Steel by combining various steel producers, including the extensive operations owned by Andrew Carnegie. By 1907, the company controlled nearly 60 percent of the nation's steel-producing capacity, making it the largest steel producer in the world *and* the world's largest corporation. Despite the recent market crash and ongoing financial panic, U.S. Steel was in robust condition. The company recently reported that its quarterly earnings had surpassed $43.8 million—the second most profitable period in its history—and that it could boast cash resources of $76 million.

Elbert Gary (known by all as "Judge" Gary for having served two terms as a county judge in Illinois) was a savvy chief executive, and he was sensitive to the money troubles facing investors and depositors. He recognized a positive role for the company to play during the crisis, especially at a time when "big business" was regularly under fire. Speaking to U.S. Steel's board of directors on Tuesday, October 29, at a meeting that included Morgan and Frick, Gary said:

> There has existed during the last week a delirium of excitement. The feeling in a large measure has been without cause, and there is already a change for the better. If all of us do everything in our power to maintain a high standard for the conduct of affairs in our charge we can be of great benefit in restoring the confidence necessary to success.[3]

In response to the crisis, on Friday, November 1, the company announced plans to pay its employees only 20 percent in cash and the remainder by check in small denominations at various banks. "This method of payment was decided upon because of the fact that the amount of currency in the banks of the country is limited," Judge Gary said.[4] It was hoped that U.S. Steel, which had a payroll of $3 million *per week*, could use its own cash hoard to provide much-needed liquidity to the system.

By 3 P.M. on Saturday, November 2, the members of U.S. Steel's finance committee had convened at the library as Morgan had requested. Judge Gary and Henry Frick were present; the lawyers for Moore & Schley were gathered in an adjoining room. Lewis Cass Ledyard, the attorney for TC&I and Morgan's friend, had suggested to Morgan at the morning meeting that perhaps U.S. Steel could save Moore & Schley if they would consider acquiring the Tennessee, Coal, Iron & Railroad Company. That was the proposal Morgan had brought them all there to discuss. Right away the lawyers from the next room brought in reports and data regarding TC&I, which the board members from U.S. Steel studied for an hour.

Tennessee Coal, Iron & Railroad Company was an independent steel producer based in northern Alabama. The company possessed coal and steel properties that extended through Alabama, Tennessee, and Georgia, and by 1907, it owned an estimated 800 million tons of iron ore and 2 billion tons of coal, plus additional reserves of limestone, dolomite, and other raw materials necessary for the manufacture of steel. Significantly, the company's ores were located within 25 miles of its ovens and furnaces—literally "sitting on its raw material"[5] —a geographic benefit many northern steel mills did not share. Given its apparent advantages, TC&I was, by some estimates, at the forefront of a movement to consolidate the disparate southern steel producers, and it was considered a potentially important competitor to U.S. Steel. Testifying to its growing influence, not long before the panic, TC&I received an order for 150,000 tons of steel rails from the railroads controlled by E. H. Harriman, an order that would typically have been granted to U.S. Steel.

Tennessee Coal, Iron, & Railroad had been among the original 12 companies that comprised the Dow Jones Industrial Average in 1896. Since then, its stock had become a notorious highflier on Wall Street, and lately rumors of mismanagement and malfeasance appeared often in the newspapers. The muckraking journalist Ida Tarbell reported that periodically TC&I was paying dividends from borrowed funds. "As for making money," Tarbell wrote, "old-timers tell you that the only department in the concern that ever ran at a profit was the company's stores!"[6] In 1906, a syndicate, which included Grant B. Schley, took over TC&I.[7] These new owners had plans to rehabilitate the company's plants, but these and other investments had depleted the company's resources completely; by 1907, the company was left with $4 million of floating debt, of which $1.5 million was about to come due.

Despite TC&I's prodigious assets, Henry Frick was vehemently and steadfastly opposed to an acquisition of TC&I by U.S. Steel. He was convinced that the firm was an inefficient producer and that its costs of production were too high to be integrated successfully with U.S. Steel. Moreover, he understood that because of the high phosphorus content of TC&I's ores, the steel it produced was generally of low quality. Morgan argued with him, saying that he felt the company's coal and iron were at least worth the company's capitalization. Even so, Elbert Gary was skeptical, too, especially because he was already familiar with the condition of both Moore & Schley and TC&I. Just recently during the panic, Moore & Schley had approached Gary himself for a loan, and he had exchanged $1.2 million of U.S. Steel gold bonds for $2 million of TC&I stock—now worth much less than what he had paid. Gary was, therefore, disinclined to extend himself or his company to aid either Moore & Schley or TC&I any further.

Finally, after a lengthy discussion, the U.S. Steel finance committee voted to make two offers to assist Moore & Schley. They would agree either to loan Moore & Schley $5 million on the equities in their loans, or U.S. Steel would buy control of TC&I for $90 per share in cash. Neither deal, however, would be sufficient to save Moore & Schley altogether. After an hour or two, Grant Schley told George Perkins to inform J. P. Morgan that his firm could not accept the proposed terms. The meeting ended with negotiations at a standstill, and they adjourned the meeting at 7 P.M. Herbert Satterlee reported that on this day Morgan did not get his customary nap and game of solitaire; that was because Morgan would be busy resolving another crisis that was gathering steam in the very next room.

Chapter 17

Modern Medici

There wasn't going to be any mistake that night.
[J. P. Morgan] intended that all should stay until the end of the party.[1]

—Recollection of Benjamin Strong Jr.
Bankers Trust Company

While Morgan was considering the problems of Moore & Schley and the disposition of the Tennessee Coal, Iron & Railroad Company on Saturday morning, conditions on the Exchange in New York remained generally quiet; the market closed as usual at noon with no extraordinary activity. Earlier in the day, the State Banking Examiner had released the weekly bank statement, but the report was so bad that it was suppressed and kept from the press. The biggest troubles were occurring at the trust companies. The situation at the Trust Company of America and the Lincoln Trust Company still continued very poorly, and there was talk that one or both of them would fail to open again on Monday because of continuing runs. The funds loaned to trust banks so far were not going to suffice and depositors were still unconvinced that their money was safe. Again, the trust company crisis was coming to a head; this time, J. P. Morgan would *not* provide the solution. He decided it was time for others to come forward.

For days, J. P. Morgan's partner, George W. Perkins, had been trying to get a complete statement from the trust companies regarding their financial condition, but he "had obtained nothing that was satisfactory."[2] The trusts would have a brief respite the next day because it would be Sunday, and Tuesday, November 5, would be Election Day, also a banking holiday. But Perkins felt it was critical that the problems with the banks and trust companies must be solved by then, or else "there was no use in making any further fight for them and that they would have to close."[3] He assigned two separate committees of examiners to ascertain the financial status of both the Trust Company of America and the Lincoln Trust.

Among the investigators he assigned to inspect the trust companies was Benjamin Strong Jr., the associate from Bankers Trust who later described working "without sleep nor leaving the building"[4] to carry out his assignment. By 9 P.M. on Saturday, November 2, Strong reported to Morgan's library to offer his final assessment of the ailing trusts. When he arrived at the building, about 40 or 50 men were already discussing both the brewing crisis and the troubles that lay in store for Monday. He noted that the presidents of the clearing-house banks were assembled in the library's East Room, while representatives from the trust companies were gathered in the West Room. Morgan, Judge Gary, Henry Frick, Lewis Cass Ledyard, and others had retired to "neutral ground"[5] in the office of Morgan's librarian at the rear of the building.

"Knowing of the Tennessee Coal and Iron situation," Strong said, "I felt satisfied that something had gone wrong."[6] Henry P. "Harry" Davison, who had established Bankers Trust, told Strong that Morgan was already convinced that $25 million would be required to deal with the trust companies in addition to an estimated $25 million to address the problems with Moore & Schley. ("[I]n those days $50 million looked very large indeed in contrast with the figures to which we are accustomed now," Strong later wrote in 1924.[7]) Morgan finally announced to his counselors in the librarian's office that he would agree to undertake the difficulties with Moore & Schley only if the trust company officials themselves would insure the needs of their weaker brethren.

For the next several hours, Strong reported that nothing but "desultory conversation"[8] took place among the bank officials. Thomas W. Lamont, another Morgan associate, was also summoned to this plenary session of bankers, and he provided an evocative description of what he saw that night at the now-famous meeting at the library:

> A more incongruous meeting place for anxious bankers could hardly be imagined: in one room—lofty, magnificent—tapestries hanging on the walls, rare Bibles and illuminated manuscripts of the Middle Ages filling the cases; in another, that collection of the Early Renaissance masters—Castagno, Ghirlandaio, Perugino, to mention only a few—the huge open fire, the door just ajar to the holy of holies where the original manuscripts were safeguarded. And, as I say, an anxious throng of bankers, too uneasy to sit down or converse at ease, pacing through the long marble hall and up and down the high-ceilinged rooms, with their cinquecento background, waiting for the momentous decisions of the modern Medici.[9]

Finally, around midnight, Edwin S. Marston, the president of the Farmers Loan and Trust Company, was summoned away from the trust company executives in the West Room to see J. P. Morgan. After meeting with Morgan for an hour, Marston—"looking very grave"[10]—returned to the room and explained to the trust presidents that Morgan had informed him of another serious situation, about which he was not at liberty to say more. Morgan told him that the problem would call for another $25 million, and he was working toward a solution. But Morgan was very concerned about the problems with the trusts and the risks they posed to this other situation. "Mr. Morgan was naturally unwilling to proceed with the other matter [i.e., the rescue of Moore & Schley]," Strong said, "with the possibility of a complete banking collapse which would render his efforts futile."[11] Clearly, this statement was an indication that Morgan was leaving the trust company problem to the trust company presidents. This time, he refused to be their rescuer, and this thrust the bankers into an utter state of consternation.

During the debates that ensued, Strong dozed off on a lounge chair next to James Stillman, the president of National City Bank. "I recall his asking me when I had last been in bed," Strong said, "and when I told him the previous Thursday night, he said the country wasn't going to smash if I went home to bed."[12] Finally, at 3 A.M., the assembled bank and trust company officials were ready to hear Benjamin Strong's full report on the faltering trust companies; by this time, there were approximately 120 men participating in the conference. Outside, a throng of reporters awaited news from the meeting, but secrecy was maintained through the night and into the morning.

Inside, Strong assured the trust presidents that the Trust Company of America was solvent and, with equity that amounted to $2 million, the firm had sufficient assets to pay off its depositors in time. Another committee organized by George Perkins reported that the Lincoln Trust was probably short of its ability to pay its depositors by at least $1 million. After concluding his report, Strong headed to leave the building; when he reached the door, he found that the library had been locked. "It was indeed true that Mr. Morgan, having assembled the men to deal with a perilous situation, had had the door to the library locked, and the key was in his own pocket," Strong wrote.[13] Even though Morgan was often not directly involved in the negotiations, clearly he was exerting powerful control over the bankers. "Mr. Morgan took no chances," Satterlee wrote. "He meant to have the situation cleared up before a single man left the building."[14]

By this time, Morgan himself had entered the discussion. He pointed to Edward King, the president of the Union Trust Company, who had been appointed the unofficial leader of his fellow trust company presidents. Morgan told him that they must take action now, and that they must provide a loan of $25 million to support the Trust Company of America, or else "the walls of their own edifices might come crumbling about their ears."[15] He told them again that the equity in the Trust Company would secure their loans and that the clearing house banks were looking after the situation elsewhere.

Even though Morgan had just told them that it was incumbent upon the trust presidents "to look after their own,"[16] they were still hesitant to take any action. They contended that in the absence of their boards of directors they lacked the authority to burden their institutions with such a heavy commitment. They were also convinced that it was their primary responsibility to conserve their assets in order to weather the financial storm that was swirling around them. Morgan understood their position and he sympathized with them, but the trenchant financier understood that the failure of the Trust Company of America could have far-reaching implications; unless it were saved that day, they risked a complete collapse of the entire banking system. "The situation must not get further out of hand," Lamont said. "It had to be saved."[17]

Several of the lawyers present had drafted a simple subscription for a loan of $25 million. As for any possible objections from the trust companies' boards of directors, Morgan told the assembled presidents that he was confident their boards would ratify whatever decision was made there that day; Morgan clearly understood the power his personal endorsement would carry. One of the lawyers read the subscription form aloud to the bankers, and he laid it on the table. Morgan waved his hand "invitingly" toward the document.

"There you are, gentlemen," Morgan said.

He waited for a few moments, and then he put his hand on the shoulder of his friend Edward King, encouraging him to come forward.

"There's the place, King, and here's the pen," Morgan said as he placed a gold pen in the hand of the Union Trust president.

King signed, followed by every other trust company president in the room.[18]

Chapter 18

Instant and Far-Reaching Relief

They must deal with it as they see fit. I have gone with it as far as I can.[1]

—J. Pierpont Morgan
November 3, 1907

A s the early morning sun rose above New York City on Sunday, November 3, 1907, the brass doors of Morgan's library were finally unlocked. After the bankers had given J. P. Morgan sufficient assurance that they would each subscribe to the new money pool to support the weaker trust companies, they were allowed to go home. As the bankers dispersed, George F. Baker, president of the First National Bank of New York, and Lewis Cass Ledyard, the attorney for the syndicate controlling the Tennessee, Coal, Iron & Railroad Company, stopped to have a few words with Morgan. "You look tired," Morgan chirped to Ledyard; their meeting at the library had been under way at least since Saturday morning. "Go home and get a good night's rest,"

Morgan added, "but be back here at nine o'clock sharp!"[2] It was then 5 A.M.

Despite the promising discussions Morgan had engineered inside his library, the city's newspaper reporters outside—and the public at large—were still largely in the dark. No statements had been released, and they were told only that the financiers were considering the general financial conditions. That was clearly insufficient. "[I]t became evident from the talk about the clubs that considerable alarm existed," observed George W. Perkins, who had also attended the all-night conference. "Stocks were being offered about town at from one to two points under the closing prices of Saturday. All sorts of rumors were flying about, and by noon it became clear that the failure of Moore & Schley on Monday and the closing of the Lincoln Trust Company would bring very general trouble."[3] The papers also reported that President Roosevelt was being urged to call for a special session of Congress to enact legislation and regulation for financial institutions. Perkins, as usual, went to see Morgan after breakfast, and they made arrangements for another conference at the library to address the still unresolved problem of the vulnerable brokerage house, Moore & Schley.

The day's first meeting convened at 4:30 P.M. "Mr. Morgan, as usual, sat in his armchair facing the blazing wood fire in the big West Room," Herbert Satterlee recalled.[4] To Morgan's right was a small table, and on the other side of this sat the city's most senior bankers and Morgan's most trusted advisers, including George Baker, James Stillman, and George Perkins. Of course, Grant B. Schley was also there, as well as Elbert H. Gary, Henry Clay Frick, and the finance committee of U.S. Steel Corporation. It was clear that should Moore & Schley suspend the next day, an indefinite number of brokerage houses and other financial institutions would come tumbling down, too. During the meeting, several bankers and financiers were intent on saving Moore & Schley, and they pressed its importance upon J. P. Morgan. Regarding the proposal for U.S. Steel to acquire TC&I, Morgan told them:

> I have done what I can. I have never been more concerned over a situation than I am over this. I think this is the most serious thing we have had to meet in this panic yet, but I cannot urge upon the Steel Corporation to take this property. I hope they will do it, but I do not

think I have the right to urge them or force it upon them if I could. They must deal with it as they see fit. I have gone with it as far as I can.[5]

Gary and Frick remained strongly opposed to the acquisition plan. They felt it was an unworthy investment that U.S. Steel did not need, and they feared such a combination would open their company to accusations of attempting to create a monopoly in steel production. At the time, U.S. Steel controlled nearly two thirds of the country's steel-producing capacity. By early evening, the issue remained unresolved, and the steel executives planned to convene again at the library later that night.

After dinner, Morgan met with Tommy Joyce and Dick Trimble, whom he had delegated the day before to perform an in-depth review of Moore & Schley's books. After working more than 24 hours straight, they presented their findings at the library privately to Morgan, Baker, and Stillman. Morgan asked Joyce how much he estimated would be needed for Moore & Schley to avoid ruin. "About seventeen or possibly eighteen millions, sir," Joyce responded.[6] With that, Morgan proclaimed that the three of them—himself, Baker, and Stillman—must raise the money at once; he announced he would take a third interest in the subscription, and he suggested that Baker and Stillman provide the remainder of the $18 million, which would be carried by their banks until U.S. Steel could arrange to take it over from them. Baker consented to Morgan's plan right away, though Stillman was unhappy.

"Why, you haven't had time to study those figures!" Stillman said.

"Well, I know my man," Morgan replied. He handed the papers back to Joyce, concluding the discussion summarily. Reluctantly, Stillman agreed.[7]

Earlier in the day, George Perkins had been conferring with Grant B. Schley of Moore & Schley and John B. Topping, the president of the Tennessee Coal, Iron & Railroad Company, to determine the exact condition of TC&I. By the time the board members of U.S. Steel reconvened at Morgan's library on Sunday evening, Perkins, Schley, and Topping had mustered significant evidence to show Gary and Frick that TC&I's condition was not as compromised as they had assumed. In particular, they demonstrated that the company had nearly completed the construction of its new rail-producing mill, which would enable TC&I

to make rails more cheaply than had been previously possible. Again, the steel executives discussed their disposition toward an acquisition of the firm.

Finally, the finance committee of United States Steel Corporation acceded to a new plan to acquire TC&I. U.S. Steel would buy a majority of the company, but not by paying cash, as had been proposed earlier. U.S. Steel would instead exchange its own bonds for shares of TC&I stock at par. Specifically, U.S. Steel would exchange each of its 60-year, 5 percent sinking fund gold bonds,* which had a par value of $11,904.76, for 100 shares of TC&I stock, which had a par value of $10,000. Gary and Frick's agreement to this deal was contingent on three important conditions being met. First, the Roosevelt administration must interpose no objections to the acquisition; second, this arrangement must "unquestionably save Moore & Schley"[8] from failure; and, third, formal arrangements must be concluded to attend to the city's struggling trust companies.

Moore & Schley's creditors were holding TC&I stock as collateral for Moore & Schley's loans—and the value of that collateral was considerably diminished as a result of the financial crisis. Therefore, the opportunity to exchange that stock for the gold-backed bonds of U.S. Steel was enormously attractive. Few other companies could have achieved such a uniquely reassuring outcome for bankers, investors, and depositors. In addition, since the acquisition would be achieved entirely through an exchange of securities, the transaction would place no further demands on the nation's already strained cash resources. With this arrangement, Grant B. Schley and the other partners of Moore & Schley could also use their new U.S. Steel securities to repay the various bank debts of the firm. Moore & Schley, numerous brokerages, the banks, and trust companies would be saved, all without the need for cash. The full board of U.S. Steel was scheduled to vote on this proposed deal in the next few days, on Wednesday, November 6. All that was required now was the willingness of the Roosevelt administration to allow the deal to occur.

Once the general terms of a deal had been determined on Sunday night, the conversation turned to whether the acquisition would be considered a breach of the Act of July 2, 1890, legislation more generally known as the Sherman Antitrust Act. The Act declared that any

---

* Gold bonds promised repayment in gold coin as opposed to silver coin or ordinary paper money.

business combination "in restraint of trade" was illegal. The law had not been invoked seriously for some years, but during the administration of President Theodore Roosevelt, the Bureau of Corporations and the attorney general of the United States had been aggressively pursuing what they felt were the anticompetitive behaviors of large corporations. Given its massive size and scope, U.S. Steel would be an obvious target of their scrutiny, and Gary and Frick were particularly sensitive to this risk.

"Before we go ahead with this," Judge Gary told Morgan, "we must consult President Roosevelt."

"But what has the president to do with it?" demanded Morgan.

"If we do this without consulting the administration," persisted Gary, "a bill in equity might stop the sale, and in that case more harm than good would be done. He cannot say that we may or may not purchase, but we ought to know his attitude since he has a general direction of the law department of the United States."

Morgan considered his point briefly. "Can you go at once?"[9]

At 10 P.M. on Sunday, Judge Gary called William Loeb, President Roosevelt's private secretary, to request an interview with the president at the earliest possible time on Monday morning. Once Loeb agreed to a meeting, Gary's men called the chief dispatcher of the Pennsylvania Railroad in Newark, New Jersey, telling him to arrange a special train comprised merely of a locomotive and a Pullman sleeper car, bound for direct travel to Washington, D.C.; all signalmen on the route would receive instructions that the one–car special would pass through during the night. After concluding their discussions on Sunday at the library, Judge Gary and Henry Frick left at midnight in their cab and raced to New Jersey for their private, waiting train.[10]

By Monday morning, November 4, cables from London already indicated that the prices of American securities were falling; if prices in New York followed suit, many brokers would be unable to meet their margin requirements, putting even more pressure on houses like the troubled Moore & Schley. After only a few hours of sleep, the 70-year-old Morgan awakened at 8:30 A.M. to await the crucial call from Washington. After breakfast, he instructed George Perkins to have a man posted at his offices at the Corner; he said that he should establish an open phone connection with the White House so they could hear Roosevelt's verdict immediately from Gary and Frick.

Gary and Frick had arrived in Washington early on Monday morning, anxious to see the president as soon as possible. For Morgan's plan to work, they must have Roosevelt's blessing for the TC&I deal *before* the stock exchange opened at 10 A.M. Upon reaching the White House at 8 o'clock, Loeb, the president's secretary, firmly refused to see the men from U.S. Steel for another hour, saying that the president would see no one before 10 o'clock. This was more than the steel men were prepared to accept.

"But this is a serious matter," pleaded Gary, "and I think that if you will tell him just what Mr. Frick and I are here for, he will see us."[11]

At that moment, James Garfield, the secretary of the interior, arrived. Gary and Frick confided their problem to him and explained their urgent need to see the president. At once, Garfield conveyed their message to the president, and Roosevelt hastily interrupted his breakfast to see them. Since the attorney general was away from the city, Roosevelt asked Elihu Root, his secretary of state, to review the matter with him.

At 9:45 A.M., Loeb told the men standing by at J. P. Morgan & Company in New York that Gary and Frick had just gone in to see the president. Right away, Perkins circulated news to Wall Street that a plan to save Moore & Schley and the trust companies was under way.

Without further news, the market opened weakly at 10 A.M. At 10:15, Judge Gary stepped out of his conference with the president to say that Roosevelt was reading the matter favorably, then he returned to the portentous meeting. Finally, at 11 A.M., Gary announced that Roosevelt was fully in favor of the proposal. "It was necessary for me to decide on the instant, before the Stock Exchange opened," Roosevelt later testified regarding this meeting, "for the situation in New York was such that any hour might be vital."[12] Gary quoted Roosevelt as replying to him, "I do not believe that anyone could justly criticize me for saying that I would not feel like objecting to the purchase under the circumstances."[13] Later Roosevelt wrote a letter to his attorney general, Charles Joseph Bonaparte, in which he clarified his reasons for acquiescing to the request from the New York businessmen:

> [Gary and Frick] feel that it is immensely to their interest, as to the interest of every responsible businessman, to try to prevent a panic and general industrial smashup at this time, and that they are willing

to go into this transaction, which they would not otherwise go into, because it seems the opinion of those best fitted to express judgment in New York that it will be an important factor in preventing a break that might be ruinous; and that this has been urged upon them by the combination of the most responsible bankers in New York who are now thus engaged in endeavoring to save the situation. But they asserted they did not wish to do this if I stated that it ought not to be done. I answered that while of course I could not advise them to take the action proposed, I felt it no public duty of mine to interpose any objection.[14]

News of U.S. Steel's new plan to acquire TC&I brought jubilation to Wall Street, saving many brokerages, banks, and trust companies. "The relief furnished by this transaction was instant and far-reaching," opined the *Commercial and Financial Chronicle*. "Institutions, whose solvency might at any moment have become impaired through the continued possession of Coal & Iron stock among their assets, have been reinstated through the conversion of the stock into bonds of the Steel Corporation. Accordingly, now their standing cannot be open to question or the object of suspicion."[15] After the first half-hour of trading, prices on the stock exchange turned upward and stayed strong for the rest of the day. It was the best day the exchange had seen since the troubles began.

Chapter 19

Turning the Corner

As a result of the refusal of the trust companies in Little Rock [Arkansas] to pay cash on depositors' checks, 10,000 miners will be paid their wages to-morrow in checks.

—*Washington Post*
October 30, 1907

The good news emanating from the nation's financial and political capitals on Monday, November 4, tempered fears in New York, but the panic still rippled across the United States, prompting banks in many cities to suspend the withdrawal of deposits. Bank suspensions—the hallmark of banking panics—immediately cut off liquidity for individuals and companies, causing hardship and spreading fear.

As had occurred in New York, many local bank clearing houses issued clearing-house loan certificates to be used as a substitute for cash. At the height of the national panic, about $250 million in these certificates had been issued, equal to about 14 percent of all the currency in circulation.[1] Unable to get cash, individuals even used cashiers' checks in trade for goods. Across the country, firms and banks resorted to a variety of substitutes for cash. Streetcar companies in Omaha and St. Louis paid their employees in nickels from the fare boxes or in five-cent fare tickets.[2] Some companies issued certified checks, scrip, or IOUs. Bank checks were useful as cash only locally, since in an environment where banks discriminated among payees, being a distant correspondent was a disadvantage. This near-money traded hands at a discount to gold coins and paper currency, reflecting fears about the solvency of banks, companies, and individuals. No region or major city was spared from the effects of the panic.[3]

News that some banks were suspending the withdrawal of deposits triggered a national wave of hoarding, the equivalent of withdrawing cash from banks to stuff it in the mattress or under the hearthstone. Reports showed that rentals of safe deposit boxes "skyrocketed."[4] All told, during the panic about $350 million[5] in deposits were withdrawn from the U.S. financial system. Of this amount, the bulk of it was simply socked away—estimates of cash hoarding ranged from $200[6] to $296[7] million. Arguably, absent the suspension of withdrawals, the amount hoarded would have been considerably greater.

Country banks learned from past experience that, during a panic, withdrawing deposits from reserve city banks could be difficult.[8] At the first news of bank runs in New York City, many country banks rushed to withdraw deposits. As a result, some reserve city banks fell below the minimum reserve requirement set in the national or state banking charters.

Some people believed that the whole episode was simply a matter of lost confidence. Local associations, such as the "Sunshine Movement" and "Prosperity League," organized to boost economic activity and employment. "Let the people resume business the way they were doing twelve months ago, start everything with a hurrah, and we will forget all about the panic in a day or two," they proclaimed.[9]

To stem the panic over the coming days, Secretary Cortelyou transferred still more cash from the vaults of the U.S. Treasury to deposits in several national banks. But by mid-November, the Treasury held only $5 million in ready cash, effectively sidelining that institution from further influence over the course of events.[10] A nation gasping for liquidity thus turned to other sources. Bank clearing houses issued their near-money certificates in rising numbers, and imports of gold began to arrive in significant volume in November.

By November 2, at least partial[11] suspension of withdrawals had spread across the country, a fast contagion given that the first suspension by the Knickerbocker occurred on October 22. Governors of Oregon, Nevada, and California declared legal holidays, which had the effect of closing the banks entirely. South Dakota, Indiana, Iowa, and Oklahoma sanctioned the payment by banks of only small amounts, such as $10. Banks discriminated in making payments. There was the perception that banks in reserve cities such as New York, Chicago, and Minneapolis–St. Paul were slow in remitting deposits back to correspondents in the South and West of the United States.

Oliver M. W. Sprague, a Harvard professor writing in 1908, argued that "The position of the banks was far from desperate, yet they had already entered the fatal and discreditable path of suspension, paying depositors at their own discretion."[12] In New York, the loss in loans and deposits was concentrated among the trust companies[13]; the banks actually conserved cash as a result of their membership in the clearing house and otherwise profited from the extension of cash to the trust companies.[14] In November, the New York banks obtained as much cash as they remitted elsewhere in the United States, prompting Sprague to scoff at the suspension of payments by them. He concluded, "The New York banks proved themselves wholly unequal to the duties of their position as the central reserve banks of the country."[15] Writing years later, the economists Milton Friedman and Anna Schwartz were more benign in their judgment, arguing that the quick restriction of payments in New York "was a therapeutic measure that almost surely kept the contraction from being even more severe and much more protracted than it was"[16] in that it cut short bank failures, prevented widespread deflation (as in 1929–1933) and minimized the decline in the stock of money.[17] Only six of 6,412 national banks failed in the panic,[18] fewer than in any other panic of the National Banking era.

After Elbert Gary and Henry Frick returned from their midnight ride to visit President Roosevelt on Monday, November 4, the general sense of crisis had begun to dissipate almost immediately. "A tremendous change for the better had taken place and at last we had one day when everyone was hopeful, and all talk of failure and collapse ceased,"[19] George Perkins said. Over the next several days and weeks, a rapid series of events finally brought the financial crisis in New York to a close, providing instant relief for the city's desperate bankers, investors, and depositors.

A pattern of calm began on Tuesday, November 5, which was Election Day for state and local races—a banking holiday. That evening at Morgan's library, the finance committee of the U.S. Steel Corporation formally ratified the plan discussed with Roosevelt to acquire the Tennessee Coal, Iron & Railroad Company. The official announcement was released to the press around 3 A.M., and the reaction was extremely positive. J. P. Morgan & Company, which served as the transfer agent for the deal, would eventually exchange more than $35.6 million of U.S. Steel's bonds for shares of TC&I stock, thereby saving Moore & Schley. The markets responded buoyantly, showing their first gains in weeks.

The next day, Wednesday, November 6, J. P. Morgan, George Perkins, and James Stillman formulated a new plan to end the persistent runs at the trust companies. They demanded that the Trust Company of America and the Lincoln Trust place 66 percent of their securities in the hands of a trustee named by Morgan. To meet their daily cash needs, the firms could use these assets as collateral for loans from a syndicate of trust companies. Morgan also required that a certain percentage of the trusts' deposits could not be withdrawn for 60 to 90 days. The impact of this plan was immediate. "On Thursday both the Trust Company of America and the Lincoln Trust Company promptly met the demands of their depositors," the *Commercial and Financial Chronicle* reported, "and yesterday the runs on both institutions, it was thought, had practically ended."[20] Eventually, the Trust Company of America and the Lincoln Trust would receive $15 million and $5 million, respectively, through this arrangement.

During the next week, President Roosevelt contributed further to these salutary measures by issuing a statement saying that the crisis had passed and announcing that no special session of Congress would be necessary to meet the needs of the present situation because the existing regulations were sufficient. The public also learned that a massive shipment of more then $12.4 million in gold had arrived from Liverpool,

England, aboard the *Lusitania*—"the richest cargo that ever came across the Atlantic on a single steamship"[21] —bringing total gold shipments to the United States from Europe to over $21 million.

By mid-November, the U.S. Treasury had virtually exhausted its cash holdings in attempting to fight the crisis. But it embarked on another tactic that had a tonic effect on confidence. On November 19, the Treasury issued about $40 million in gold bonds to national banks—this was ostensibly to finance ongoing construction of the Panama Canal. By buying these bonds, the banks could use them as a basis for additional bank note circulation, thus further alleviating the liquidity drought. Reports even surfaced that efforts were under way to form a depositors' committee to reopen the Knickerbocker Trust Company. In the coming months, the Knickerbocker would be resuscitated, though not before Charles T. Barney, the trust company's former president who became embroiled in the schemes of F. Augustus Heinze and Charles W. Morse, committed suicide in his Park Avenue home on November 14, 1907.

Chapter 20

Ripple Effects

Worried over the belief that he had lost $20,000, his balance in the Knickerbocker Trust Company of New York, Valentine Hayerdahl of Mount Vernon committed suicide yesterday afternoon by shooting himself through the head at his home, 53 Rich Avenue, Chester Hill. Mr. Hayerdahl, who was formerly a salesman for the Haviland China Company of New York, resigned a short time ago to go into business for himself. All the money Mr. Hayerdahl owned was on deposit in the trust company. He told several friends that he believed that his life's earnings were gone.

—*New York Times*
November 27, 1907

The crash and panic of 1907 reverberated in markets, governments, and the lives of individuals throughout the United States and around the world. Commodity prices fell 21 percent, eliminating virtually the entire increase from 1904 to 1907.[1] Industrial production dropped more than in any other U.S. panic up to 1907.[2] The dollar volume of bankruptcies declared in November spiked up by 47 percent over a year earlier—the panic would be associated with the second worst volume of bankruptcies up to 1907.[3] Gross earnings by railroads fell by 6 percent in December,[4] production fell 11 percent from May 1907 to June 1908, wholesale prices fell 5 percent and imports shrank 26 percent.[5] Unemployment rose from 2.8 percent to 8 percent,[6] a dramatic increase in a short space of time. Immigration, which had reached 1.2 million people in 1907, dropped to around 750,000 by 1909; it would not reach 1 million again until 1910.

The *Commercial and Financial Chronicle* wrote, "It is probably no exaggeration to say that the industrial paralysis and the prostration was the very worst ever experienced in the country's history."[7] Economists Milton Friedman and Anna Schwartz concluded that the recession was "among the five or six most severe."[8] In characteristic understatement, Jack Morgan wrote to his partners in London, "I do not think that 1907 was a good year anywhere, from what I can make out."[9] Indeed, the U.S. crisis in 1907 has been associated with financial crises in Egypt (January to May), Hamburg (October), Chile (October), Holland and Genoa (September), and Copenhagen (winter).[10] Contemporary Wall Street observer, Alexander Dana Noyes, wrote,

> The case simply was that the crisis affected the world at large, part of the world passing through the acute stage before our own markets did. . . . the strain on the financial world was so severe a character that it was bound to result in a break in the chain of credit, wherever the link was weakest or the wherever the strain was greatest. The link was weakest, no doubt, in markets such as Egypt and Chile; the strain was incalculably greatest in New York, where credit had been so grossly abused, and where inflation of prices had prevailed on such as scale of magnitude as to render the situation, despite the country's immense resources, more vulnerable than that of any other in the long chain of connecting markets.[11]

A case in point was the impact of the crash and panic of 1907 on Mexico, a country heavily dependent on mineral and agricultural prices, and on flows of investment capital from the United States. Historian Kevin Cahill noted:

> In 1906 over $57 million of foreign investment poured directly into Mexican banks, but when this influx ceased at the end of 1907, money

became scarce. . . . The loss of foreign investment caused the total assets of Mexican banks to plummet from $360 million in 1907 to $305 million in 1908 . . . New bank loans also declined . . . A large majority of borrowers were unable to repay their loans. Two consecutive years of drought curtailed agricultural production, making it impossible for the commercial farmers to repay their debts. Moreover, individuals throughout the republic had borrowed money to buy stocks on margin. The collapse of the economy caused stock prices to decline, and many of these investors faced bankruptcy. The inability of the banks to collect their debts produced profound difficulties for banks at all levels.[12]

Cahill suggested that the financial strains in Mexico had political consequences and that the panic and subsequent depression were among the catalysts for the Mexican Revolution. "[Scholars] contend that because Mexico depended heavily on foreign markets and capital, particularly that of the United States," Cahill wrote, "the U.S. depression crippled the Mexican Economy. Generating widespread dissatisfaction with President Porfirio Diaz's government, it thus was one of the factors that provoked the Maderistas and other revolutionaries to rebellion in 1910."[13]

In January 1908, banks finally lifted their suspension of payments.[14] The subsequent recession ended in June 1908, followed by buoyant economic growth in the United States for the next 18 months. By late 1909, the stock market and industrial production recovered to prepanic levels (see Figure 20.1a and b), and the economic cycle peaked in January 1910, though it slumped again until January 1912.

Despite the massive upheaval and anxiety that plagued the nation in 1907, the financial system returned to a remarkably stable condition until the commencement of World War I, when trading in equities was interrupted by the closing of the New York Stock Exchange from August through November 1914. The reaction that ensued during those critical intervening years would significantly shape the financial system as we know it today.

Responding to the anxieties created by 1907's liquidity drought, on May 30, 1908, the U.S. Congress passed the Aldrich-Vreeland Act. This legislation enacted an emergency currency scheme to afford a method

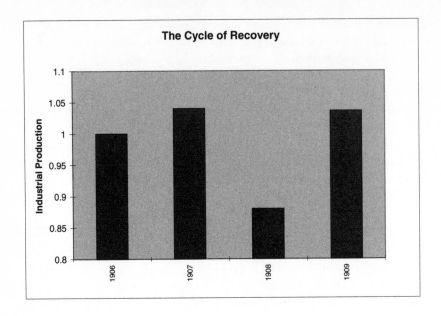

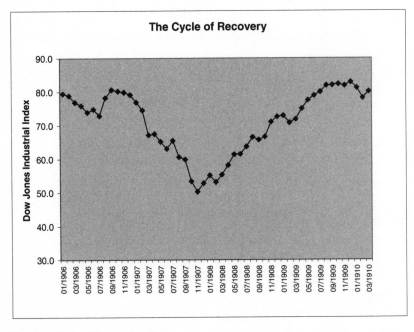

Figure 20.1   The cycle of recovery.
SOURCE: Authors' Figure, Based on Monthly Index of Stock Prices, Cowles Foundation, Yale University.

of issuing currency based on the reserves in banks. The Act also created a National Monetary Commission to study the adequacy of the financial system in the United States. Political wrangling ensued.[15] The co-chairs of the commission were Senator Nelson W. Aldrich and Representative Edward B. Vreeland, old-line Republicans identified with the financial community. Democrats and progressive Republicans scoffed that the Commission would design a system to the advantage of Wall Street. Indeed, as emerged years later, a secret conference of financiers and politicians on Jekyll Island, Georgia, in November 1910 produced a design for a "National Reserve Bank" that made its way into the final report of the National Monetary Commission. Senator Aldrich claimed the design was his, though it was strikingly similar to a plan advocated by Paul Warburg, partner in the firm, Kuhn, Loeb, earlier in the decade.

Warburg was present at Jekyll Island, as was Frank A. Vanderlip, then president of National City Bank, who is credited with drafting the proposal to emerge from that conference. Others at the conference were A. Piatt Andrew (assistant secretary of the treasury), Henry P. Davison (partner in J. P. Morgan & Company), Charles D. Norton (president of First National Bank of New York), and Benjamin Strong (president of Bankers Trust). These successors to Morgan, Stillman, and Baker essentially designed the Federal Reserve System. Ironically, the Fed, one of the landmark achievements of the Progressive Era, was a child of the "money trust" that the Progressives feared, though President Woodrow Wilson, Treasury Secretary Carter Glass, and the Democrats would later claim the credit for establishing the Fed.[16]

The National Monetary Commission published its report on January 11, 1911. The essence of the 24-volume report was to repudiate the National Banking System as a cause of panics and "inelastic" currency, and to recommend the establishment of a "National Reserve Association" that would promote cooperation among banks. In stumping for adoption of such legislation, Frank Vanderlip said in Chicago, "The whole world is united in agreement that we have about the worst system of banking that there is anywhere in existence. It makes of us ... an international nuisance."[17] In effect, the report advocated reversing the monetary system in the United States, founded on the vision of an agrarian society held by President Thomas Jefferson and the antipathy toward a central bank held by President Andrew Jackson.

Unfortunately for Aldrich and Vreeland, the Congressional elections of 1910 returned the Democrats to a majority. The Commission's proposals sprouted debates over the degree of independence of the central bank, its control and governance, and its geographic structure. The Democratic legislators recalled perhaps Thomas Jefferson's warning:

> I believe that banking institutions are more dangerous to our liberties than standing armies. If the American people ever allow private banks to control the issue of their currency, first by inflation and then by deflation, the banks and the corporations that will grow up around them will deprive the people of all property until their children wake up homeless on the continent their fathers conquered.[18]

In November 1912, voters elected Woodrow Wilson as president. Representative Carter Glass, chairman of the House Banking Committee, took up the National Monetary Commission's report in 1912 and called a series of hearings. Wilson asked Glass to speed up the work. Glass found it challenging to forge a coalition in support of a specific design—bankers and conservatives had strong views, as did William Jennings Bryan, an agrarian populist and former Democratic presidential candidate, now Wilson's secretary of state.

On December 22, 1913, both houses of Congress passed the Federal Reserve Act. Wilson signed it into law immediately. The large scope of this legislation is suggested by its title, *An act to provide for the establishment of Federal Reserve Banks, to furnish an elastic currency, to afford means of rediscounting commercial paper, to establish a more effective supervision of banking, and for other purposes*. An organizing committee, chaired by the secretaries of treasury and agriculture, promptly embarked on the task of staffing and structuring the Federal Reserve System. They drew boundaries for 12 districts, each with a regional reserve bank. Benjamin Strong, president of Bankers Trust, was appointed to be the first governor of the Federal Reserve Bank of New York.

Historian Robert Wiebe wrote: "The panic of 1907 acted as a catalyst in the [political] ferment. Most obviously, it convinced almost everyone, including the bankers, that financial reform was imperative ... the panic released countless little pockets of pressure, turning concerned but comfortable citizens into active reformers and opening many more to the calls for change."[19] Indeed, with the end of the panic, the political landscape had changed: political coalitions were re-forming and a change of leadership was in the public mind.

■   ■   ■

On December 7, 1907, Roosevelt had launched the American "Great White Fleet" on a 'round-the-world voyage that asserted the role of the United States as a world power. Ironically, the president who launched the fleet was at his zenith, from which he would decline. At the end of 1907, Theodore Roosevelt was a "lame duck" president, having announced in 1904 that he would not seek another term. This may have exposed him to the enmity of critics who claimed that his approval of the merger of Tennessee Coal & Iron into U.S. Steel was a "sell-out" to Wall Street interests. Congress held hearings on the deal. These concluded without issue, though they provided a platform for airing charges that the panic had actually been engineered by New York financiers to serve their own interests.* As the end of his term approached, the unusual coalition of Republicans and reformers began to splinter. Roosevelt took a year-long tour through Europe and Africa following Taft's election (prompting J. P. Morgan to raise a toast that "America expects that every lion will do his duty"[20]). The absence had not mellowed Roosevelt's politics; Taft's policies proved to be a disappointment.

Voters elected William Howard Taft to be president in 1908. This commenced a conservative reaction in Washington against the progressivism of Roosevelt's administration. Where Roosevelt believed the president could do whatever the Constitution did not expressly forbid, Taft believed the president could do only what the Constitution expressly allowed.[21] This difference explained the growing divide between conservative and progressive Republicans. Various issues in 1909 and 1910 served to widen the split. In May 1911, the Supreme Court decided that the Standard Oil and American Tobacco Companies violated the Sherman Act and ordered their dissolution. In the fall of 1911, Taft's Justice Department began antitrust suits against U.S. Steel and International Harvester. The charge against U.S. Steel was that it had violated

---

* Our review of letters, cables, diaries, memoranda, and other archival material by these financiers affords no evidence that this was the case, and the veracity of the specific charges of self-dealing in this case has never been proven.

the Sherman Antitrust Act when it acquired Tennessee Coal & Iron—in this move, Taft appeared to rebuke Roosevelt for his earlier approval of the deal. The attack on U.S. Steel was the last straw[22] for Roosevelt, who thereafter moved to compete for the Republic nomination for president.

In other respects, Taft's administration was marked more by inaction compared to Roosevelt's muscular activism. Disgusted with Taft's inability to sustain his progressive legacy, Roosevelt first attempted to wrest the Republican nomination in 1912; failing that, he formed the Progressive Party—colloquially called the "Bull Moose" party after Roosevelt's indomitable stamina—and ran as an independent candidate.

In 1912, Congressman Arsene Pujo of Louisiana commenced hearings on competition in the financial community. Arguably, these hearings represented the high-water mark of the Progressives' distrust of high finance. The objective of the hearings was to determine the existence of a "money trust," a financial analogue to the large industrial trusts—like Standard Oil—that had been formed in the late nineteenth century. Progressives feared that through the workings of a money trust, investment capital in the United States would be channeled to the advantage of a few oligarchs and that by this means they would control the country. The Pujo hearings were a forerunner to the modern concern with "crony capitalism" and "club deals."[23] The hearings gained testimony from numerous prominent financiers, including J. P. Morgan. The investigation yielded no solid evidence of collusion among financiers, only circumstantial evidence—the banks and financial houses did some business together.

Ultimately, the final Pujo report found ". . . there exist[ed] an established and well defined identity and community of interest between a few leaders of finance, created and held together through stock ownership, interlocking directorates, partnerships and joint account transactions, and other forms of domination over banks, trust companies. . .and industrial corporations, which resulted in a great and rapidly growing concentration of the control of money and credit in the hands of a few men."[24] The evidence in support of this was a matrix of corporate directorships. The committee found that officers of the First National Bank were board directors in 49 corporations, with capital of $11.5 billion. For National City Bank, the figures were 41 corporations and $10.5 billion. J. P. Morgan & Company's officers were directors in

112 corporations with capital of $22.5 billion. Writing in 1914, Louis Brandeis estimated that the total capitalization of the New York Stock Exchange was only $26.5 billion. Brandeis concluded:

> The operations of so comprehensive a system of concentration neces-sarily developed in the bankers overweening power. And the bankers' power grows by what it feeds on. Power begets wealth; and added wealth opens ever new opportunities for the acquisition of wealth and power. The operations of these bankers are so vast and numerous that even a very reasonable compensation for the service performed by the bankers, would, in the aggregate, produce for them incomes so large as to result in huge accumulations of capital. . . . We must break the Money Trust or the Money Trust will break us.[25]

Progressivism reached its peak in 1912. That year, the three-way presidential campaign resulted in the election of a Democrat—only the second since the Civil War. Woodrow Wilson had been president of Princeton University and then a reform-minded governor of New Jersey. As president of the United States, he picked up the torch of Progressivism and kindled important initiatives in a variety of areas including financial sector regulation, the income tax, direct election of senators, lowering the tariff, and establishing the Federal Trade Commission.

After 1913, the Progressive movement began to wane as the country slipped into another recession. Fearing political gains by the Republicans, Wilson moved deftly to the right on the political spectrum. Public opinion became distracted by the World War—the New York Stock Exchange was closed for more than four months at the outset of the war in 1914, from the end of July to early December.[26] Anyway, it seemed that the major reforms had been achieved. In 1917, America entered World War I, and war concerns diverted resources and attention from social issues to foreign policy. Fears of political radicals surfaced in response to the privations of war and to the Russian Revolution—this resulted in a welling of antiradical legislation.

Republicans regained control of Congress in 1918. The war ended on November 11, 1918, but not before Congress passed the Espionage Act of 1918, which formally suspended wartime civil liberties. Anarchists reacted to this and other measures used to suppress radicals with a spree of bombings. Five days after Sacco and Vanzetti, two anarchists, were indicted for armed robbery and murder, anarchists exploded a bomb outside the new offices of J. P. Morgan & Company at 23 Wall Street, killing 33 people and injuring 400.[27] The explosion on September 16, 1920, closed the New York Stock Exchange for a day and left some scars on the side of the building that are visible a century later, but otherwise barely interrupted the work in the financial community. On the left wing of American politics, liberals recoiled from the resurgence of violence by radicals on the far left. With the death of Roosevelt in 1919 and Wilson in 1924, Progressivism lost its most prominent champions.

The presidential election of 1920 displaced Progressivism as the dominant idea in American politics. From 1920 to 1932, conservative Republicans occupied the White House, overseeing a period of remarkable growth. But in October 1929, a market crash stimulated a scenario similar to 1907: panic, bank failures, economic contraction, and outcry for government intervention.

After the 1932 election of President Franklin D. Roosevelt and a new Congress, the political pendulum swung back to an activist executive branch and comprehensive state intervention. In 1933, Congress passed regulations covering a raft of ills, not least those perceived of Wall Street in the first decade of the century. Fearing that a "money trust" was at the heart of market abuses in the 1920s, Congress passed the Glass–Steagall Act of 1933 that required the separation of commercial banking and investment banking (the same act established federal deposit insurance that would help to quell bank depositors' fears). Financial institutions were no longer allowed to both take deposits and underwrite securities offerings. This proved to be a pivotal event in American financial markets that forced J. P. Morgan & Company to choose to limit its activities strictly to commercial banking. Morgan partner Henry S. Morgan (son of J. Pierpont Morgan) led several J. P. Morgan & Company partners into forming the investment bank, Morgan Stanley. The division of the financial services industry held until 1999 when Congress repealed the provisions of Glass–Steagall separating commercial and investment banking.

Lessons

Financial Crises as a Perfect Storm

Education consists mainly in what we have unlearned.

—Mark Twain[1]

The financial crisis that embraced the panic and crash of 1907 lasted 15 months, from the stock market's peak in September 1906 to its trough in November 1907. During that time, the value of all listed stocks in the United States declined 37 percent (see Figure L.1), making it among the most damaging financial crashes of the nineteenth and twentieth centuries, affecting virtually every industrial sector. The sharpest part of this massive market downturn coincided with the banking panic in October and November 1907, resulting in the failure of at least 25 banks and 17 trust companies.[2] The events of 1907 stand out both for the grave threat to the financial system and for the role of a small group of business leaders in trying to organize collective action to fight it. The immediate effects of this crisis produced an "extremely severe"[3] and "extraordinarily violent"[4] economic contraction, leading to an "intense" depression[5] in 1908.

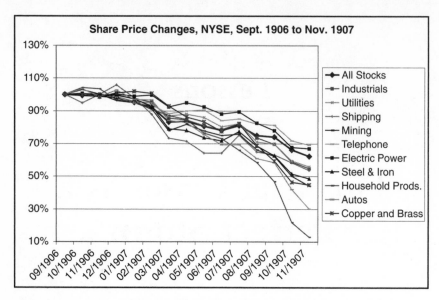

Figure L.1   Share price changes, New York Stock Exchange, September 1906 to November 1907.
SOURCE: Authors' figure, based on data from Monthly Index of Stock Prices, Cowles Foundation, Yale University.

Thus, we end our story about 1907 as we began—with a question: Why do markets crash and bank panics occur? Any single case study, such as the one we have presented here, is subject to a range of interpretations and we encourage the reader to draw one's own conclusions from the foregoing narrative. Yet we think that the story of the panic and crash of 1907 inspires consideration that major financial crises can be the result of a convergence of certain unique forces—the forces of the market's perfect storm—that cause investors and depositors to react with alarm.

The recounting of the events of 1907 suggests that the storm gathers as follows. It begins with a highly complex financial system, whose very complexity makes it difficult for anyone to know what might be going wrong; by definition, the multiple parts of the financial system are linked, which means that trouble in one institution, city, or region can travel easily and quickly to others. Buoyant growth in the economy makes the financial system more fragile, in part due to the demand for capital and in part due to the tendency of some institutions to take on more risk than is prudent. Leaders in government and the financial sector implement policies that advertently or inadvertently elevate the exposure to risk of crisis. An economic shock hits the financial system. The mood of the market swings from optimism to pessimism, creating a self-reinforcing downward spiral. Collective action by leaders can arrest the spiral, though the speed and effectiveness with which they act ultimately determines the length and severity of the crisis.

Reflecting on the crash and panic of 1907 consider each of these forces and the nature of their interplay.

1. System-Like Architecture

In 1907, the United States held about 16,000[6] financial institutions (compared to about 7,500 in 2007), all without a central bank or regulator. The vast majority of these were small "unit" banks having no branches. The market for financial services was highly fractionalized and localized. The suppliers were, on average, small enterprises. This collection of financial intermediaries in the economy is a system. Fundamental to the definition of any system is that its parts are linked and that they interact—such as in a household heating system (the furnace and thermostats interact), the digestive system (the body's organs are interdependent and operate for the benefit of all), and a telecommunications system (a network increases in utility as connectivity with other people increases). Thus it is in a financial system: Various institutions may be linked through the same investors and depositors; and these intermediaries (banks, trust companies, brokerage firms) may be lenders and creditors to each other by virtue of the cash transfers that they facilitate.

A financial system has two vitally important characteristics that can serve as the foundations for financial crises. First, the very existence of a system means that trouble can travel. The difficulties of one financial intermediary can spread to others. Second, the complexity of a financial system means that it is difficult for all participants in the financial system to be well informed—this is called an "information asymmetry" and may motivate perverse behavior that can trigger or worsen a financial crisis. Consider the nature of the system's linkages first.

The financial system was global as early as the Renaissance, in the sense of institutions in different countries being linked through

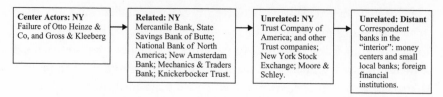

Figure L.2   Some linkages among financial institutions in 1907.

transactions and deposits. As noted earlier, bank deposits in 1907 could be "pyramided," a practice that amplified the sensitive linkage among financial institutions, especially between interior and money center institutions. The formation of bank clearing houses in selected cities in the nineteenth century ensured the linkage among banks in those cities, but they also served to dampen the spread of the panic.

The economic historian, Charles Kindleberger, noted that over time the waves of financial crises have had a strong international dimension to them because of such linkages. Alexander Noyes, a financial journalist writing shortly after the panic of 1907, argued that liquidity problems in Egypt were contemporaneous with liquidity problems in Hamburg, Chile, Holland, Genoa, and Copenhagen; he wrote, "The crisis affected the world at large, part of the world passing through the acute stage before our own markets did."[7] Stock market crises thus spread globally through the asset holdings of international investors.[8] In 1907, the systemic nature of financial crises can be seen in the chain of linkages as the panic spread, beginning on October 16, from one institution to many others in New York City and beyond (see Figure L.2).

An important insight of the field of system dynamics is that systems can display surprising nonlinearities—this means that orderly systemic structures may produce unpredictable behavior. Feedback loops, time delays, and other factors can affect the behavior of entire systems. In recent years, the study of complex systems has evolved into an advanced interdisciplinary field.[9] The application of concepts from system dynamics to the study of financial markets is relatively new.*

---

* In his 2003 book, *Why Stock Markets Crash,* Didier Sornette wrote (p. 16) that the approach of looking at systems wholistically rather than in parts yields important insights in science, engineering, and business. Importantly, this "complex systems" approach illuminates aggregate behaviors reflecting interconnections, relationships and feedbacks among the components. Truly, the whole is much greater than the collection of parts.

The other relevant aspect of the complexity of financial systems has to do with the opacity of information. Some participants in a market have an information advantage over others—this is called information asymmetry. This condition may lead to a situation in which better-informed people might exploit the poorly informed—a problem known as *adverse selection*.*

In 1983, two economists, Douglas Diamond and Phillip Dybvig[10] suggested that bank panics are simply randomly occurring events. Bank runs occur when depositors fear that some kind of shock will force the bank into costly and time-consuming liquidation. To be the last in line to withdraw deposited funds exposes an individual to the risk of loss. Therefore, a run is caused simply by the fear of random deposit withdrawals and the risk of being last in the queue.[†] In the mid-1980s, a long line in front of a Hong Kong pastry shop adjacent to a bank triggered a bank run. Depositors assumed that the line was headed into the bank; word spread rapidly; soon, the bank was mobbed.[11]

A different theory is that bank runs are explained by asymmetric information: the problem of adverse selection can motivate panic selling or withdrawal of deposits. Economists Charles Calomiris, Gary Gorton, and others[12] have suspected that runs could begin when some depositors observe negative information about the value of bank assets and withdraw their deposits. Unable to discriminate perfectly between sound and unsound banks and observing a wave of withdrawals, other depositors follow suit. A run begins. In a world of unequally distributed information, some depositors will find it costly to ascertain the solvency of their banks. Thus, runs might be a rational means of monitoring the performance of banks, a crude means of forcing the banks to reveal to depositors the adequacy of their assets and reserves.

Calomiris and Gorton reasoned that if the information asymmetry theory were true, panics would be triggered by real asset shocks that cause the decline in collateral values underpinning bank loans. They

---

* Economist George Akerlof has described this phenomenon as the "lemons" problem in which the market for used cars features imperfect pricing. Michael Spence extended these insights by drawing on the labor market. Joseph Stiglitz focused on credit markets. Akerlof, Spence, and Stiglitz received the Nobel Prize in economics in 2001 for their groundbreaking work in this area.
† One researcher, Glenn Donaldson, found some evidence in support of this "random withdrawal" theory: Interest rates during a panic were much higher than in nonpanic times. See Donaldson (1992), pp. 278, 298.

found that bank panics originated in areas of real shocks and that the cause in these regions was a decline in asset values. In particular, panics have tended to follow sharp declines in the stock markets and tended to occur in the spring and the fall. They also reasoned that the resolution of a bank panic could be created by the elimination of an important aspect of the information asymmetry: gaining clarity as to which banks were solvent and insolvent would stop the runs on solvent banks.

Studies have considered how well information asymmetry explains panics, by looking at whether deposit losses predict panics, the yield spreads between low- and high-risk bonds peak at the panic, and real declines in the stock market are greater in panic years than nonpanic years. Generally, these findings are affirmed[13] though they are not uniformly supportive.[14],*

Information asymmetry played a major role in the events of 1907. Viewed from a century later, one is struck by how little the average depositor—or even J. P. Morgan himself—could know about the condition of financial institutions. To resolve this asymmetry, Morgan had privately chartered audits of the assets of various institutions and debtors. But he must have known that the more serious asymmetry lay not between him and the institutions, but between the public and the institutions—therefore, Morgan attempted to use the press, and even the pulpits, to shape public perceptions about the safety and soundness of the financial system.

Perhaps Morgan's most meaningful action to fight the panic was the commitment of his own firm's capital in support of threatened institutions—today, there is a large research literature that confirms the important role of experts to *certify* the veracity of conditions to a larger and less well-informed audience. The industry of certified public

---

* Looking at the evidence across the financial crises in the nineteenth century, economist Frederic Mishkin (1991) saw this pattern: "... most of the financial crises begin with a rise in interest rates, a stock market decline and the widening of the interest rate spread. Furthermore, a financial panic frequently is immediately preceded by a major failure of a financial firm, which increases uncertainty in the marketplace. The increase in uncertainty and the rise in interest rates would magnify the adverse selection–lemons problem in the credit markets while the decline in the stock market increases agency as well as adverse selection problems, both of which are reflected in the rise in the spread between interest rates for low and high-quality borrowers. The increase in adverse selection and agency problems would then lead to a decline in investment activity and aggregate economic activity."[15]

accountants is a prime example of this certification function. Closer to home for Morgan would be the role of securities underwriters who risk their firms' capital and reputation in bringing new companies to the public markets.

To summarize, the first condition of financial crises is the system-like architecture of the financial services industry—this system creates *linkages* by which trouble can spread; and it creates *complexity* that makes it difficult to know the location and nature of the trouble. It would be impossible to derive the benefits of the financial services industry without the systemic effects it carries. The best we can do is to understand better how such systems can behave. We should worry about feedback effects in the financial system; whether the feedback amplifies or dampens the output of the system; and whether the responses of the system are linear or nonlinear. There is considerably more work to be done in this area.

In-depth case studies, such as our history of the events of 1907, can illuminate the behavior of financial systems in crisis. Much of the re-search on complex systems today, at places such as the Santa Fe Institute or Max Planck Institute, focus on theoretical modeling or the explo-ration of very large data sets. In his excellent book on the application of complex systems theory to economics, *The Origin of Wealth* (2006), Eric Beinhocker describes such systems as having collective and dy-namic attributes that are "better understood through a *bottoms-up holistic approach*"[16] (italics added). *Collective* refers to the fact that the parts of the system interact with each other. *Dynamic* means that the condition of the system changes through time, largely through the interaction of the parts. Arguably, the events up to and including the panic of 1907 are an example of positive self-reinforcing feedback that builds to an intolerable level that triggers a massive shutdown or wave of negative feedback. The architecture of the system sets the stage for the crisis. The triggers, feedback, and actors are sketched in the next six factors.

2. Buoyant Growth

A rapidly-changing environment is a precursor to financial instability. Indeed, change in the form of buoyant economic growth may be espe-cially pernicious since it engenders false optimism about the stability of markets and institutions. Every major financial panic has occurred after an episode of rapid economic growth[17] though not all panics are associated with recessions.[18] Of special interest is not the fact of growth, but rather the cause of the inflection, the downturn from boom to slump. Rapid economic growth creates a demand for money that eventually imposes liquidity strains on the financial system (see Figure L.3).

The crash and panic of 1907 punctuated a period of very rapid economic growth in the United States. This growth created a massive demand for external finance and meant the financial system within the U.S. had a low level of capital relative to the recent rate of demand.[19] New capital—nearly $100 million in gold imported in 1907—was obtained from Europe, through borrowings denominated not in U.S. dollars, but in sterling, francs, and marks—large borrowings denominated in foreign currencies have also been associated with financial crises.[20]

Responding to the widespread unemployment and economic malaise resulting from the stock market crash of 1929 and the ensuing Great Depression, economists John Maynard Keynes and Joseph Schumpeter wrestled with the sources of economic recession and pointed their fingers toward the nature of the boom that preceded it. The dominant implications of their message are that downturns of some kind are inevitable following growth, and that we should be less surprised by crashes and panics than by the booms, bubbles, and manias that precede them.

Keynes' classic book, *The General Theory of Employment, Interest and Money* (Macmillan, London: 1936), focused on why economies were given to cycles. He argued that a complex interplay of changes in consumption and investment drive business cycles. During the rising part of the business cycle (the "boom"), businesses invest in new production in order to meet rising demand. The investment creates jobs, which stimulates consumption. But consumption and investment are rarely synchronous. Eventually, business investment will outpace consumer demand—Keynes calls this the "insufficiency of effective demand." Businesses reduce their investment and employment.[21] Investors prefer to hold cash rather than consume or make long-term investments—the reduction in investment and preference for liquidity throws the economy into a stall. This triggers a pernicious self-reinforcing cycle:

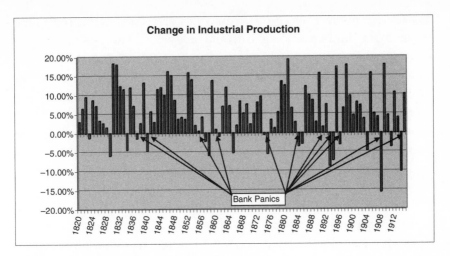

Figure L.3   Banking panics and business cycles.
SOURCE: Graph prepared by authors. Bank panics identified in Calomiris and Gorton (2000), p. 99.
Data on industrial production from Davis (2004), the Davis Industrial Production Index, downloaded
from NBER web site.

Businesses reduce investment and employment, causing less consumption, which triggers a reduction in investment and employment, and so on. Eventually, consumption will bottom out and the economy will return to equilibrium—but at a high social cost. Keynes argued for the socialization of business cycle risk by having governments spend liberally in the troughs of the business cycle to maintain employment and pump-prime recoveries.*

In contrast to Keynes, Schumpeter saw investment opportunities—rather than consumption—as the primary driver of the economic cycle. The relentless invention of new goods, services, and forms of organization continued to overwhelm the old. This was Schumpeter's assertion of "Creative Destruction" as the central fact of capitalism.[22] Nevertheless,

---

* Politicians gladly embraced Keynes's recommendation in the mid-twentieth century—they were pleased to spend not only in the troughs, but also in the booms. By the early 1980s, the ill effects of deficit spending had discredited Keynes' policy recommendations. By spending during the boom years, governments may actually hasten the slumps by preempting the flow of capital into profitable private-sector investments to divert capital to the public sector. To be fair, Keynes advocated only that governments should spend what they can raise over one complete economic cycle rather than carry debt from one cycle to the next. Today, neoclassical economics disputes the ability of Keynesian prescriptions to stabilize the economic cycle.

growth and business success sow the seeds of a slump. Disruptive new technologies displace existing firms and industries[23] Success draws imitators who draw off some of the profits from invention.[24] New technology and new competitors trigger rounds of destructive price competition[25] In addition, entrepreneurs are fallible: sometimes they start businesses that cannot be sustained. During the expansion phase of a business cycle, conditions may be forgiving. Then eventually the mass of these business mistakes aggregates to a point where they can be sustained no longer. Finally, expansion eventually breeds speculation and the inappropriate use of debt to finance expansion.

For Schumpeter, the inflection point at which the business cycle turns downward occurs when there is an exhaustion of investment opportunities to sustain the rapid rate of expansion. Households, squeezed by debt, reduce their consumption in order to repay loans. Businesses must liquidate inventories and close unprofitable operations. Entrepreneurs must abandon innovations of marginal worth. The recession is the time to wash away these mistakes and lay the foundations for the next expansion. Contraction was, for Schumpeter, a cold shower for the economic system.[26]

Keynes, Schumpeter, and their descendants help to explain the business cycle tipping point that seems to be associated with panics and crashes. Keynes described the inflection as a saturation of demand. Schumpeter saw it as a saturation of investment opportunities and displacement of old products and processes by new ones. Business-cycle theories lend color to the environment that accompanies crises, but they say little about the specific triggers of a crisis or the mechanism by which a crisis radiates through an economy. There is more to the story.

3. Inadequate Safety Buffers

The business cycle is associated with a cycle of credit expansion and contraction that significantly amplifies changes in markets and economic growth. The boom part of the credit cycle erodes the shock absorbers that cushion the financial system in the slump. Some banks, eager to make profits, unwisely expand their lending to less and less creditworthy clients as the boom proceeds. Then some external shock occurs and the bank directors awaken to the inadequacy of their capitalization relative to the credit risks they have taken; banks reduce or cut off the new loans available to their clients. This triggers a liquidity crisis that drives both a stock market crash and depositor panic. Hyman Minsky, a doctoral student of Schumpeter's and a prominent scholar of Keynesian economics, argued that this behavior on the part of the financial system would create phases of "expansion," "remorse," and "disgrace."

The prime cause of economic slumps was the credit cycle, the expansion and contraction of loans for businesses and consumers. Easy credit amplifies the boom, and tight credit amplifies the contraction—in this view, Minsky followed Keynes. Minsky also argued for government intervention to reduce the amplitude of the cycle: more aggressive lending by the government during contractions and tighter regulation of bank lending standards during the booms. Economic slumps would be associated with financial crises by means of the loss of discipline. Through the boom, banks would overreach and extend loans to riskier clients. The buoyancy of economic booms causes riskier creditors to approach banks for loans—a problem of adverse selection. Some banks succumb to the temptation to make loans to these creditors, perhaps in the belief that luck or a bank clearing house will see them through—this is a problem of moral hazard.[27] Adverse selection and moral hazard ultimately earn their just reward. Decline in asset values causes a decline in collateral for loans; therefore, banks tighten their lending practices.[28] As the slump worsens, the banks with the riskiest clients turn illiquid and then insolvent.

The fragility of such a system stems not only from the behavior of some banks. It also grows from the structure of the industry. A system with many small and undiversified banks—such as existed in the United States in 1907—is more prone to panics.[29] In addition, the absence of systemic shock absorbers such as bank clearing houses[30] and cooperative agreements will increase exposure to crises.[31]

The events of 1907 are consistent with an explanation for crises based on the instability of financial intermediaries. We noted instability among trust companies generally, and specifically in the cases of the Knickerbocker and the Trust Company of America. Brokerage firms, too, featured prominently: the failure of Otto Heinze & Co. and the near failure of Moore and Schley marked major turning points in the episode. The economists Ellis Tallman and Jon Moen (1990) found that the trust companies were a key source of instability leading up to the panic of 1907. The unequal regulation of banks and trust companies led to a concentration of riskier assets in trusts. The trusts took advantage of opportunities from which the banks were restricted. Moreover, the trusts were able to concentrate their portfolios more.*

In a system, trouble spreads unless shock absorbers exist to stop it. In 1907, such shock absorbers were evident in the insurance companies, which paid claims on the San Francisco earthquake and fire damage; the Bank of England and U.S. Treasury, which sought to promote a sufficient supply of currency; and the local clearing houses. Today, we would include among the safety buffer the Fed, the International Monetary Fund, the World Bank, and central banks around the world. Still, research suggests that financial crises will occur where "financial markets are opaque, when regulation and supervision are poor, and when lending is based on collateral rather than expected cash flow due to poor accounting standards. Countries that suffer from longer, costlier, and more systematically destabilizing crashes tend also to suffer from poor transparency, weak macroeconomic policies, and microstructural weaknesses in advance of the asset price bubble."[32]

In 1907, the difficulty facing banks and the financial system was how to forestall the spread of the crisis throughout the country and abroad. Some banks resorted to advertising the probity and connections of their directors, their financial record, and the size of their equity capital base.[33] One common remedy to the brittleness of the financial system was to create local clearing houses, each of which would mutually guarantee the cash settlement of checks drawn on its members. Like insurance companies, the clearing houses pooled the risks of the individual members—and they offered the monitoring function that regulators would eventually assume. The use of clearing house certificates was widespread in 1907—the dollar volume of certificates issued exceeded

---

* Innovations in the design of financial institutions continue to be a source of concern, as recent debates about hedge funds have shown.

the volume of certificates issued in the previous great panic (1893) by a factor between two and four times.[34]

The whole question is whether the safety buffers in existence are adequate to prevent the spread of potential shocks. The question of adequate sufficiency must be tested *relative* to the size of the available assets and the size of the shocks, which the buffer is meant to absorb. Over time, the size and complexity of the economy will outgrow the sophistication of static financial safety buffers. The modern measure of shock absorption, *value at risk*, is one way to estimate this effect. A long-term trend in global financial markets has been toward more transparency, deregulation, and liberalization of entry. Some critics have asserted that these trends have increased the fragility of the financial system, though recent research suggests not.[35] The sobering recent book, *A Demon of Our Own Design*, by Richard Bookstaber (New York: John Wiley & Sons, 2007) argues that tight coupling within financial markets makes them "built to crash."

4. Adverse Leadership

Adding to the stew of uncertainty that leads up to the financial crisis is the action of political and economic leaders who advertently or inadvertently elevate the risk of crisis. Like rapid growth, the mistakes of leadership can help to create an environment vulnerable to shocks.

In 1907, Theodore Roosevelt was on the warpath against anticompetitive business practices. He wielded the power of the Department of Justice and the Sherman Antitrust Act, and he used the bully pulpit to excoriate the "malefactors of great wealth." State governments followed suit with new legislation to limit railroad rates; New York State employed a young prosecutor, Charles Evans Hughes, to investigate the insurance industry. The Supreme Court imposed a massive fine on Standard Oil for rate fixing.

Two weeks after Roosevelt's "malefactors of great wealth" speech, *The Commercial and Financial Chronicle* bemoaned the President's aggressive stance and warned of their vituperative power: "The complete and final danger in class hatreds—and even in 'classes' which are themselves foreign to the genius of this country—is that, once aroused, they have no stopping place short of exhaustion, and make no discriminations."[36] In November, *Harper's* commented, "The President has talked too much and threatened too much, and his words have produced direful effects."[37] The *Boston Traveler* opined: "The constant fulminations of the President induced a condition of suspicion and unrest, and was an element—an important factor—in the precipitation of the panic."[38]

Should Roosevelt and the Progressives really be implicated in the crash? Financial markets withstand political bluster fairly well—were Roosevelt's speeches just empty rhetoric, we might absolve him. But markets are highly sensitive to changes in government policy (such as rate regulation, taxation, and antitrust enforcement) that affect the underlying drivers of value. By late 1906, the radical shift in government policy was apparent. Roosevelt's speeches only confirmed the shift. He was both messenger and message and thus deserves a place among the drivers of these events.

Management of the nation's money supply is another means by which leadership influences a crisis. In their book, *A Monetary History of the United States* (1963), Milton Friedman and Anna Schwartz emphasized the importance of leadership in managing financial system liquidity during a crisis:

> The detailed story of every banking crisis in our history shows how much depends on the presence of one or more outstanding individuals willing to assume responsibility and leadership. It was a defect of the financial system that it was susceptible to crises resolvable only with such leadership. . . . In the absence of vigorous intellectual leadership by the [Federal Reserve] Board or of a consensus on the correct policy in the community at large or of Reserve Bank governors willing and able to assume responsibility for an independent course, the tendencies of drift and indecision had full scope. Moreover, as time went on, their force cumulated. Each failure to act made another such failure more likely.[39]

In the absence of a central bank, financial system liquidity was a constant source of concern to financial leaders. In an effort to sustain the dollar, Treasury Secretary George Cortelyou and his predecessor L. M. Shaw sought to build government gold reserves for more than a year before the crash in March 1907. This took liquidity *out* of the financial system at a time when economic growth and the San Francisco earthquake and fire created an urgent demand for more cash.[40] Correspondence within J. P. Morgan & Company noted the dearth of liquid funds with which to finance corporate needs.

With the crash in March 1907, Cortelyou deposited a large volume of gold into the financial system that had the effect of flooding the market with liquidity and inordinately reducing the cost of funds, yet this was not sufficient—and then in June and July he returned to attempting to build government reserves. That summer funds flowed abroad in the form of gold exports, into the Treasury, and to the interior of the United States in anticipation of the crop harvest.[41] Figure L.4 shows that liquid assets held by banks on behalf of the public and Treasury started declining in June.

As research has subsequently revealed, that summer the recession was in full bloom; it was hardly a time to take liquidity from the system. This, unfortunately, was a pattern to be repeated again, most notably by the U.S. Federal Reserve between 1930 and 1933.[42] Economist Glenn Donaldson has noted that "market liquidity, or the lack thereof, is a primary element—perhaps the primary element—in determining the length and severity of a panic."[43]

5. Real Economic Shock

Research on financial crises acknowledges the role of some triggering event. Financial crises require a spark. As the history of 1907 suggests, however, there may be several candidates. Was it the suspension of payments to depositors by the Knickerbocker Trust? Or was it the failure of Otto Heinze & Company? But that failure was caused by the collapse of the Heinzes' attempted corner in United Copper, which was possible owing to the depressed share values prevailing after the market crash in March and/or the speculative behavior of short-sellers. Adverse court rulings, rising regulation, and outlandish rhetoric affected the atmosphere of business confidence. The San Francisco earthquake and fire in April 1906 triggered a global liquidity crunch. Then, in the

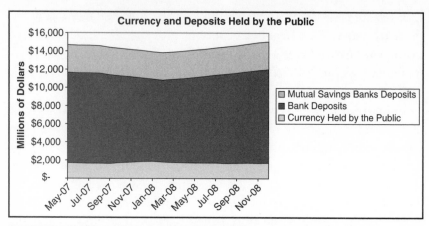

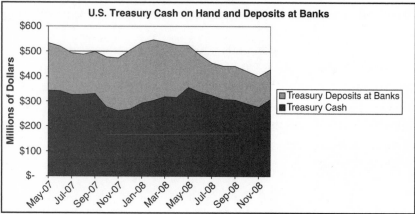

Figure L.4   Volumes of cash and deposits, May 1907 to December 1908.
Source: Authors' figures. Data from Milton Friedman and Anna Jacobson Schwartz, *A Monetary History of the United States*, NBER, 1963, pages 706 and 750.

summer of 1907, the Bank of England compounded problems by dramatically curtailing the acceptance of American finance bills in London. Which of these sparked the crisis?

The answer is a matter of judgment. If markets are rational, the shock that triggers a financial crisis will probably have these attributes:

- **Real, not cosmetic.** A "real" event is one that affects economic fundamentals: a variation in agricultural harvest, the introduction of new technology or some other disruptive innovation, labor unrest, the opening of new markets, deregulation or reregulation, or an earthquake.[44]

- **Large and costly.** The trigger of a major financial crisis must be meaningful enough to shake the system. It must cause a material downward shift in outlook among most investors.

- **Unambiguous.** A shock is a signal to investors. In order for it to cause a major shift in expectations among investors, the event must stand apart from the noise in the marketplace. And most investors must agree on its implications. Moreover, the signal must be authentic and impossible for a casual participant to send.

- **Surprising.** For an event to qualify as a "shock," it must be unanticipated, by definition. Indeed, it is the surprise that causes the sudden shift in expectations that triggers the crisis. Predicting shocks is an impossibility.[45]

From the perspective of these attributes, the trigger for the crisis in 1907 occurred well before the actual panic in the fall. Two events stand forth as real, large and costly, unambiguous, and surprising: the San Francisco earthquake and fire, and the Bank of England's restriction on finance bills.

6. Undue Fear, Greed, and Other Behavioral Aberrations

The events of 1907 suggest an emotional influence on the occurrence and severity of financial crises. Our history recounts suicides, letters describing overly buoyant or depressed markets, anxiety among depositors and bank executives, animated crowds in the streets of New York's financial district, use of public relations and the press in an attempt to build investor confidence—indeed, the very word *panic* suggests a suspension of rationality. In *The Psychology of the Stock Market*, published in 1912, G. C. Selden wrote:

> Both the panic and the boom are eminently psychological phenomena. This is not saying that the fundamental conditions do not warrant sharp declines in prices and at other times equally sharp advances. But the panic, properly so-called, represents a decline greater than is warranted by conditions usually because of an excited state of the public mind

accompanied by exhaustion of resources; while the term "boom" is used to mean an excessive and largely speculative advance. . . . It is really astonishing what a hold the fear of a possible panic has on the minds of many investors. The memory of the events of 1907 undoubtedly operated greatly to lessen the volume of speculative trade from that time to the present.[46]

This echoes the perspective of a range of authors whose books' very titles argue the case: *Irrational Exuberance* (Robert Shiller); *Extraordinary Popular Delusions and the Madness of Crowds* (Charles Mackay); *The Crowd: A Study of the Popular Mind* (Gustave Le Bon); *Manias, Panics, and Crashes* (Charles P. Kindleberger). In his classic text for investors, *Reminiscences of a Stock Operator*, Edwin Lefevre wrote, "A speculator's deadly enemies are ignorance, greed, fear, and hope."[47] In his analytic exploration, *Why Markets Crash*, Didier Sornette has argued that the root of aberrant market trends is one of the best-documented findings: people tend to be overconfident. His analysis of crashes suggests that herding and imitative behavior by investors lead to self-reinforcing market trends that are ultimately sharply reversed.

Optimism or pessimism is defined *relative* to those prices consistent with underlying fundamentals.[48] The extent to which market prices depart from those dictated by economic fundamentals remains a topic of keen debate at the frontier of economics. The concept of an emotional market "panic" challenges fundamental economic assumptions about the rationality of economic decision makers. Rationality assumes that prices today reasonably reflect an expectation of prices tomorrow and that markets are efficient in impounding news into asset prices. On balance, large markets in standard assets appear to be rational on average and over time. But crashes and panics are the exceptions to such "average" assumptions. To suspend the assumption of rationality admits the possibility of a great deal of bizarre behavior.[49]

7. Failure of Collective Action

The events of 1907 illustrate how collective action might address a bank panic. Most vividly, we see J. P. Morgan and his circle of influential New York bankers asserting that "the trouble stops here" with their support for the Trust Company of America. Morgan also forced the chief executives of the largest New York trust companies to form their own association to support the Trust Company of America and other institutions. Even so, Professor O. M. W. Sprague later criticized the collective efforts of trust companies: "The steps taken, however, were slow, and the means adopted were not sufficiently clear in import to renew general confidence."[50]

Throughout the United States in 1907, bank clearing houses functioned to monitor their members and assure depositors of convertibility. If it were necessary to suspend convertibility, the clearing houses issued scrip. Ultimately, the legacy of the crash and panic was to nationalize collective action by means of founding the Federal Reserve Bank. Several scholars have highlighted the important role of collective action as a brake on the severity of financial crises.[51]

Was the collective action in 1907 a success? The panic of 1907 was among the worst on record, hardly consistent with successful collective action. Our account here focuses principally on the New York City financial community and the role that a small circle of leaders played there. But the panic extended to all commercial centers in the United States. The true benchmark for collective action is the outcome *that might have been*. It seems reasonable to guess that the panic of 1907 would have been much worse without the collective action by Morgan and others.

Until 1914, the United States was a laboratory for systems of voluntary collective action. In the absence of a central bank that would set standards, monitor members, and be the lender of last resort, local and regional associations of bankers formed to perform these functions. Elmus Wicker studied the flows of funds among banks generally in the panics after the Civil War. He concluded that especially in 1907, "rent-seeking" behavior by individual banks prevented the New York Clearing House from functioning adequately to combat the panic. Wicker argued that these associations failed because they were voluntary (members could quit in a crisis), communication and information were limited, and incentives were perverse.[52]

These are the conditions of the classic game-theory problem, "the prisoner's dilemma,"[53] which illustrates how opportunism and the absence of joint action result in least desirable outcomes. The model has been used to explain a wide range of phenomena in business and finance. The key here is in anticipating the probabilities and actions of other players in the game.

The decision facing an equity investor during a crash or a bank depositor during a panic is: Should I exit now? The diagram in Figure L.5 casts the prisoner's dilemma into a financial crisis setting. Here, two shareholders contemplate immediately liquidating their holdings in a firm for $70 per share, were only one to sell, while the other would continue to hold shares that fall to $55 per share. If both sell simultaneously, they will both realize $40 per share. If neither sells, the firm's shares will stabilize at $100. Shareholders face the payoffs shown in the cells of the diagram, associated with either selling immediately, or waiting.

If the shareholders act in concert and wait, they may obtain better information and a better price for their firm (quadrant I.) If some sell into the tender offer while others wait, those who sell may obtain a better deal than those who wait and wind up with a lower share value. Absent joint action and communication, if all shareholders sell into the crash, everyone is worse off. The essence of this prisoner's dilemma is

		Investor B	
		Wait	Sell Now
Investor A	Wait	I. A gets $100/share B gets $100/share	II. A gets $60/share B gets $80/share
	Sell Now	III. A gets $80/share B gets $60/share	IV. A,B each get $70/share

Figure L.5 Example of the prisoner's dilemma as applied to investor or depositor behavior in a panic.

that in the absence of coordination, investors will tend to rush for the exits simultaneously, producing the worst-case outcome.

To the extent that crashes and panics conform to this model, the prisoner's dilemma has important implications for depositors and shareholders:

- Depositors and shareholders lose by the asymmetric structure of payoffs, and the difficulty of taking joint action. The very desire to avoid loss triggers the selling action that produces a slump in share price.
- A key problem for depositors and shareholders is to assess the probability of others' actions. In this sense, crises are like games.
- Collective action among depositors and shareholders may lead to better outcomes. Such is manifestly illustrated by the leadership group that collected around J. P. Morgan in 1907. The appearance of clearing houses is also an example of collective action.
- Today, computer-automated program trading and other rigid, formula-based approaches to investing that are known to be favored by some hedge funds and institutional investors remove human discretion from the unfolding crisis, and therefore may frustrate attempts at collective action.
- Time is very valuable to depositors and shareholders. Conducting research, organizing pools of liquid capital, coordinating action, and communicating information to the public takes time. At several points during the panic of 1907, the help arrived within a hair's breadth of collapse. In modern terms, exchanges are now governed by "circuit-breaker" rules that suspend trading temporarily to permit Keynes' "animal spirits" to subside and allow investors to analyze and disseminate information.

Most of the crises of the nineteenth century had been unfettered panics; 1907 was more limited in its devastation because of Morgan's leadership of the collective effort. Leadership is the decisive resource in collective action. What is the nature of such leadership? Conferred power and authority may be useful but are insufficient. Secretary Cortelyou had both but was distant from the work of organizing the collective effort.

Morgan, however, had earned his authority by virtue of his years in the business and his leadership of earlier collective efforts, such as in responding to the financial crisis of 1893. He displayed other qualities of leadership as well: the ability to recognize problems and opportunities, to shape a vision and strategy for responding and to engage others in them, to persuade, and to organize action.

Coda: Can It Happen Again?

Almost certainly, it can. In the early twenty-first century, the United States is protected by a regulatory system vastly stronger than the weak form of oversight that existed in 1907. The Fed, deposit insurance, advanced reporting systems and the like, grant a higher degree of confidence in the financial system than was afforded J. P. Morgan and his contemporaries. Yet, as Alan Greenspan, former Chairman of the Fed, has said, "Highly leveraged institutions, such as banks, are, by their nature periodically subject to seizing up as difficulties in funding leverage inevitably arise. The classic problem of bank risk management is to achieve an always elusive degree of leverage that creates an adequate return on equity without threatening default. The success rate has never approached 100 percent. . . ."[54]

Regulatory and institutional reforms in the twentieth century have ameliorated but not completely prevented financial crises: the twentieth century saw 15 stock market crashes.[55] We have seen serious financial market instability over the last 25 years in equities (1987, 2001), currencies (Mexico in 1994, Asia in 1997), government debt (Russia in 1998), and various financial institutions (the failure of Continental Illinois National Bank in 1984, the rash of savings and loan failures in 1987–1989, and the failure of Long-Term Capital Management in 1998). These are events of "the first magnitude"[56] and ignore a larger number of brief and/or localized events, yet they all resulted in decline of asset values, constriction of credit, and damage to financial institutions.[57] It seems unlikely that we will completely prevent these kinds of events in the future. However, understanding the cause of financial market crises may help to forearm investors, regulators, and chief executives.

One's perspective on the cause (or causes) of financial crises will have big implications for the actions necessary to avoid them. Charles Kindleberger and Hyman Minsky saw crises as inevitable products of economic expansion. This betokens the "animal spirits" to which John Maynard Keynes referred and to which many behavioral economists have been drawn. If irrational behavior is the whole story of crises, then the equivalent of a "good cold shower" would be a remedy. On the other hand, Charles Calomiris and a new generation of information economists point to the impact of real shocks and poor transparency as the basis for the propagation of crises. This seems closer to what we observed in the events of 1907. Certainly, improving system transparency would forestall some of the panic behavior one sees in crises.

Our seven elements embrace these and other factors. This approach, drawn from a detailed history of one crisis, is broadly consistent with some of the large-scale assessments of financial crises,[58] encompassing a wide range of other explanations. Much as one might prefer a "silver bullet," single explanation, the research evidence remains imperfect enough to exclude with confidence all factors but one. Therefore, in hopes of promoting thoughtful anticipation and response to financial crises, we choose to highlight the broader range suggested by 1907.

At any moment, many of the seven drivers of crises reside in the economic environment. Though it is uncertain when and where they will align in ways to produce a crisis, history emphasizes that financial crises occur without respect to the nature of regulations or the institutions they govern. One of the most dangerous statements in the markets is, "This time it's different." We doubt that history will repeat itself in exactly the same way as 1907, but the drivers we generalized from that crisis can and do recur. The economic situation in the early twenty-first century thus offers some arresting parallels to 1907:

- **System-like architecture.** The global financial system in the twenty-first century is vastly larger and more complicated owing to economic growth, proliferation of products and services, entry of new players (such as hedge funds and institutions from emerging countries), cross-listing of securities among global markets, arbitrage among markets, and so on. New credit derivatives and other exotic contracts might help to reduce risk, but they have never sustained a live test: No one knows whether they will dampen or amplify a crisis.

- **Buoyant growth.** The world economy has been growing at historically rapid rates for some time, owing significantly to explosive growth in emerging countries, such as China, India, Brazil, and Russia. Rapid growth can absorb the liquidity in the financial system and fuel a mentality of speculation. Newly minted millionaires may not bring to their investing the discipline and long experience necessary to weather a crisis.

- **Inadequate safety buffers.** Instant telecommunications and computer-based trading strategies eliminate the delays that existed in 1907—time to think and assess has dwindled. Today, money travels at the speed of light. Though regulatory safety buffers (such as the Basel Accords) are much stronger, their enforcement remains largely at the national and local levels. The largest financial institutions are supranational, and some fear, beyond the detailed oversight of any one regulatory jurisdiction. Have prudential banking practices been maintained in the Middle East, South America, and Asia? The "Asian flu" crisis of 1997 sprouted in part from concerns about the capital adequacy of banks in Thailand. Rumors circulate about the soundness of banks in China and other East Asian countries. The roughly 9,000 hedge funds in the world are unregulated and control over $1 trillion in investment capital directly and, depending on the degree of leverage they employ, perhaps a total of $4 to $10 trillion—many of these funds are conservatively managed; but we should worry about the aggressive funds that employ extreme leverage, well above the industry average. In the United States, a spike in real estate prices grew from low interest rates and aggressive lending practices such as adjustable-rate mortgages and the waiver of down payments. Enron, the Detroit automakers, and numerous corporations demonstrated that when off-balance-sheet items such as special-purpose entities, pensions, and health care obligations were taken into account, the firms were very highly levered. Generally, the huge imbalance of trade between the United States and the rest of the world impairs confidence in the dollar—virtually no one expects the dollar to strengthen against other currencies, thereby reducing the country's macroeconomic flexibility.

- **Adverse leadership.** Two leaders, Vladimir Putin, president of Russia, and Hugo Chavez, president of Venezuela, dramatically weakened the respect for private capital in their countries through attacks on wealthy individuals, confiscation of corporate assets, and use of oil output and other natural resources as instruments of foreign policy. The failure of the Doha Round of trade-liberalization negotiations triggered an outpouring of antiinvestor sentiment, aimed mainly at the developed nations. In most emerging nations, the indifference with which leaders view official corruption and disrespect for the sanctity of contracts and rights of investors eats like rust at the investor confidence in those countries. Protectionist sentiment seems to be rising—not merely toward commercial trade, but also toward flows of investment capital. In 2005, Franz Muntefering, head of a major political party in Germany, criticized foreign private equity investors as "swarms of locusts that fall on companies, stripping them bare before moving on."[59] In 2006, Korea considered enacting laws that would prevent hostile takeovers by foreign firms. In the United States, rhetoric and policy proposals by political leaders can impair investor confidence—consider recent headlines on such topics as foreign trade, job and industrial protection, national health care, government deficits, "soak-the-rich" tax schemes, CEO pay, and the growing gap between the richest segment of the population and the rest.

- **Real economic shock.** A shock can be identified only in hindsight. It takes but a little imagination to derive some possibilities: a pandemic of avian flu, an oil price spike to $100 a barrel, a major terrorist strike on the order of 9/11, the outbreak of major (read: nuclear) war (India/Pakistan, Iran/Israel), and an implosion of a major financial institution, such as a hedge fund. The stability of the hedge fund industry has been of special interest since the failure of Long-Term Capital Management in 1998. Amaranth Capital Partners, a $6 billion fund, failed in 2006. Andrew Lo and others[60] have highlighted the growing integration between hedge funds and banks that can lead to greater systemic risk. Of vital importance is the correlation or linkage among these institutions to cause trouble to radiate through the system. Hedge funds may take significant risks in their trading strategies; their use of leverage amplifies those risks dramatically; their linkages with banks could cause instability to travel.

- **Undue fear, greed, and other behavioral aberrations.** Market sentiment changes continuously and is sometimes at variance from what rational pricing and trading would suggest, as blogs and financial newspapers attest daily. Two notable shifts from buoyant optimism to fear occurred during the respective boom and slump in Internet stocks in 1998–2001 and real estate in 2002–2006. The extent to which these shifts were consistent with changes in economic fundamentals remains a subject of research, though conventional wisdom seems to hold that these swings were aberrations rather than rational movements in the markets.

- **Failure of collective action.** The prompt leadership by the New York Federal Reserve bank to organize a group of institutions to take over the investment positions of Long-Term Capital Management in 1998 was reminiscent of J. P. Morgan's leadership in 1907. The Bank for International Settlements has organized a Committee on the Global Financial System that monitors the stability of global markets for the G10 countries.[61] But in a globally complex financial system, will such collective action be possible if the crisis is triggered beyond the reach of any of today's regulators?

The events of 1907 suggest that these seven factors are mutually reinforcing. Rapid growth leads to optimism that for a time may stimulate more growth. Insufficient information fuels optimism and delays collective action. Imperfect information and optimism promote a tendency to discount the effect of real shocks to the system when they occur. Real shocks, absence of shock absorbers, and lack of collective action may amplify the conditions of instability. The factors come and go in the economy; at any point in time, a few of them are almost certainly present, and their presence individually is insufficient to cause financial market instability. Rather, it is the convergence of some or all of the forces that produces the crisis. The panic of 1907 thus offers us lessons, but also insights for action: the importance of transparency, feedback to decision makers, encouragement of collective action, the establishment of safety buffers in the global financial system, and the duty of leaders to serve their constituencies.

APPENDIX A

Key Figures after the Panic

The following provides an epilogue for many of the prominent individuals for whom the crash and panic of 1907 proved to be pivotal.

George F. Baker rose from president of First National Bank of New York, which he cofounded in 1863 (when he was 23), to chairman of the board in 1909. He was a director in 22 corporations and a philanthropist. His gifts founded Harvard Business School and Baker Library at Dartmouth. Baker remained chairman until 1926. He died May 2, 1931, at age 91.

Charles T. Barney, who died from a self-inflicted gunshot wound on November 14, 1907, was survived by his wife, Lily Whitney Barney, and their two sons. Lily Barney sold their home in Manhattan's Murray Hill district in 1912.

George B. Cortelyou remained as secretary of the treasury until the end of the Roosevelt administration in 1908. He threw his support to the concept of a central bank for the United States since, based on his experience, the Treasury did not have the power to maintain stability of the financial system during a crisis. After leaving government, he became the chief executive officer of Consolidated Gas Company. He died on October 23, 1940, in New York.

Henry P. Davison became a senior partner at J. P. Morgan & Company in 1909. In testimony at the Pujo hearings, Davison was one of the most articulate defenders of bankers as stewards of the public interest. Davison argued that the banker should be a director of corporations because of

> ... his moral responsibility as sponsor for the corporation's securities, to keep an eye upon its policies and to protect the interests of investors in the securities of that corporation ... in general [bankers] enter only those boards which the opinion of the investing public requires them to enter, as evidence of good faith that they are willing to have their names publicly associated with the management.[1]

In August 1914, Davison successfully persuaded the governments of France and Britain to grant J. P. Morgan & Company a monopoly franchise on underwriting bonds issued by those governments in the United States. During World War I, he raised funds for the American Red Cross to supply ambulances to the American Army in France. He pressed for the formation of the International Red Cross, an association of the national Red Cross organizations, a goal that was achieved in 1919. Following two unsuccessful operations to excise a brain tumor, he died in 1922 at the age of 55.

F. Augustus Heinze met his downfall with the panic and crash of 1907. After the failed attempt to corner the stock of United Copper Company and his ouster from the Mercantile National Bank, the firm of Otto Heinze & Company and Heinze himself were financially ruined. According to his brother Otto, Augustus maintained that he was blameless and that "the old line of bankers were bringing about a money panic in order to get rid of the new class of financiers and the new trust companies."[2] In the wake of the panic, Heinze's firm was placed in the hands of a receiver and he was indicted on 16 counts of financial malfeasance and various breaches of banking law. Heinze's case dragged on in the courts for years, and in a stunning reversal he was completely exonerated in 1909. Nonetheless, Heinze's firm was destroyed, his mining interests had collapsed, his relationships with his brothers had dissolved, and his health suffered. Only 44 years old, the garrulous *bon vivant* died alone on November 4, 1914, at his home in Saratoga, New York, from cirrhosis of the liver.[3]

Thomas W. Lamont stayed with J. P. Morgan & Company for his entire career, becoming a partner in 1910 and rising to the position of chairman of the board in 1943. He was acting head of the firm on "Black Thursday," October 24, 1929, when he committed the company to large purchases of stocks in an effort to instill confidence in the market. And he served on various semiofficial assignments for the U.S. government, including the 1919 Paris Peace Negotiations that led to the Treaty of Versailles. He died on February 2, 1948. His son, Corliss Lamont, was a philosophy professor at Columbia and a socialist. His other son, Thomas Stillwell Lamont, rose to vice chairman of Morgan Guaranty Trust Company. His grandson, Ned Lamont, was the antiwar candidate for U.S. Senate in Connecticut in 2006.

J. P. "Jack" Morgan Jr. arrived in Europe at the height of the panic, to assist his father with the attempt to arrange gold loans from the central bank of France to U.S. banks. The French, concerned about the deepening crisis, insisted on a guarantee of the loan from the U.S. government. Roosevelt refused on grounds that this would set the precedent for government guarantees of private deals. The effort to acquire gold from France stalled and then, by late November 1907, was unnecessary. Jack was back in the United States by January 1908. He worked in the shadow of his famous father and the luminous financiers at J. P. Morgan & Company, such as George Perkins, Henry Davison, Thomas Lamont, and Charles Steele. Jack's work at the firm proceeded quietly. In 1910, he was active in organizing the London affiliate, Morgan, Grenfell. Later that year, he sustained a partial nervous breakdown that removed him from business for some months. (Like his father, Jack suffered bouts of "the blues," as he called them.)

Jack followed the build-up to the Pujo hearings and then counseled his father in preparing to testify. Upon Pierpont's death in 1913, Jack became the senior partner of the firm. The firm advanced to be the sole financier for French and British purchases in the United States during World War I. In 1915, a German sympathizer attempted to assassinate Jack, almost killing him with two shots in the abdomen. This generated popular sympathy for Morgan. Upon his return to work, a crowd gathered to applaud him. In the following years, he assisted the war effort, helped to reorganize General Motors, financed corporate growth in the 1920s, reorganized J. P. Morgan & Company in the 1930s, and rationalized his father's massive art collection. Though he was a senior partner of the firm, Jack relied increasingly upon Thomas W. Lamont as, in effect, chief executive. Jack died of a heart attack on March 13, 1943, at the age of 75. His biographer, John Forbes, said, "Morgan was a team player and submerged his own personality in the firm, where he managed with consummate skill to hold together a group of highly skilled and individualistic partners and make maximum use of their separate gifts to achieve very substantial results."[4]

J. Pierpont Morgan emerged from the panic of 1907 lauded by some and hated by others even more than before. Letters and cables of congratulations for his leadership poured in. He and his firm enjoyed a robust volume of corporate financing buoyed by his reputation in the crisis. In 1910, Harvard granted him an honorary doctorate. By 1912, he was slowing down, gradually withdrawing from the daily grind of business to focus on philanthropy and his beloved collection of books and art.

And yet, the panic pricked a longstanding blister of suspicion among Progressives that Morgan's success was due to anticompetitive behavior. Morgan, the organizer of large corporate combinations, was famous for combating "ruinous competition." Thus, the Pujo hearings, nominally covering the structure of corporate finance in America, was focused particularly on J. P. Morgan & Company, and its senior partner, Pierpont. He testified in the hearings on December 18 and 19, 1912. Reading it a century later, the transcript conveys tension and combat between Pierpont and the chief investigator, Samuel Untermyer. Morgan was unable to recall particulars of his firm's deals and operations. Untermyer's questions appeared to lead the witness, yet Morgan resisted. He remained calm and respectful on the stand. On the chief point of the hearings, Morgan remained adamant that money or credit could not be controlled by a small cabal of financiers:

Untermyer: Is not commercial credit based primarily upon money or property?

Morgan: No, sir. The first thing is character.

Untermyer: Before money or property?

Morgan: Before money or anything else. Money cannot buy it.

Untermyer: If that is the rule of business, Mr. Morgan, why do the banks demand, the first thing they ask, a statement of what the man has got, before they extend him credit . . . He does not get it on his face or character?

Morgan: Yes, he gets it on his character . . . Because a man I do not trust could not get money from me on all the bonds in Christendom.[5]

He left for Europe on January 7, 1913, shortly after giving testimony in the Pujo hearings. Touring through Egypt, he became ill on February 13 with what his doctor said was "general physical and nervous exhaustion resulting from prolonged excessive strain in elderly subject."[6] Pierpont died in Rome on March 31, 1913, age 75. Thomas Lamont wrote that the effect of the Pujo hearings "upon Mr. Morgan's physical powers was devastating."[7]

   Charles W. Morse, the confederate of F. Augustus Heinze, was the vice president of Mercantile National Bank when it suspended operations. He has been described as "physically ugly, amoral, rich beyond reason," rapacious, and shady.[8] In January 1910, Morse was convicted of misappropriating bank funds from the Bank of North America (a bank controlled by Heinze and Morse) and sentenced to 15 years in prison. He began his sentence at the federal penitentiary in Atlanta, where he met Charles Ponzi, who would later become famous for the eponymous pyramid scheme; Ponzi was serving a two-year sentence on a charge of sponsoring illegal immigrants.

   Morse believed that he had done nothing wrong that did not occur daily in the financial community. Therefore, he launched a vigorous effort to spring himself, with the assistance of lawyers, lobbyists to the White House, and journalists such as Clarence W. Barron. Mysteriously, Morse grew ill; it was feared that he would die quickly. President Taft commuted Morse's sentence in January 1912 and released him from prison. Thereupon, Morse fled to Europe, after which it was revealed that Morse's "illness" was due to eating soap shortly before his medical exams.[9] In the fall of 1912, Morse returned to the United States and formed a new steamship company, having been forced to sell off his Consolidated Lines to J. P. Morgan at a steep discount in 1907. With the advent of World War I, he bid on ship construction projects for his U.S. shipping company, and won contracts for 36 vessels. In 1922, Morse was indicted for fraud and war profiteering but was acquitted.[10]

George W. Perkins retired from J. P. Morgan & Company in 1910, at the age of 48. He worked for Theodore Roosevelt's presidential campaign in 1912 and continued as a political adviser thereafter. During World War I, he worked to organize food supplies for the army and assisted the YMCA in raising money for relief work among soldiers. He also raised funds to create Palisades Park. Perkins died June 18, 1920, following a nervous breakdown in May. Papers reported that he contracted influenza in France and had not fully recovered when he resumed work. The *New York Tribune* said that he died from "acute inflammation of the brain, the result of complete nervous exhaustion due to intense and continuous overwork."[11]

His early retirement from J. P. Morgan & Company was described by his family as a desire to "devote most of his time to public work."[12] But early retirement for public work was not something Morgan partners, such as Henry Davison, did. Throughout Perkins's career, he had been ambitious for power. Perhaps the shift to electoral politics was intended to fill that need. But thereafter he subsided from public view, a remarkable change for one of the most creative and effective players in the New York financial community. Perkins had been perhaps the chief architect of the combinations that created International Harvester and U. S. Steel, and he had lifted New York Life Insurance Company to the top echelon of its industry by daringly eliminating middlemen in the distribution of life insurance services in the United States.

Theodore Roosevelt acknowledged that he was "gravely harassed and concerned" over the panic of 1907.[13] He was sensitive to the charges that his policies had triggered the panic. He wrote, "I do not think that my policies had anything to do with producing the conditions which brought on the panic; but I do think that very possibly the assaults and exposures which I made, and which were more or less successfully imitated in the several States, have brought on the panic a year or two sooner than would otherwise have been the case. The panic would have been infinitely worse, however, had it been deferred."[14] His other sensitivity about the panic concerned his approval of the Tennessee Coal

& Iron acquisition by U.S. Steel. His critics argued that the merger was unnecessary to stem the panic and that it was a ruse to profit Morgan and his circle. Thus, six years later, Roosevelt wrote, "It offered the only chance for arresting the panic and it did arrest the panic. . . . The panic was stopped, public confidence in the solvency of the threatened institution being at once restored."[15]

Roosevelt was an original item. No previous president offered the combination of massive energy, moral suasion, charisma, and belief in a very strong executive branch. He changed U.S. politics, though un-like the other faces sculpted into the side of Mount Rushmore, he is remembered more for his style, rather than substance. He was a charis-matic leader, among the most popular of presidents, as reflected in his landslide election in 1904 and his significant poll in the 1912 election, running as a third-party candidate.

The biographer, H. W. Brands, wrote, "The frustrating fact for Roo-sevelt was that, as much as Americans loved him, they didn't particularly heed him." [16] After 1908, Roosevelt never regained the "bully pulpit" of powerful elected office. His political influence lay chiefly in the stream of speeches, articles, and books he produced in retirement. His proposal for Progressive programs foreshadowed numerous initiatives of presidents later in the twentieth century. After his electoral defeat in 1912, he em-barked on a dangerous exploration of the River of Doubt in Brazil that left him weakened from exertion and disease. An ardent advocate for the projection of U.S. power abroad, he reviled Wilson's policy of neutrality at the outbreak of World War I. When the United States did join the fight in 1917, his four sons volunteered. The youngest boy, Quentin, was killed in 1918, when his airplane was shot down. This plunged Roosevelt into depression that muted, but did not totally suppress, his public voice. He died on January 6, 1919, in his sleep and was buried at his home, Sagamore Hill, on Oyster Bay, Long Island, New York.

James Stillman was president of National City Bank from 1891 to 1909 and chairman of the board from 1909 to 1919. A biographer once described Stillman as a "carefully-dressed, smallish man, with the tall hat and the inevitable cigar, who didn't answer sometimes for twenty minutes, but fixed one with his clear, dark eyes and his air of immense dignity, presented a really fascinating enigma. His mental power was as great as his shyness and, like many shy people who inspire fear in others, he preferred those who were not afraid of him. . . . Throughout his day's work, there was manifest intensity visible in the concentration, in the careful calculation of each problem, in the dislike of hearing any details discussed, while yet expecting them to be carefully watched."[17]

Stillman fashioned a strategic alliance with the Rockefeller interests through a double marriage of his daughters into the Rockefeller family and through an equity investment by the Rockefellers into National City Bank. He and his junior associate, Frank Vanderlip, were the leaders of a major transformation of the bank from the one-person operation of Moses Taylor, the president from 1856 to 1882, to an institution with a broader strategic intention. Taylor was both an industrialist and a banker; in contrast, Stillman focused exclusively on banking and foresaw the massive economic changes in America and resolved to position City Bank to take advantage of them. Stillman envisioned that National City Bank would provide "any service" that the new large corporations would require. In February 1907, Stillman wrote to Vanderlip:

> I firmly believe ... that the most successful banks will be the ones that can do something else than the mere receiving and loaning of money. That does not require a very high order of ability, but devising methods of serving people and [of] attracting business without resorting to unconservative or unprofitable methods, that opens limited fields for study, ability and resourcefulness and few only will be found to do it.[18]

Thereafter, National City Bank broadened its range of services, expanded its service to institutions and individuals, and reached to new locations. Stillman implemented a decentralized, multi-divisional structure. Historians Harold Cleveland and Thomas Huertas have argued that by the start of the twentieth century, National City was a truly "modern" corporation, a leader firm in its industry. Stillman died, still chairman, in March 1918. In 1955, National City Bank merged with First National Bank of New York to form Citibank, forerunner of Citigroup, the largest American financial institution as of 2007.

Benjamin Strong rose to president of Bankers Trust and served in that capacity until 1914, when he was appointed the first governor of the Federal Reserve Bank of New York. He served in this capacity until October 1928, when he died at age 55 of an intestinal abscess. He was the "prime mover ... dominant figure" of the Federal Reserve System from its inception.[19] He had grasped the need for international coordination to assist Europe's recovery from World War I and was a leading proponent of "easy money" policies that drove the boom in the stock market in the 1920s and its eventual reckoning in 1929.[20]

In a note to another governor written shortly before his death, Strong advocated aggressive use of open market operations to flood the market with liquidity in the event of another financial crisis. Unfortunately, Strong's successors ignored the advice and for three years pursued deflationary policies with disastrous effect. Economists Friedman and Schwartz attribute the severity of the Great Depression to "the shift of power within the System and the lack of understanding and experience of the individuals to whom the power shifted."[21] The *Wall Street Journal* eulogized him: "His services were of the highest value and conditions today might have been different if his health had permitted undivided attention to his office for the past three months."[22]

Frank A. Vanderlip worked for National City Bank from 1904 until his retirement. His most important contribution to the aftermath of the panic of 1907 was to be the ghostwriter of the "Aldrich Plan," in which he drafted proposed legislation to establish the modern Federal Reserve System.[23] Vanderlip rose to president of National City Bank in 1909. His important innovation was the founding of the first foreign branch of any major commercial bank for National City, in Buenos Aires. He also led the organizing of American International Corporation in November 1915 for the purpose of making foreign investments. Vanderlip chafed under Stillman's voting control of National City Bank and sought from Stillman an option to buy his shares. Stillman refused. Poor in health, Stillman spent much of 1917 in Paris.

Vanderlip continued to promote the internationalization of the bank and made the unfortunate decision to open a branch in Moscow, just after the Russian Revolution. The branch's assets were soon nationalized leaving National City Bank exposed to repay deposits in that branch from dollars in New York—an exposure equal to 40 percent of the bank's capital. Stillman returned to New York, placed Vanderlip on leave, and died soon thereafter. Control of the bank passed to Stillman's son. Vanderlip resigned in June 1919. Stillman's son proved to be an incompetent executive and resigned in May 1921, turning management of the company over to a new cadre of professional executives who demanded, and were given, an equity interest in the bank. Frank Vanderlip died on June 29, 1927.[24]

APPENDIX B

Definitions

A close reading of the extensive literature on financial crises reminds one of Humpty Dumpty's exchange with Alice in Lewis Carroll's *Through the Looking-Glass*:

"When I use a word," Humpty Dumpty said, in a rather scornful tone, "it means just what I choose it to mean, neither more nor less."

"The question is," said Alice, "whether you can make words mean so many different things."

"The question is," said Humpty Dumpty, "which is to be master— that's all.

Good analysis of events begins with careful definitions—philosophers tell us that these will refer to essential features, avoid circularity, apply to the thing defined neither more nor less, avoid figurative or obscure language, and describe what it *is* as opposed to is not.[1] To assist the analyst of financial crises as they may arise in the future, this appendix offers an overview of some relevant terms:

Crash typically refers to a sharp decline in equity prices. For instance, the classic treatise on the subject, by Charles Kindleberger and

Robert Aliber, defines a crash as "a collapse of the prices of assets or perhaps the failure of an important firm or bank."[2] This is not a very specific definition: How much of a collapse is required to meet the definition? Frederic Mishkin and Eugene White wrote, "On the face of it, defining a stock market crash or collapse is simple. When you see it, you know it."[3]

Panic refers to a sudden fear-driven withdrawal of bank deposits that triggers a liquidity crisis for banks or the entire financial system. Kindleberger and Aliber define panic as "'a sudden fright without cause' (from the god Pan, known for causing terror), which may occur in asset markets or involve a rush from less liquid securities to money or government securities—in the belief that governments do not go bankrupt because they can always print more money."[4] Charles Calomiris adds a crucial point: that the rush to withdraw overwhelms a bank or system to the extent that it suspends convertibility of deposits into cash—thus, banks either close their doors, honor only a fraction of each withdrawal request, or start issuing IOUs in the form of scrip or clearing house certificates.[5] Noyes wrote, "The characteristics which distinguish a panic [of the first magnitude] from those smaller financial convulsions and industrial set-backs which are of constant occurrence on speculative markets, are five in number: First a credit crisis so acute as to involve the holding back of payment of cash by banks to depositors, and the momentary suspension of practically all credit facilities. Second, the general hoarding of money by individuals through withdrawal of great sums of cash from banks. ... Third, such financial helplessness that gold has to be bought or borrowed instantly in huge quantity from foreign countries. ... Fourth, the shutting down of manufacturing enterprises, suddenly and on large scale. ... Fifth, ... disappearance of the buying demand throughout the country."[6]

Financial crisis is a general term that may embrace crashes and panics and indicates great stress on the financial system of banks and other financial intermediaries usually resulting in prominent institutional failures and sharp contraction in the national economy. Such were the events of 1907. Mishkin and White defined a financial crisis as: "A disruption to financial markets in which adverse selection and moral hazard problems become much worse, so that financial markets are unable to efficiently channel funds to those who have the most productive investment opportunities. As a result, a financial crisis can drive the economy away from an equilibrium with high output in which financial markets perform well to one in which output declines sharply."[7]

Insolvency occurs where the liabilities of a firm or bank exceed its assets. To be declared insolvent is a condition of bankruptcy.

Illiquidity describes the circumstance in which a firm is unable to pay its creditors (or a bank is unable to pay its depositors) when obligations are presented for payment. Illiquidity refers to the unavailability of ready cash. A firm or bank may be illiquid but not insolvent.

Mania. Kindleberger and Aliber offer general hints at the definition of *mania:* "dramatic but they have been infrequent . . . have been associated with the expansion phase of the business cycle"[8]; ". . . involves increases in the prices of real estate or stocks or a currency or a commodity in the present and nature future that are not consistent with the prices of the same real estate or stocks in the distant future"[9]; "emphasizes irrationality"[10]; "a loss of touch with rationality, something close to mass hysteria."[11]

Bubble. Kindleberger and Aliber define *bubble* as "a generic term for the increases in asset prices in the mania phase of the cycle"[12]; "foreshadows that some values will eventually burst. Economists use the term *bubble* to mean any deviation in the price of an asset or a security or a commodity that cannot be explained in terms of the 'fundamentals.' . . . an upward price movement over an extended period of fifteen to forty months that then implodes."[13] In his book on tulip mania, Mike Dash defines *bubble* as "booms in which a commodity's price quite outstrips what is actually worth to anyone other than a speculator."[14] Robert Shiller defined "speculative bubble" as "a situation in which temporarily high prices are sustained largely by investors' enthusiasm rather than by consistent estimation of real value."[15] Shiller added, "The traditional notion of a speculative bubble is, I think, a period when investors are attracted to an investment irrationally because rising prices encourage them to expect, at some level of consciousness at least, more price increases. A feedback develops—as people become more and more attracted, there are more and more price increases. The bubble comes to an end when people no longer expect the price to increase, and so the demand falls and the market crashes."[16]

Palgrave's *Dictionary of Political Economy* published in 1926 defined *bubble* as "Any unsound undertaking accompanied by a high degree of speculation."[17] Peter Garber notes "bubble ... is a fuzzy word filled with import but lacking a solid operational definition ... if we have a serious misforecast of asset prices we might then say that there is a bubble. This is no more than saying that there is something happening that we cannot explain, which we normally call a random disturbance. In asset pricing studies, we give it a name—bubble—and appeal to unverifiable psychological stories."[18] Some economists, such as Allan Meltzer[19] and Olivier Blanchard,[20] allow that some deviations from fundamentals may be rational, as for instance, where a market price depends on its own expected rate of change. That is, perhaps the changes in asset prices will be self-fulfilling. Meltzer has written, "Bubble phenomena are what remain unexplained by [some rational hypothesis]. In this sense, bubbles are a name assigned to phenomena that may be explained by an alternative hypothesis ... 'bubble' is a name we assign to events that we cannot explain with standard hypotheses."[21]

As an alternative approach to defining the term, the following list presents some characteristic conditions that have been observed near the peak of a bubble in asset prices[22]:

- Dramatic rise in prices reflected in aggressively high valuation multiples and transactions.
- Buoyant demand for the assets: oversubscribed initial public offerings in equities, numerous participants in auctions for companies, natural resources, and real estate.
- Optimism about the sustainability of future price increases.

- Entry into the market by naïve, inexperienced, and unsophisticated investors. Bernard Baruch sold his stocks in early 1929 when he started receiving unsolicited stock tips from his shoeshine boy.
- Talk of a "new paradigm" rendering long-standing investment maxims invalid. Such was the case during the Internet boom. "This time it's different" is one of the most dangerous attitudes in investing.
- Jumbo deals. These deals change the competitive landscape and/or frame of reference for investors. Travelers Insurance acquired Citicorp in 1998, signaling the end of the regulatory ban on universal banking. The audacity of jumbo deals serves to reinforce "new paradigm" thinking.
- Innovations in deal design, new securities, technology, and goods and services. Leading up to 1907 were the creation of trusts, new national consumer-branded products, and the spread of the telephone, automobile, and household electricity. Joseph Schumpeter heavily emphasized the role of the inventor and entrepreneur in triggering new phases in economic cycles.
- Aggressive financing. Banks lower their credit standards to the benefit of borrowers who avail themselves of the cheap credit.
- Regulators and other watchdogs relax their monitoring of financial intermediaries and investor behavior.
- Positive economic news. A recent stretch of growth.
- Media hype and considerable popular interest. Rising prices, huge profits, jumbo deals, often to the benefit of Everyman and Everywoman, garner front-page stories.

Irrational exuberance. At the core of the foregoing definitions is a sense of psychological instability. Alan Greenspan, chairman of the U.S. Federal Reserve Board expressed the concern on December 5, 1996, coined the phrase *irrational exuberance* in suggesting that prices in the stock market might not be reflecting economic fundamentals.[23] Robert Shiller defined *irrational exuberance* as "wishful thinking on the part of investors that blinds us to the truth of our situation."[24] After the stock market had risen considerably further, on February 23, 1999, Greenspan was asked whether he still thought the market displayed irrational exuberance. He replied that irrationality is "something you can only know after the fact."

Peter Garber criticizes such definitions as "fuzzy" and "poor" and notes that describing a period in financial market history analysts tend simply to refer to price movements and not to the state of mind (irrationality) on which they depend. But behavioral economists now have instruments for gauging the sentiment of investors. Robert Shiller has constructed a bubble expectations index that is based on assessments about the height of asset prices and the outlook for future increases.[25] His metrics suggested buoyant optimism in stocks in 1999 and in real estate in early 2006.

The key problem is that not all explosive movements in prices are bubbles, manias, or evidence of irrational exuberance. As Alan Meltzer has pointed out, asset prices exploded in Germany in the 1920s in response to the Reichsbank's monetary expansion.[26]

References

Primary Research Sources

Our research into the events of 1907 drew on diaries, letters, cables, memoranda, notes, newspaper clippings, and memoirs in the following archives:

- Benjamin Strong Papers, Federal Reserve Bank of New York, New York.
- George W. Perkins Papers, Rare Book and Manuscript Library, Columbia University, New York, New York.
- Herbert L. Satterlee Papers, Morgan Library and Museum, New York, New York.
- J. S. Morgan & Company Papers, Guildhall Library, London, United Kingdom.
- Morgan Grenfell & Company Papers, Guildhall Library, London, United Kingdom.
- Morgan Family Papers, Morgan Library and Museum, New York, New York.
- Thomas W. Lamont Papers, Baker Library, Harvard Graduate School of Business Administration, Boston, Massachusetts.

- Frank A. Vanderlip Papers, Butler Library, Columbia University, New York, New York.
- Otto C. Heinze Papers, Butte-Silver Bow Public Archives, Butte, Montana.

Three periodicals provided an excellent stream of contemporary reporting and opinion:

- *Commercial and Financial Chronicle,* volume 84, 1907.
- *New York Times,* 1907.
- *Wall Street Journal,* 1907.

For a factual perspective on life in the first decade of the twentieth century, we consulted *Encyclopedia Britannica*, 11th ed. (1910), Cambridge: Cambridge University Press.

Contemporary accounts were supplemented by the published documents from the various congressional hearings (National Monetary Commission, 1910, Pujo Investigation, 1912–1913, and Federal Reserve Act, 1913). Also, we drew on histories and biographical accounts written by contemporary observers of the events of 1907—see the works by Satterlee, Clews, and Tarbell. The records of Theodore Roosevelt were especially valuable concerning his thinking before, during, and after the panic:

- E. E. Morison, ed., *The Letters of Theodore Roosevelt*, volumes 2–6, Cambridge, Mass.: Harvard University Press.

Finally, we obtained quantitative data on manufacturing output, and prices and trading volumes for stocks, bonds, call money, and commodities, from the *Commercial and Financial Chronicle* editions and from these sources:

- National Bureau of Economic Research, databases on economic output.
- International Finance Center, Yale University School of Management, original databases on security prices.

Published Writings Consulted

Akerlof, George 1970. "The Market for Lemons: Qualitative Uncertainty and the Market Mechanism." *Quarterly Journal of Economics* 84: 488–500.

Allen, Frederick Lewis, 1935. *The Lords of Creation*. New York: Harper & Row.

———. 1949. *The Great Pierpont Morgan*. New York: Harper & Brothers Publishers.

———. 1952. *The Big Change: America Transforms Itself 1900–1950*. New York: Harper & Brothers.

Andrew, A. Piatt 1908a. "Hoarding in the Panic of 1907." *Quarterly Journal of Economics* 22: 290–299.

———. 1908b. "Substitutes for Cash in the Panic of 1907." *Quarterly Journal of Economics* 22: 488–498.

———. 1910. *Statistics for the United States, 1867–1909. National Monetary Commission*. 61st Congress, 2nd Session, Senate, Doc. 570. Washington, D.C.: U.S. Government Printing Office.

Anonymous. 1908. *"Bonum Meritum." A War of Words between President Roosevelt and J. Pierpont Morgan Concerning Railroad, Tariff, and Trust Questions and the Panic of 1907 as Supposed by the Author*. Chicago: M. A. Donohue & Company.

Baker, Malcolm, Richard S. Ruback, and Jeffrey Wurgler 2004. "Behavioral Corporate Finance: A Survey." In Espen Eckbo (ed.). 2006. *Handbook of Corporate Finance: Empirical Corporate Finance*. New York: Elsevier/North Holland.

Barry, John M. 2004. *The Great Influenza: The Epic Story of the Deadliest Plague in History*. New York: Viking.

Beard, Patricia, 2003. *After the Ball: Gilded Age Secrets, Boardroom Betrayals, and the Party That Ignited the Great Wall Street Scandal of 1905*. New York: Harper-Collins.

Beinhocker, Eric 2006. *The Origin of Wealth: Evolution, Complexity, and the Radical Remaking of Economics*. Boston: Harvard Business School Press.

Bernanke, Benjamin, 2006. "Hedge Funds and Systemic Risk" speech. Downloaded from www.federalreserve.gov/Boarddocs/speeches/2006/200605162/default.htm.

Blum, John Morton 1977. *The Republican Roosevelt*. Cambridge, Mass.: Harvard University Press.

Bookstaber, Richard 2007. *A Demon of Our Own Design*. New York: John Wiley & Sons.

Bordo, Michael D. 1985. "The Impact and International Transmission of Financial Crises: Some Historical Evidence, 1870–1933." *Revista di storia economica*, 2nd ser., vol. 2: 41–78.

———. 2000. "Are Financial Crises Becoming Increasingly Contagious? What Is the Historical Evidence on Contagion?" Rutgers University, working paper, downloaded at www1.worldbank.org/economicpolicy/managing%20volatility/contagion/documents/Bordo-Murshid.pdf.

Bordo, Michael D., and Christopher M. Meissner 2005, "Financial Crises, 1880–1913: The Role of Foreign Currency Debt." Cambridge, Mass.: National Bureau of Economic Research, working paper 11173.

Boyer, Brian H., Tomomi Kumagai, and Kathy Yuan. "How Do Crises Spread? Evidence from Accessible and Inaccessible Stock Indices." *Journal of Finance* 61: 957–1003, and downloaded from SSRN (January 2005). AFA 2003 Washington, D.C. Meetings. Available at SSRN: http://ssrn.com/abstract=341940.

Brandeis, Louis. 1914. *Other People's Money*, downloaded from http://library.louisville.edu/law/brandeis/opm-ch1.html.

Brands, H.W. 1997. *TR: The Last Romantic.* New York: Basic Books.

Brown, Clair, John Haltiwanger, and Julia Lane. 2006. *Economic Turbulence: Is a Volatile Economy Good for America?* Chicago: University of Chicago Press.

Brownlee, W. Elliot. 1979. *Dynamics of Ascent: A History of the American Economy,* 2nd ed. New York: Knopf.

Bulmer, Martin, Kevin Bales, and Kathryn Kish Sklar (eds.). 1991. *The Social Survey in Historical Perspective, 1880–1940.* Cambridge, U.K.: Cambridge University Press.

Burr, Anna Robeson. 1927. *The Portrait of a Banker: James Stillman 1850–1918.* New York: Duffield & Company.

Cahill, Kevin J. 1998. "The U. S. Bank Panic of 1907 and the Mexican Depression of 1908–1909." *The Historian* 60: 795–785.

Calomiris, Charles W. 2000. *U.S. Bank Deregulation in Historical Perspective.* Cambridge, U.K.: Cambridge University Press.

Calomiris, Charles W., and Gary Gorton. 1991. "The Origins of Banking Panics: Models, Facts, and Bank Regulation." In R. Glenn Hubbard (ed.), *Financial Markets and Financial Crises.* Chicago: University of Chicago Press. This was also published as a chapter by the same title in Charles W. Calomiris (ed.). (2000). *U.S. Bank Regulation in Historical Perspective.* Cambridge, U.K.: Cambridge University Press.

Calverley, John P. 2004. *Bubbles and How to Survive Them.* London: Nicholas Brealey Publishing.

Cannon, James G. 1910. "Clearing House Loan Certificates and Substitutes for Money Used During the Panic of 1907," speech delivered before the Finance Forum, New York City, March 30, 1910. Baker Library, Harvard Business School.

Capen, E.C., R.V. Clapp, and W.M. Campbell. 1971. "Competitive Bidding in High-Risk Situations," *Journal of Petroleum Technology* (June): 641–645.

Carlson, Mark. Undated. "Causes of Bank Suspensions in the Panic of 1893." Washington, D.C.: U.S. Federal Reserve Board, working paper.

Carosso, Vincent P. 1970. *Investment Banking in America*. Cambridge, Mass.: Harvard University Press.

———. 1987. *The Morgans: Private International Bankers, 1854–1913*. Cambridge, Mass.: Harvard University Press.

Chan, Nicholas, Mila Getmansky, Shane Haas, and Andrew Lo. 2005. "Systemic Risk and Hedge Funds," manuscript prepared for NBER Conference on Risks of Financial Institutions, dated August 1, 2005. To appear in M. Carey and R. Stulz, eds., *The Risks of Financial Institutions and the Financial Sector*. Chicago: University of Chicago Press. Downloaded at http://web.mit.edu/alo/www/Papers/systemic2.pdf.

Chandler, Lester V., 1958. *Benjamin Strong: Central Banker*. Washington, D.C.: The Brookings Institution.

Chapin, Robert Coit. 1909. "The Standard of Living among Workingmen's Families in New York City." New York City Charities publication committee, Russell Sage Foundation.

Chernow, Ron. 1990. *The House of Morgan: An American Banking Dynasty and the Rise of Modern Finance*. New York: Atlantic Monthly Press.

———. 1998. *Titan: The Life of John D. Rockefeller Sr.* New York: Random House.

Cleveland, Harold van B., and Thomas F. Huertas. 1985. *Citibank, 1812–1970*. Boston: Harvard University Press.

Clews, Henry. 1973. *Fifty Years in Wall Street*. New York: Arno Press (originally published in 1908).

Cohen, Lizabeth. 1990. *Making a New Deal, Industrial Workers in Chicago, 1919–1939*. Cambridge, U.K.: Cambridge University Press.

Cooper, John Milton. 1983. *The Warrior and the Priest: Woodrow Wilson and Theodore Roosevelt*. Cambridge, Mass.: Belknap Press of Harvard University Press.

Corey, Lewis. 1930. *The House of Morgan: A Social Biography of the Masters of Money*. New York: G. Howard Watt.

Cotter, Arundel. 1916. *The Authentic History of the United States Steel Corporation*. New York: Brody Magazine and Book Company.

Cowan, Ruth Schwartz. 1983. *More Work for Mother: The Ironies of Household Technology from the Open Hearth to the Microwave*. New York: Basic Books.

Crocker, Ruth Hutchinson. 1992. *Social Work and Social Order: The Settlement Movement in Two Industrial Cities, 1889–1930*. Urbana and Chicago: University of Illinois Press.

Crowther, Samuel. 1933. *Life of George W. Perkins*. Unpublished biography found among the papers of J. P. Morgan, Jr., Box 107.

Curran, Thomas J. 1975. *Xenophobia and Immigration, 1820–1930*. Boston: Twayne Publishers, a division of G. K. Hall & Co.

Daniels, Roger. 2004. *Guarding the Golden Door: American Immigration Policy and Immigrants since 1882*. New York: Hill and Wang.

Dash, Michael. 1999. *Tulipomania*. New York: Three Rivers Press.

Davis, Allen F. 1967. *Spearheads for Reform: The Social Settlements and the Progressive Movement, 1890–1914*. New York: Oxford University Press.

Davis, Emry. 1913. *Important Issues of the Day*. New York: Author.

Davis, Joseph H. 2004. "A Quantity-Based Annual Index of U.S. Industrial Production, 1790–1915," *Quarterly Journal of Economics* 119: 1177–1215.

De Long, J. Bradford. 1991. "Did Morgan's Men Add Value? An Economist's Perspective on Financial Capitalism." In *Inside the Business Enterprise: Historical Perspectives on the Use of Information*. Chicago: University of Chicago Press.

Deutsch, Sarah. 2000. *Women and the City, Gender, Space, and Power in Boston, 1970–1940*. New York: Oxford University Press.

Diamond, Douglas W., and Philip H. Dybvig. 1983. "Bank Runs, Deposit Insurance, and Liquidity." *Journal of Political Economy* 91(June): 401–419.

Diner, Stephen J. 1998. *A Very Different Age: Americans in the Progressive Era*. New York: Hill & Wang.

Dodd, Donald B. 1993. *Historical Statistics of the States of the United States: Two Centuries of the Census, 1790–1990*. Westport, Conn.: Greenwood Press.

Donaldson, R. Glenn. 1992. "Sources of Panics: Evidence from the Weekly Data." *Journal of Monetary Economics* 31: 277–305.

———. 1993. "Financing Banking Crises: Lessons from the Panic of 1907." *Journal of Monetary Economics* 31: 69–95.

Eisenach, Eldon J. 1994. *The Lost Promise of Progressivism*. Lawrence: University of Kansas.

Ethington, Philip J. 1996. *The Public City: The Political Construction of Urban Life in San Francisco, 1850–1900*. Cambridge, U.K.: Cambridge University Press.

Ewen, Elizabeth. 1985. *Immigrant Women in the Land of Dollars: Life and Culture on the Lower East Side, 1890–1925*. New York: Monthly Review Press.

Fink, Leon (ed.). 2001. *Major Problems in the Gilded Age and the Progressive Era*, 2nd ed. New York: Houghton Mifflin.

Fitzgerald, Keith. 1996. *The Face of the Nation, Immigration, the State, and the National Identity*. Stanford, Calif.: Stanford University Press.

Fitzpatrick, Ellen. 1990. *Endless Crusade: Women Social Scientists and Progressive Reform*. Oxford: Oxford University Press.

Forbes, John Douglas. 1981. *J. P. Morgan, Jr. 1867–1943*. Charlottesville: University of Virginia.

Friedman, Milton, and Anna Schwartz. 1963. *A Monetary History of the United States, 1867–1960*. Princeton: Princeton University Press.

Gage, Beverley. 2006. *The Day Wall Street Exploded*. Oxford: Oxford University Press.

Garber, Peter M. 2001. *Famous First Bubbles: The Fundamentals of Early Manias*. Cambridge, Mass.: MIT Press.

Garraty, John A. 1957. *Right-Hand Man: The Life of George W. Perkins*. New York: Harper & Brothers.

Geisst, Charles R. 1997. *Wall Street: A History*. Oxford: Oxford University Press.

Gordon, John Steele. 1999. *The Great Game: The Emergence of Wall Street as a World Power 1653–2000*. New York: Scribner.

Gordon, Linda. 1994. *Pitied but Not Entitled, Single Mothers and the History of Welfare*. Cambridge, Mass.: Harvard University Press.

Gorton, Gary, and Lixim Huang. 2002. "Banking Panics and the Origin of Central Banking," Cambridge, Mass.: National Bureau of Economic Research, working paper 9137.

Gould, Lewis L. 2001. *America in the Progressive Era 1890–1914*. London: Pearson Education Limited.

Graham, Otis L. 1971. *The Great Campaigns: Reform and War in America, 1900–1928*. Englewood Cliffs, N.J.: Prentice Hall.

Harbaugh, William Henry. 1963. *The Life and Times of Theodore Roosevelt*. New York: Collier Books.

Harris, Larry. 2003. *Trading & Exchanges: Market Microstructure for Practitioners*. Oxford: Oxford University Press.

Hart, Albert B., and Herbert R. Ferleger. 1941. *Theodore Roosevelt Cyclopedia*. New York: Roosevelt Memorial Association.

Harvey, George. 1928. *Henry Clay Frick: The Man*. Washington, D.C.: BeardBooks.

Hays, Samuel P. 1964. "The Politics of Reform in Municipal Government in the Progressive Era," *Pacific Northwest Quarterly* 55(4) (October): 157–169.

Horwitz, Steven. 1990. "Competitive Currencies, Legal Restrictions, and the Origins of the Fed: Some Evidence from the Panic of 1907." *Southern Economic Journal* 56: 639–649.

Hoyt, Edwin P. Jr. 1966. *The House of Morgan*. New York: Dodd, Mead & Company.

———. 1967. *The Guggenheims and the American Dream*. New York: Funk & Wagnalls.

Hunter, William C., George G. Kaufman, and Michael Pomerleano (eds.). 2003. *Asset Price Bubbles: The Implications for Monetary, Regulatory, and International Policies*. Cambridge, Mass.: MIT Press.

Huston, James L. 1987. *The Panic of 1857 and the Coming of the Civil War*. Baton Rouge: Louisiana State University Press.

Issel, William. 1988. "'Citizens Outside the Government': Business and Urban Policy in San Francisco and Los Angeles, 1890–1932." *Pacific Historical Review* 57(2) (May): 117–145.

Kaminski, Graciela, and Sergio Schmukler. 1999. "On Booms and Crashes: Stock Market Cycles and Financial Liberalization." George Washington University and The World Bank, working paper.

Kemmerer, E. W. 1910. *Seasonal Variations in the Relative Demand for Money and Capital in the United States*. National Monetary Commission. 61st Cong. 2d Sess. Senate Doc. 588. Washington D.C.: U.S. Government Printing Office.

Keynes, John Maynard. 1909. "Recent Economic Events in India," *Economic Journal* 19 (March): 51–67.

———. 1936. *The General Theory of Employment, Interest and Money*. London: Macmillan.

Kindleberger, Charles. 1978. *Manias, Panics, and Crashes: A History of Financial Crises*. New York: Basic Books. This book has been revised and published to the most recent edition (5th) dated 2005 that lists Charles P. Kindleberger and Robert Aliber as co-authors.

Kloppenberg, James T. 1986. *Uncertain Victory*. Oxford: Oxford University Press.

Lacey, Michael J., and Mary O. Furner (eds.). 1993. *The State and Social Investigation in Britain and the United States*. Cambridge, U.K.: International Center for Scholars and Cambridge University Press.

Lamont, Thomas W. 1975. *Henry P. Davison: The Record of a Useful Life*. New York: Arno Press, A New York Times Company.

Leiby, James. 1978. *A History of Social Welfare and Social Work in the United States*. New York: Columbia University Press.

Lissak, Rivka Shpak. 1989. *Pluralism & Progressives: Hull House and the New Immigrants, 1890–1919*. Chicago: University of Chicago Press.

Lowenstein, Roger. 2004. *The Origins of the Crash: The Great Bubble and Its Undoing*. New York: Penguin Press.

Mandelbrot, Benoit. 2004. *The (Mis)Behavior of Markets: A Fractal View of Risk, Ruin, and Reward*. New York: Basic Books.

Mason, Alpheus T. 1975. "The Case of the Overworked Laundress." In John A. Garraty (ed.), *Quarrels that Have Shaped the Constitution*. New York: Harper & Row.

Massachusetts State Department of Health. 1917. *The Food of Working Women in Boston*. Boston: Wright & Potter Printing Co.

McCormick, Richard L. 1981. *From Realignment to Reform: Political Change in New York State 1893–1910*. Ithaca, N.Y.: Cornell University Press.

———. 1986. *The Party Period and Public Policy: American Politics from the Age of Jackson to the Progressive Era*. Oxford: Oxford University Press.

McGerr, Michael. 2003. *A Fierce Discontent: The Rise and Fall of the Progressive Movement in America*. Oxford: Oxford University Press.

McNelis, Sarah. 1968. *Copper King at War: The Biography of F. Augustus Heinze*. Missoula, Mont.: University of Montana Press.

Mills, A. L. 1908. "The Northwest in the Recent Financial Crisis," *Annals of the American Academy of Political and Social Science* 1(31): 113–119.

Mishkin, Frederic S. 1990. "Asymmetric Information and Financial Crises: A Historical Perspective," Cambridge, MA: National Bureau of Economic Research, working paper 3400; and in R. Glenn Hubbard (ed.). 1991. *Financial Markets and Financial Crises*. Chicago: University of Chicago Press.

———. 1991. "Anatomy of a Financial Crisis." Cambridge, MA: National Bureau of Economic Research, working paper 3934, 4; published under. "Anatomy of a Financial Crisis." *Journal of Evolutionary Economics* 2(2): 115–130.

Mishkin, Frederic S., and Eugene N. White. 2003. "U.S. Stock Market Crashes and Their Aftermath: Implications for Monetary Policy," in William C. Hunter, George G. Kaufman, and Michael Pomerleano (eds.), *Asset Price Bubbles*. Cambridge, Mass.: MIT Press.

Moen, Jon, and Ellis W. Tallman. 1992. "The Bank Panic of 1907: The Role of Trust Companies." *Journal of Economic History* 52: 611–630.

More, Louise Bolard. 1907. *Wage Earners' Budgets: A Study of Standards and Costs of Living in New York City*. New York: H. Holt.

Morison, Elting E. (ed.). 1952. *The Letters of Theodore Roosevelt*, vols. 1–8. Cambridge, Mass.: Harvard University Press.

Morris, Edmund. 2001. *Theodore Rex*. New York: Random House.

Muncy, Robyn. 1991. *Creating a Female Dominion in American Reform, 1890–1935*. Oxford: Oxford University Press.

Noyes, Alexander D. 1909a. "A Year after the Panic of 1907." *Quarterly Journal of Economics* 23: 185–212.

———. 1909b. *Forty Years of American Finance*. New York: G. P. Putnam's Sons, The Knickerbocker Press.

Odell, Kerry A., and Marc D. Weidenmier. 2002. "Real Stock, Monetary Aftershock: The San Francisco Earthquake and the Panic of 1907," Cambridge, Mass.: National Bureau of Economic Research, working paper 9176.

O'Grada, Cormac, and Eugene N. White. 2002. "Who Panics during Panics? Evidence from a Nineteenth Century Savings Bank." Cambridge, Mass.: National Bureau of Economic Research, working paper 8856.

O'Toole, Patricia. 2005. *When Trumpets Call: Theodore Roosevelt After the White House*. New York: Simon & Schuster.

Parthemos, James. 1988. "The Federal Reserve Act of 1913 in the Stream of U.S. Monetary History." *Economic Quarterly* 74 (July/August): 19–28.

Payne, Elizabeth Anne. 1988. *Reform, Labor, and Feminism: Margaret Dreier Robins and the Women's Trade Union League*. Urbana, Ill.: University of Illinois Press.

Perkins, Dexter. 1956. *Charles Evans Hughes and American Democratic Statesmanship*. Boston: Little, Brown and Company.

Pringle, Henry F. 1931. *Theodore Roosevelt: A Biography*. New York: Harcourt, Brace and Company.

———. 1939. *The Life and Times of William Howard Taft: A Biography*. New York: Farrar & Rinehart, Inc.

Raftery, Judith. 1994. "Los Angeles Clubwomen and Progressive Reform," in William Deverell and Tom Sitton (eds.), *California Progressivism Revisited*. Berkeley and Los Angeles: University of California Press.

Ramirez, Carlos. 1995. "Did J. P. Morgan's Men Add Value? Corporate Investment, Cash Flow, and Financial Structure at the Turn of the Century." *Journal of Finance* 50: 661–678.

Ranciere, Romain, Aaron Tornell, and Frank Westermann. 2005. "Systemic Crises and Growth." CESifo working paper 1451. Downloaded from http://SSRN.com/abstract=708994.

Ripley, William Z. 1916. *Trusts, Pools, and Corporations*. Boston: Ginn and Company.

Roberts, Priscilla. 2000. "Benjamin Strong, the Federal Reserve, and the Limits to Interwar American Nationalism." *Economic Quarterly* (March 22).

Rockoff, Hugh 2000. "Banking and Finance, 1789–1914." Chapter 14, in Stanley L. Engerman and Robert E. Gallman (eds.), *The Cambridge Economic History of the United States*, vol. II, "The Long Nineteenth Century." Cambridge, U.K.: Cambridge University Press.

Rodgers, Daniel T. 1992. "Republicanism: The Career of a Concept," *Journal of American History* 79(1) (June): 11–38.

Roll, Richard. 1986. "The Hubris Hypothesis of Corporate Takeovers." *Journal of Business* 59(2): 197–216.

Roosevelt, Theodore. 1913. *An Autobiography*. New York: Charles Scribner and Sons.

Sandel, Michael. 1996. *Democracy's Discontent: America in Search of a Public Philosophy*. Cambridge, Mass.: Belknap Press of Harvard University Press.

Satterlee, Herbert L. 1939. *J. Pierpont Morgan: An Intimate Portrait*. New York: MacMillan.

Schumpeter, Joseph A. 1976. *Capitalism, Socialism and Democracy*. New York: Harper & Row (originally published in 1942).

———. 2004. *The Theory of Economic Development*. New Brunswick, N.J.: Transaction Publishers (originally published in 1934).

Scott, Anne Firor. 1991. *Natural Allies: Women's Associations in American History*. Urbana: University of Illinois Press.

Silber, William L. 2006. *When Washington Shut Down Wall Street: The Great Financial Crisis of 1914 and the Origins of America's Monetary Supremacy*. Princeton, NJ: Princeton University Press.

Sklar, Katheryn. 1993. "The Historical Foundations of Women's Power in the Creation of the American Welfare State, 1830–1930," in Seth Koven and Sonya Michel (eds.), *Mothers of a New World: Maternalist Politics and the Origins of Welfare States*. New York: Routledge.

Skocpol, Theda. 1992. *Protecting Soldiers and Mothers: The Political Origins of Social Policy in the United States*. Cambridge, Mass.: Belknap Press of Harvard University Press.

Smith, Dennis. 2005. *San Francisco Is Burning: The Untold Story of the 1906 Earthquake and Fires*. New York: Viking Press.

Sobel, Robert. 1988. Panic on Wall Street: A Classic History of America's Financial Disasters—with a New Explanation of the Crash of 1987. New York: E. P. Dutton, Truman Talley Books (originally published in 1968).

Sprague, O. M. W. 1908. "The American Crisis of 1907," *Economic Journal* (September): 353–372.

———. 1910. *A History of Crises under the National Banking System*. National Monetary Commission. Washington. D.C.: U.S. Government Printing Office.

Sornette, Didier. 2003. *Why Stock Markets Crash: Critical Events in Complex Financial Systems*. Princeton, N.J.: Princeton University Press.

Stiglitz, Joseph. 2003. *The Roaring Nineties*. New York: Norton.

Strouse, Jean. 1999. *Morgan: American Financier*. New York: Random House.

Swiss Re. 2006. "A Shake in Insurance History: The 1906 San Francisco Earthquake" (January).

Taft, William H. 1908. *Present Day Problems: A Collection of Addresses Delivered on Various Occasions*. New York: Dodd, Mead & Company.

Taleb, Nassim Nicholas. 2004. *Fooled by Randomness: The Hidden Role of Chance in Life and in the Markets*. New York: Random House.

Tallman, Ellis W., and Jon R. Moen. 1990. "Lessons from the Panic of 1907." *Economic Review* 75(May/June): 2–13.

———. 1995. "Private Sector Responses to the Panic of 1907: A Comparison of New York and Chicago." *Economic Review* 80(March): 1–9.

Tarbell, Ida. 1933. *The Life of Elbert H. Gary: A Story of Steel.* New York: D. Appleton-Century Company, Inc.

Thomas, Gordon, and Max Morgan Witts. 1971. *The San Francisco Earthquake.* New York: Stein and Day.

Tichenor, Daniel J. 2002. *Dividing Lines: The Politics of Immigration Control in America.* Princeton, N.J.: Princeton University Press.

Torpey, John. 2003. "Passports and the Development of Immigration Controls in the North Atlantic World During the Long Nineteenth Century." Chapter 5, in Andreas Fahrmeir, Olivier Faron, and Patrick Weil (eds.), *Migration Control in the North Atlantic World: The Evolution of State Practices in Europe and the United States from the French Revolution to the Inter-War Period.* New York, Oxford: Berghahn Books.

Unger, Nancy C., 2000. *Fighting Bob LaFollette: The Righteous Reformer.* Chapel Hill: University of North Carolina.

U.S. Bureau of the Census. 1949. *Historical Statistics of the United States, 1789–1945.* Washington, D.C.: U.S. Department of Commerce.

U.S. House of Representatives, Subcommittee of the Committee on Banking and Currency. 1913. *Money Trust Investigation: Investigation of Financial and Monetary Conditions in the United States under House Resolutions No. 429 and 504.* Washington, D.C.: U.S. Government Printing Office.

U.S. Department of the Treasury. 1908. *Response of the Secretary of the Treasury to Senate Resolution No. 33 of December 12, 1907, Calling for Certain Information in Regard to Treasury Operations, United States Depositaries, the Condition of National Banks, etc.* Washington, D.C.: U.S. Government Printing Office, 60th Congress, 1st Session, Senate, Doc. 208.

Van Kleeck, Mary. 1906–07. "Working Hours of Women in Factories." *Charities and Commons* 17: 13–21.

———. 1913 *Artificial Flower Makers.* New York: Survey Associates, Inc., Russell Sage Foundation.

Varaiya, Nikhil P., and Kenneth R. Ferris. 1987. "Overpaying in Corporate Takeovers," *Financial Analysts Journal* 43 (May/June) 3: 64–70.

Warsh, David. 2006. *Knowledge and the Wealth of Nations: A Story of Economic Discovery.* New York: Norton.

Wicker, Elmus. 2000. *Banking Panics of the Gilded Age.* New York: Cambridge University Press.

Wiebe, Robert H. 1959. "The House for Morgan and the Executive, 1905–1913." *American Historical Review* 65: 49–60.

———. 1967. *The Search for Order 1877–1920*. New York: Hill & Wang.

———. 1995. *Self Rule: A Cultural History of American Democracy*. Chicago: University of Chicago Press.

Wister, Owen. 1930. *Roosevelt: The Story of a Friendship 1880–1919*. New York: MacMillan.

Wyman, Mark. 1993. *Round Trip to America: The Immigrants Return to Europe, 1880–1930*. Ithaca, N.Y.: Cornell University Press.

Zeidel, Robert F. 2004. *Immigrants, Progressives, and Exclusion Politics: The Dillingham Commission, 1900–1927*. DeKalb: Northern Illinois University Press.

Zuckoff, Mitchell. 2005. *Ponzi's Scheme: The True Story of a Financial Legend*. New York: Random House.

Notes

Prologue

1. Contemporary accounts of the death of Charles Barney, which included numerous details of the shooting and the subsequent events of the day, appeared in a number of daily newspapers, including the *New York Times*, the *Washington Post*, the *Chicago Daily Tribune*, and the *Wall Street Journal*. The level of detail appears to have been reported for its relevance to the banking panic then under way, but also (of course) for its titillating value. Most of this particular reportage appeared in the aforementioned publications on November 15, 16, and 17, 1907.

2. *New York Times*, November 15, 1907, p. 1.

3. *Chicago Daily Tribune*, November 16, 1907, p. 2.

4. *Washington Post*, November 17, 1907, p. 3.

5. Higgins later recanted this statement, claming he was misquoted. *Washington Post*, November 16, 1907, p. 1.

6. *New York Times*, November 15, 1907, p. 1.

7. Strouse (1999), p. 575.

8. *Washington Post*, October 22, 1907, p. 3.

9. See note 6.

10. Ibid.

11. Ibid.

12. Ibid.

13. *Washington Post*, November 16, 1907, p. 1.

Introduction

1. Quotation popularly attributed to Mark Twain without specific citation.

2. Calomiris and Gorton (2000), p. 99, lists the panics from 1814 to 1914 and ranks them in order of severity and type: a) suspensions (1873, 1893, 1907, 1914), b) coordination to forestall suspensions (1884, 1890), and a perceived need for coordination (1896).

3. Details on the history of panics and crashes are drawn from Mishkin (1991) and Carlson (undated).

4. The concept of a "perfect storm" or convergence of large forces was popularized in Sebastian Junger's book by the same name (New York: W. W. Norton, 1997).

Chapter 1: Wall Street Oligarchs

1. Allen (1949).

2. The analysis of growth rates draws on indices of U.S. industrial production drawn from "U.S. Industrial Production Index" of the National Bureau of Economic Research, downloaded from www.nber.org/data/industrial-production-index/.

3. Lamoreaux, N. R. 1985. *The Great Merger Movement in American Business, 1895–1904.* Cambridge: Cambridge University Press, p. 2.

4. DeLong (1991), p. 3.

5. Carosso, *Investment Banking* (1970), p. 99.

6. Quoted in Harbaugh (1963), pp. 157–158.

7. Ibid., p. 159.

8. Allen (1952), p. 79.

9. Quoted in Carosso (1987), p. 452, citing Sheridan A. Logan, *George Fisher Baker and His Bank, 1840–1955: A Double Biography* (St. Joseph, Mo.: Author, 1981), p. 163.

10. Burr (1927).

11. De Long (1991), p. 14.

12. Carosso (1987), p. 288.

13. Information on J. P. Morgan's support for Thomas Edison is drawn from Carosso (1987), p. 270–271.

14. See note 8.

Chapter 2: A Shock to the System

1. U.S. Bureau of the Census. 1949. *Historical Statistics of the United States, 1789–1945:* a supplement to *Statistical Abstract of the United States.* Washington, D.C.: U.S. Department of Commerce, p. 224.

2. Our discussion of the economic impact of the San Francisco earthquake draws on the research by Odell and Weidenmier (2002).

3. The company later reorganized, offering its claimants a payment of half cash and half stock in the new company.

4. The facts about insurance companies are drawn from Odell and Wiedenmier (see note 2), and from Thomas, Gordon, and Max Morgan Witts. 1971. *The San Francisco Earthquake.* New York: Stein and Day.

5. Private Cables, Morgan Grenfell Archives, Guildhall Library, London. Used with permission of Deutsche Bank.

6. W. S. Burns to G. W. Perkins, October 20, 1906: "Cause of advance in Bank rate is to prevent withdrawals of gold, £2,000,000 out today, said for Egypt, and fear further requirements US of America." Private Cables, Morgan Grenfell Archives, Guildhall Library, London. Used with permission of Deutsche Bank.

7. Bank of England, historical statistics web site, http://213.225.136.206/mfsd/iadb/Repo.asp?Travel=NIxIRx, accessed October 29, 2006.

8. The discussion of Bank of England's actions in the fall of 1906 draws from Tallman and Moen (1995), Odell and Weidenmier (2002), and the *Commercial and Financial Chronicle.*

9. Series of telegrams from Private Cables (see note 5).

10. Letter from J. P. Morgan Jr. Letterpress book. December 18, 1906. Quotation courtesy of the Morgan Library and Museum.

11. Letter from J. P. Morgan Jr. Letterpress book. December 24, 1906. Quotation courtesy of the Morgan Library and Museum.

12. Letter from J. P. Morgan Jr. Letterpress book. January 22, 1906. Quotation courtesy of the Morgan Library and Museum.

13. Clews (1973), p. 783.

14. Noyes (1909a).

Chapter 3: The "Silent" Crash

1. Letter from J. P. Morgan Jr. to Edward Grenfell, March 14, 1907, Morgan Library and Museum, Box 5, letterpress book 3, January 24, 1907, to January 15, 1908. Used with permission.

2. E. C. Grenfell to J. P. Morgan Jr., March 6, 1907. Used with permission of Deutsche Bank.

3. J. P. Morgan Jr. to E. C. Grenfell, March 6, 1907. Used with permission of Deutsche Bank.

4. Three telegrams between E. C. Grenfell and J. P. Morgan Jr., March 13, 1907. Used with permission of Deutsche Bank.

5. *Commercial and Financial Chronicle*, March 9, 1907, p. 534.

6. J. P. Morgan Jr., March 14, 1907. Used with permission of Morgan Library and Museum.

7. J. S. Morgan & Company to J. P. Morgan Jr., March 22, 1907. Used with permission of Deutsche Bank.

8. J. P. Morgan Jr. to J. S. Morgan & Company, March 23, 1907. Used with permission of Deutsche Bank.

9. *Commercial and Financial Chronicle*, March 23, 1907, p. 654.

10. J. P. Morgan Jr. to J. S. Morgan & Company, March 29, 1907. Used with permission of Morgan Library and Museum.

11. *Commercial and Financial Chronicle*, March 30, 1907, p. 716.

12. *Commercial and Financial Chronicle*, April 13, 1907, p. 832.

13. *Commercial and Financial Chronicle*, April 20, 1907, p. 851.

14. *Commercial and Financial Chronicle*, May 4, 1907, p. 1020.

15. Private Cables, Morgan Grenfell Archives, Guildhall Library, London. Used with permission of Deutsche Bank.

16. Few of the most important works on this period are: McGerr (2003); Diner (1998); Wiebe (1967); Rodgers, Daniel. 1982. "In Search of Progressivism," *Reviews in American History*, No. 10, McCormick (1986), particularly Chapter 7, "Progressivism: A Contemporary Reassessment," and chapter 8, "Prelude to Progressivism: The Transformation of New York State Politics, 1890–1910"; and Eisenach (1994).

17. Essay by E. E. Morison and J. M. Blum in Morison (1952), Vol. 5, p. xvi.

18. Cooper (1983), p. 83.

19. McGerr (2003), pp. 156–158.

20. Ibid.

21. *Commercial and Financial Chronicle*, June 1, 1907, p. 1270.

22. Ibid., p. 1276.

23. *Commercial and Financial Chronicle*, March 9, 1907, p. 534.

Chapter 4: Credit Anorexia

1. Private cables, Morgan Grenfell Archives, Guildhall Library, London. Used with permission of Deutsche Bank.

2. *Commercial and Financial Chronicle*, May 24, 1907, p. 16.

3. J. P. Morgan Jr. to J. S. Morgan & Company, June 21, 1907. Used with permission of Morgan Library and Museum.

4. Sprague (1910), p. 241.

5. Odell and Weidenmier (2002), pp. 12, 14.

6. Tallman and Moen (1990), p. 4.

7. *Commercial and Financial Chronicle*, June 29, 1907, p. 1514.

8. J. P. Morgan Jr. to J. S. Morgan & Company, July 19, 1907. Used with permission of Morgan Library and Museum.

9. *Commercial and Financial Chronicle*, July 27, 1907, p. 184.

10. *Commercial and Financial Chronicle*, August 3, 1907, p. 248.

11. *Commercial and Financial Chronicle*, June 1, 1907, p. 1351.

12. Leroy-Beaulieu quoted in Noyes (1909), p. 199.

13. Clews (1973, p. 787) makes the point of the small book value of equity relative to the large fine imposed.

14. *Commercial and Financial Chronicle*, August 24, 1907, p. 28.

15. Ibid., p. 440.

16. *Commercial and Financial Chronicle*, September 7, 1907, p. 550.

17. J. S. Morgan & Company to Jack Morgan, August 27, 1907. Used with permission of Deutsche Bank.

18. *Commercial and Financial Chronicle*, September 21, 1907, p. 681.

19. Odell and Weidenmier (2002), p. 14.

Chapter 5: Copper King

1. *Current Literature*, January 1908.

2. McNelis (1968), p. 27.

3. *McClure's Magazine*, May 1907.

4. Ibid.

5. McNelis (1968), p. 21.

6. See note 1.

7. *Cosmopolitan*, January 1904.

8. Ibid.

9. See note 1.

10. Ibid.

11. McNelis (1968), p. 209.

12. *Current Literature*, February 1910.

13. *New York Times*, October 20, 1907, p. 1.

14. Ibid.; see note 12.

15. *Wall Street Journal*, November 30, 1907, p. 6.

16. Tallman and Moen (1990), p. 5; and McNelis (1968), p. 153.

17. Ibid.

18. McNelis (1968), p. 117.

19. Ibid., p. 156.

20. *Wall Street Journal*, October 19, 1907, p. 1; *Wall Street Journal*, January 19, 1907; *New York Times*, April 13, 1907.

21. McNelis (1968), pp. 156–157.

Chapter 6: The Corner and the Squeeze

1. Many of the details about the Heinzes' attempted corner of United Copper stock and the resultant fallout were gathered from contemporary accounts in the following publications: *The Arena*, the *Chicago Daily Tribune*, the *Commercial and Financial Chronicle*, *Cosmopolitan*, *Current Literature*, *Leslie's Monthly Magazine*, *McClure's Magazine*, the *New York Times*, the *Wall Street Journal*, and the *Washington Post*. Other contemporary references are cited below, in addition to a number of books that provide brief glimpses of and various perspectives on the events of October 1907, as well as the personal histories of F. Augustus Heinze and Charles W. Morse. The biography of F. Augustus Heinze by Sarah McNelis, who personally interviewed Otto Heinze, was especially helpful.

2. McNelis, (1968), p. 157; and *New York Times*, May 3, 1910, p. 20.

3. Tallman and Moen, (1990), pp. 5–6.

4. McNelis (1968), p. 157.

5. Ibid.

6. *New York Times*, May 3, 1910, p. 20.

7. *Wall Street Journal*, October 17, 1907, p. 3.

8. Ibid.

9. *Chicago Daily Tribune*, October 15, 1907, p. 4; and *Wall Street Journal*, October 15, 1907, p. 8.

10. Ibid.

11. *New York Times*, October 15, 1907, p. 11; and *Wall Street Journal*, October 15, 1907, p. 8.

12. McNelis (1968), p. 158.

13. Ibid.

14. *Chicago Daily Tribune*, October 17, 1907, p. 2.

15. *New York Times*, October 17, 1907, p. 1.

16. See note 14.

17. See note 15.

18. *Wall Street Journal*, October 17, 1907, p. 3; and *New York Times*, October 16, 1907, p. 13.

19. *Wall Street Journal*, October 16, 1907, p. 4.

20. *Wall Street Journal*, October 17, 1907, p. 3.

21. Ibid., pp. 3, 4.

22. See note 20.

23. Ibid.

24. See note 15.

Chapter 7: Falling Dominoes

1. *New York Times*, October 17, 1907, p. 1.

2. *Washington Post*, October 18, 1907, p. 4.

3. See note 1.

4. *Washington Post*, October 17, 1907, p. 3.

5. *Chicago Daily Tribune*, October 17, 1907, p. 2.

6. See note 4.

7. See note 1.

8. See note 5.

9. *Wall Street Journal*, October 18, 1907, p. 7.

10. See note 1.

11. Ibid.

12. See note 2.

13. *Washington Post*, October 18, 1907, p. 11.

14. *Wall Street Journal*, October 19, 1907, p. 2.

15. See note 2.

16. See note 14.

17. See note 13.

18. See note 2.

19. *New York Times*, October 18, 1907, p. 1.

20. *New York Times*, October 18, 1907, p. 4; see note 13.

21. See note 13.
22. See note 19.
23. See note 1.
24. Ibid.
25. See note 19.
26. See note 1.
27. See note 19.

Chapter 8: Clearing House

1. Rockoff (2000), p. 652.
2. Ibid., pp. 676–677. This is based on the statistic that the United States had 1,504 trusts in 1909.
3. U.S. Bureau of the Census (1949), chart Series N 135–140, Bank Suspensions—Number of Suspensions: 1864–1945, p. 273. Between 1892 and 1897, 964 banks had suspensions. In 1907, there were 90 bank suspensions: 58 state banks, 12 national banks, and 20 private banks (most of these occurred in the fall, after the failure of the Knickerbocker Trust Company in October). In 1908, 153 bank suspensions were recorded: 83 state banks, 51 private banks, and 19 national banks.
4. *Commercial and Financial Chronicle*, January 4, 1907, p. 6.
5. *New York Times*, October 18, 1907, p. 1.
6. *Wall Street Journal*, October 19, 1907, p. 1.
7. See note 5.
8. Ibid.
9. *New York Times*, October 19, 1907, p. 1.
10. *Chicago Daily Tribune*, October 19, 1907, p. 4.
11. Ibid.
12. *New York Times*, October 20, 1907, p. 1.
13. Ibid.
14. Ibid.
15. See note 10.
16. See note 12.

17. Ibid.

18. *Washington Post*, October 21, 1907, p. 1.

19. *Wall Street Journal*, October 22, 1907, p. 1; and *Washington Post*, October 22, 1907, p. 3.

20. *Washington Post*, October 22, 1907, p. 3s.

21. See note 9.

22. *New York Times*, October 22, 1907, p. 2.

23. Ibid.

24. *Wall Street Journal*, October 22, 1907, p. 1.

Chapter 9: Knickerbocker

1. Satterlee (1939), p. 455. Reprinted with the permission of Scribner, an imprint of Simon & Schuster Adult Publishing Group, from *J. Pierpont Morgan: An Intimate Portrait* by Herbert L. Satterlee. Copyright © 1939 by Herbert L. Satterlee; copyright renewed, © 1967 by Mabel Satterlee Ingalls. All rights reserved.

2. The descriptions of the Knickerbocker Trust Company and many of the details about the run on the Knickerbocker and its subsequent suspension appeared originally in various contemporary accounts in the following periodicals: the *Bankers' Magazine*, the *Chicago Daily Tribune*, the *Commercial and Financial Chronicle*, the *Independent*, the *New York Times*, the *Wall Street Journal*, and the *Washington Post*. The intervention of J. P. Morgan during this early phase of the crisis of 1907 has been ably told in several Morgan biographies, especially those by Chernow, Satterlee, and Strouse. The best details and primary source material of the actions of the bankers were the personal recollections of George W. Perkins and Benjamin Strong, which were accessed by Robert F. Bruner at the Morgan Library and Museum and the archives of the Federal Reserve Bank of New York, respectively.

3. This location would later become the site for the Empire State Building.

4. *Wall Street Journal*, November 2, 1903, p. 4.

5. Ibid.; and *Bankers' Magazine*, November 1903, p. 719.

6. *Bankers' Magazine*, August 1907, p. 207.

7. Carosso (1970), pp. 98–99.

8. Moen and Tallman (1992), pp. 612–614.

9. Notably, many trust companies still abstained from these connections since the clearinghouse association usually imposed a cash reserve requirement on any trust companies that cleared through a member bank. See Moen and Tallman (1992), pp. 620–621.

10. Satterlee (1939), pp. 464–465. Reprinted with the permission of Scribner, an imprint of Simon & Schuster Adult Publishing Group, from *J. Pierpont Morgan: An Intimate Portrait* by Herbert L. Satterlee. Copyright © 1939 by Herbert L. Satterlee; copyright renewed, © 1967 by Mabel Satterlee Ingalls. All rights reserved.

11. Ibid., p. 455; and *Bankers' Magazine*, November 1903, p. 719.

12. See note 1.

13. Ibid. Reprinted with the permission of Scribner, an imprint of Simon & Schuster Adult Publishing Group, from *J. Pierpont Morgan: An Intimate Portrait* by Herbert L. Satterlee. Copyright © 1939 by Herbert L. Satterlee; copyright renewed, © 1967 by Mabel Satterlee Ingalls. All rights reserved.

14. *New York Times*, November 15, 1907, p. 1.

15. See note 1. Reprinted with the permission of Scribner, an imprint of Simon & Schuster Adult Publishing Group, from *J. Pierpont Morgan: An Intimate Portrait* by Herbert L. Satterlee. Copyright © 1939 by Herbert L. Satterlee; copyright renewed, © 1967 by Mabel Satterlee Ingalls. All rights reserved.

16. Sprague (1908), p. 359.

17. Calomiris and Gorton (1991), p. 156.

18. *New York Times*, October 22, 1907, p. 1.

19. Ibid.

Chapter 10: A Vote of No Confidence

1. Satterlee (1939), pp. 464–465.

2. *New York Times*, October 22, 1907, p. 1.

3. *Wall Street Journal*, October 23, 1907, p. 1.

4. See note 2.

5. Ibid.

6. *Chicago Daily Tribune*, October 22, 1907, p. 1.

7. Ibid.

8. Ibid.

9. Ibid.

10. Ibid.

11. *New York Times*, October 6, 1907, p. 12.

12. See note 6.

13. Strouse (1999), p. 575 (footnote).

14. Satterlee (1939), pp. 455–458.

15. See note 1.

16. See note 2.

17. Satterlee (1939), p. 456.

18. See note 6.

19. *Washington Post*, October 25, 1907, p. 2.

20. *New York Times*, October 23, 1907, p. 2.

21. Account by Perkins in Crowther (1933), unpublished manuscript.

22. Ibid.

23. Strouse (1999), p. 577.

Chapter 11: A Classic Run

1. Diary of Marion Satterlee, pp. 13, 14.

2. *Washington Post*, October 23, 1907, p. 2.

3. Ibid.

4. *New York Times*, October 23, 1907, p. 2.

5. Ibid.

6. Ibid.

7. Ibid.

8. Ibid.

9. Ibid.

10. Ibid.

11. Ibid.

12. *Wall Street Journal*, October 23, 1907, p. 1.

13. See note 2; see note 4.

14. See note 4.

15. Ibid.

16. Ibid.

17. Ibid.

18. Ibid.

19. Satterlee (1939), p. 466. Reprinted with the permission of Scribner, an imprint of Simon & Schuster Adult Publishing Group, from *J. Pierpont Morgan: An Intimate Portrait* by Herbert L. Satterlee. Copyright © 1939 by Herbert L. Satterlee; copyright renewed, © 1967 by Mabel Satterlee Ingalls. All rights reserved.

20. See note 4.

21. Ibid.

22. See note 2.

23. See note 4.

24. Ibid.

Chapter 12: Such Assistance as May Be Necessary

1. *Washington Post*, October 23, 1907, p. 2.

2. *New York Times*, October 23, 1907, p. 2; ibid.

3. Satterlee (1939), p. 465.

4. Strong (1924), 22-page letter to Thomas W. Lamont, Benjamin Strong Papers, Federal Reserve Bank of New York, New York.

5. *Washington Post*, October 23, 1907, p. 1.

6. See note 1.

7. Ibid.

8. Ibid.

9. See note 5.

10. *New York Times*, October 23, 1907, p. 1.

11. *Wall Street Journal*, October 23, 1907, p. 1.

12. Ibid.

13. Ibid.; see note 5.

14. Satterlee (1939), p. 466.

15. Ibid., p. 456.

16. Strong (1924), 22-page letter to Thomas W. Lamont, Benjamin Strong Papers, Federal Reserve Bank of New York, New York; and *Bankers' Magazine*, May 1905, p. 624.

17. *Wall Street Journal*, June 22, 1905, p. 8.

18. Strouse (1999), p. 577.

19. See note 5.

20. Account by Perkins in Crowther (1933), unpublished manuscript.

21. See note 10.

22. Strong (1924), 22-page letter to Thomas W. Lamont, Benjamin Strong Papers, Federal Reserve Bank of New York, New York.

23. Satterlee (1939), p. 467.

24. Ibid., p. 468.

25. Strong (1924), 22-page letter to Thomas W. Lamont, Benjamin Strong Papers, Federal Reserve Bank of New York, New York.

26. Ibid.

27. Ibid.

Chapter 13: Trust Company of America

1. Strong (1924), 22-page letter to Thomas W. Lamont, Benjamin Strong Papers, Federal Reserve Bank of New York, New York.

2. Account by Perkins in Crowther (1933), unpublished manuscript.

3. *New York Times*, October 24, 1907, p. 10.

4. Satterlee (1939), p. 470.

5. See note 2.

6. See note 1.

7. Ibid.

8. Ibid.

Chapter 14: Crisis on the Exchange

1. Recounted in Satterlee (1939), p. 477. Reprinted with the permission of Scribner, an imprint of Simon & Schuster Adult Publishing Group, from *J. Pierpont Morgan: An Intimate Portrait* by Herbert L. Satterlee. Copyright © 1939 by Herbert L. Satterlee; copyright renewed, © 1967 by Mabel Satterlee Ingalls. All rights reserved.

2. Ibid., p. 473. Reprinted with the permission of Scribner, an imprint of Simon & Schuster Adult Publishing Group, from *J. Pierpont Morgan: An Intimate Portrait* by Herbert L. Satterlee. Copyright © 1939 by Herbert L. Satterlee; copyright renewed, © 1967 by Mabel Satterlee Ingalls. All rights reserved.

3. Ibid. Reprinted with the permission of Scribner, an imprint of Simon & Schuster Adult Publishing Group, from *J. Pierpont Morgan: An Intimate Portrait* by Herbert L. Satterlee. Copyright © 1939 by Herbert L. Satterlee; copyright renewed, © 1967 by Mabel Satterlee Ingalls. All rights reserved.

4. Quoted in the *New York Times*, October 25, 1907, p. 7.

5. Account by Perkins in Crowther (1933), unpublished manuscript.

6. Satterlee (1939), p. 474. Reprinted with the permission of Scribner, an imprint of Simon & Schuster Adult Publishing Group, from *J. Pierpont Morgan: An Intimate Portrait* by Herbert L. Satterlee. Copyright © 1939 by Herbert L. Satterlee; copyright renewed, © 1967 by Mabel Satterlee Ingalls. All rights reserved.

7. See note 5.

8. Ibid.

9. Ibid.

10. Satterlee (1939), p. 476. Reprinted with the permission of Scribner, an imprint of Simon & Schuster Adult Publishing Group, from *J. Pierpont Morgan: An Intimate Portrait* by Herbert L. Satterlee. Copyright © 1939 by Herbert L. Satterlee; copyright renewed, © 1967 by Mabel Satterlee Ingalls. All rights reserved.

11. See note 5.

12. Ibid.

13. Ibid.

14. Satterlee (1939), p. 479. Reprinted with the permission of Scribner, an imprint of Simon & Schuster Adult Publishing Group, from *J. Pierpont Morgan: An Intimate Portrait* by Herbert L. Satterlee. Copyright © 1939 by Herbert L. Satterlee; copyright renewed, © 1967 by Mabel Satterlee Ingalls. All rights reserved.

15. See note 5.

Chapter 15: A City in Trouble

1. *New York Times*, October 26, 1907, p. 1.
2. *New York Times*, October 27, 1907, p. 5.
3. *New York Times*, October 26, 1907, p. 1.
4. *New York Times*, October 29, 1907, p. 2.
5. *New York Times*, October 27, 1907, p. 2.
6. *New York Times*, October 28, 1907, p. 1.
7. *New York Times*, October 24, 1907, p. 6.
8. *New York Times*, October 23, 1907, p. 5.
9. Morison (1952), p. 823.
10. *New York Times*, October 29, 1907, p. 1.
11. Account by Perkins in Crowther (1933), unpublished manuscript.
12. Ibid.
13. Ibid.
14. Ibid.
15. Ibid.
16. U.S. Department of the Treasury (1908), pp. 15 and 16.

Chapter 16: A Delirium of Excitement

1. *New York Times*, October 30, 1907, p. 3.
2. Wicker (2000), p. 96, quoting U.S. House of Representatives, Stanley Hearings, 1911, vol. 2, p. 936.
3. *New York Times*, October 30, 1907, p. 3.
4. *New York Times*, November 3, 1907, p. 3.

5. Cotter (1916), p. 71.
6. Tarbell (1933), p. 197.
7. Among the owners from whom TC&I was purchased was Oakleigh Thorne, the president of the struggling Trust Company of America; by 1907, in fact, the Trust Company held about $640,000 worth of TC&I stock.

Chapter 17: Modern Medici

1. Strong (1924), 22-page letter to Thomas W. Lamont, Benjamin Strong Papers, Federal Reserve Bank of New York, New York.
2. Account by Perkins in Crowther (1933), unpublished manuscript.
3. Ibid.
4. See note 1.
5. Satterlee (1939), p. 485.
6. See note 1.
7. Ibid.
8. Ibid.
9. Lamont (1975), p. 81.
10. See note 1.
11. Ibid.
12. Ibid.
13. Ibid.
14. See note 5.
15. See note 9.
16. Lamont (1975), p. 82.
17. Ibid.
18. Ibid.

Chapter 18: Instant and Far-Reaching Relief

1. Tarbell (1933), pp. 199–200.
2. Satterlee (1939), p. 486.

3. Account by Perkins in Crowther (1933), unpublished manuscript.

4. See note 2.

5. See note 1.

6. Satterlee (1939), p. 487. Reprinted with the permission of Scribner, an imprint of Simon & Schuster Adult Publishing Group, from *J. Pierpont Morgan: An Intimate Portrait* by Herbert L. Satterlee. Copyright © 1939 by Herbert L. Satterlee; copyright renewed, © 1967 by Mabel Satterlee Ingalls. All rights reserved.

7. Ibid. Reprinted with the permission of Scribner, an imprint of Simon & Schuster Adult Publishing Group, from *J. Pierpont Morgan: An Intimate Portrait* by Herbert L. Satterlee. Copyright © 1939 by Herbert L. Satterlee; copyright renewed, © 1967 by Mabel Satterlee Ingalls. All rights reserved.

8. See note 3.

9. This entire exchange between Morgan and Gary was recounted in Tarbell (1933), p. 200.

10. Pringle (1931), pp. 441–442.

11. Tarbell (1933), p. 201.

12. Pringle (1931), p. 443, quoting Stanley Committee, p. 1371.

13. Pringle (1931), p. 442.

14. Morison (1952), no. 4484, p. 831.

15. *Commercial and Financial Chronicle*, November 9, 1907, p. 1176.

Chapter 19: Turning the Corner

1. The estimate of clearing house loan certificates issued is from Cannon (1910). The amount this represented as a percentage of all cash in the hands of the public is calculated by the authors and draws the denominator, $1.784 billion, from Friedman and Schwartz (1963), p. 706.

2. Horwitz (1990), p. 643 wrote: "In Omaha, Nebraska, a streetcar company was forced to pay its workers with 600,000 nickels from its fareboxes. The St. Louis streetcar company had earlier done its Omaha counterpart one better by paying employees with five-cent fare tickets that could be used in exchange for checks or goods at local stores.

The fare tickets circulated fairly widely for several weeks, evidently because they had a redemption value as streetcar rides. . . . The essence of money is its general acceptability. Historically, stones, shells, tobacco, cigarettes and cattle have all served as money. Indeed, as Mises put it, something can become money only 'through the practice of those who take part in commercial transactions.'"

3. Cannon (1910) identifies the use of clearing house loan certificates in the following cities: New York, NY; Augusta, GA; Baltimore, MD; Buffalo, NY; Canton, OH; Chicago, IL; Cincinnati, OH; Denver, CO; Des Moines, IA; Detroit, MI; Fargo, ND; Fort Wayne, IN; Grand Rapids, MI; Harrisburg PA; Kansas City, MO; Little Rock, AR; Los Angeles, CA; Omaha, NE; Philadelphia, PA; Portland, OR; St. Joseph, MO; St. Louis, MO; St. Paul, MN; Salt Lake City, UT; San Francisco, CA; Savannah, GA; Seattle, WA; Sioux City, IA; South Bend, IN; Spokane, WA; Tacoma, WA; Topeka, KS; Wichita, KA; Wheeling, WV. Casual review of newspapers and other publications that year suggests that this list is not exhaustive.

4. Andrew (1908), p. 294.

5. Sprague (1908), p. 367.

6. Ibid.

7. Cited in Noyes (1909a), p. 188.

8. Andrew (1908), p. 298.

9. Noyes (1909a), p. 211.

10. U.S. Department of the Treasury (1908), page 19.

11. Sprague (1908), p. 364, notes that "the extent to which suspension was carried cannot be accurately determined."

12. Sprague (1908), p. 365.

13. Tallman and Moen (1990), p. 61.

14. Donaldson (1993), p. 87.

15. Sprague (1908), p. 366.

16. Friedman and Schwartz (1963), p. 163.

17. Ibid., p. 167.

18. Calomiris and Gorton (1991), p. 150.

19. Account by Perkins in Crowther (1933), unpublished manuscript.

20. *Commercial and Financial Chronicle*, November 9, 1907, p. 1177.

21. *New York Times*, November 9, 1907, p. 2.

Chapter 20: Ripple Effects

1. Noyes (1909a), p. 207.

2. Calomiris and Gorton (1991), p. 156.

3. Ibid.

4. These developments are discussed in detail in Sprague (1908), p. 368–371.

5. Noyes (1909a), p. 208.

6. Cahill (1998), p. 296.

7. Ibid.

8. Friedman and Schwartz (1963), p. 156.

9. J. P. Morgan Jr. Papers, ARC 1216, Box 5, letterpress book #4, January 16, 1908, to January 28, 1909, Morgan Library and Museum. Letter dated January 16, 1908.

10. Both Noyes (1909a), pp. 202–206, and Kindleberger (1977) mention that the panic of 1907 occurred in a context of financial instability in foreign cities. The notion of contagion, or spread, of financial crises has been documented in the financial crises of the late twentieth century. But the global contagion in 1907 is not as fully documented. Flows of gold into and out of the United States in 1907 are well discussed in contemporary and recent writings on the panic. It remains to be shown how these flows (or other mechanisms) actually transmitted the financial crisis globally in 1907.

11. Noyes (1909a), p. 206.

12. Cahill (1998), p. 795.

13. Ibid.

14. Calomiris and Gorton (1991), p. 161, date the end of suspension at January 4, 1908. Friedman and Schwartz (1963), p. 163, discuss that the U.S. Treasury resumed demanding payments in cash in December, but that some banks continued to restrict payments through January.

15. Chapter 2 of James Neal Primm's *A Foregone Conclusion: The Founding of the Federal Reserve Bank of St. Louis* (Federal Reserve Bank of St.

Louis, 1989), gives a detailed and entertaining history of the legislative process that produced the Federal Reserve Act of 1913. This chapter may be downloaded at http://stlouisfed.org/publications/foregone/chapter_two.htm. See also Friedman and Schwartz (1963), pp. 168–173 for a critical discussion of the banking reform efforts.

16. This is discussed in Friedman and Schwartz (1963), p. 171, footnote 59, who refer to a table in Paul M. Warburg, *The Federal Reserve System: Its Origins and Growth* (New York: Macmillan, 1930, vol. 1, chapters 8 and 9).

17. Speech by Frank A. Vanderlip (undated), "The Aldrich Plan for Banking Legislation," given to the Commercial Club of Chicago. Attributed by references in the text to about 1911. Used with permission of the Columbia University Rare Book and Manuscript Library.

18. Letter from Thomas Jefferson to the secretary of the treasury, Albert Gallatin, 1802.

19. Wiebe (1967), p. 201.

20. Brands (1997), p. 646.

21. The sense of this difference was offered by Gould (2001), p. 54.

22. Gould (2001), p. 61, highlights the antitrust case against U.S. Steel as the trigger for Roosevelt's run for the Presidency in 1912.

23. See Dennis K. Berman and Henny Sender, "Probe Brings 'Club Deals' to Fore," *Wall Street Journal*, October 11, 2006, p. C1.

24. Final report of Pujo Money Trust Committee (1912), p. 129.

25. Brandeis (1914), downloaded from http://library.louisville.edu/law/brandeis/opm-ch1.html.

26. See Silber (2006) for details on the closing of the NYSE.

27. See Gage (2006) for details on the anarchist bombing at 23 Wall Street in 1920.

Lessons: Financial Crises as a Perfect Storm

1. Quoted in Alex Ayres, ed. 2005. *The Wit and Wisdom of Mark Twain.* New York: Harper & Row, p. 67.

2. Wicker (2000), pp. 86–87.

3. Friedman and Schwartz (1963), p. 156.

4. Noyes (1908), p. 211, wrote, "The truth regarding the industrial history of 1908 is that reaction in trade, consumption, and production, after the panic of 1907, was so extraordinarily violent that violent recovery was possible without in any way restoring the actual status quo. At the opening of the year, business in many lines of industry was barely 28 percent of the volume of the year before; by mid-summer it was still only 50 percent of 1907; yet this was astonishingly rapid increase over the January record. Output of the country's iron furnaces on January 1 was only 45 percent of January, 1907; on November 1 it was 74 percent of the year before."

5. *Commercial and Financial Chronicle*, quoted in Cahill (1998), p. 796.

6. This figure, cited in Sprague (1908), p. 358, includes savings banks.

7. Noyes (1909a), pp. 202–206.

8. Boyer, Kumagai, and Juan (2005), p. 957.

9. *Science*, vol. 284. no. 5411 (1999), offered several attributes of complex systems, which are paraphrased here: a high degree of structure; evolution is sensitive to starting conditions and to small variations in conditions over time. This implies many possible paths along which evolution of the system might occur; the design or function of the system is difficult to understand and verify; components interact in multiple ways; constant evolution over time.

10. See Diamond, Douglas, and Phillip Dybvig. 1983. "Bank Runs, Liquidity, and Deposit Insurance." *Journal of Political Economy* 91:401–419.

11. We thank our colleague, Professor Wei Li, for this example of a Diamond-Dybvig bank run.

12. See Gorton (1985), Chari and Jagannathan (1988), Jacklin and Battacharya (1988), Calomiris and Schweikart (1991), and Calomiris and Gorton (1992).

13. See Gorton (1987), Donaldson (1992), Mishkin (1991), and Carlson (undated).

14. Carlson (undated), p. 4, tests the asymmetric information theory as explainer of panics and bank suspensions—as opposed to Diamond and Dybvig's random withdrawal theory. He finds the results to favor the asymmetric information theory when tested using state-level data, but indeterminate when using local level data.

15. Mishkin (1991), p. 27. Reprinted from Chapter 3, "Asymmetric In-formation and Financial Crises: A Historical Perspective," by Frederic S. Mishkin, in *Financial Markets and Financial Crisis*, R. Glenn Hub-bard, ed. Published by The University of Chicago Press, © 1991 by the National Bureau of Economic Research. All rights reserved.

16. Beinhocker (2006), p. 45.

17. Ranciere, Tornell, and Westermann (2005), p. 1: "We document the fact that countries that have experienced occasional financial crises have, on average, grown faster than countries with stable financial conditions. . . . Financial liberalization policies that facilitate risk-taking increase leverage and investment. This leads to higher growth, but also to a greater incidence of crises."

18. Gorton and Huang (2002), p. 7, found that a ". . . regularity concern-ing banking panics is that there is an important business cycle and, possibly, seasonal component to the timing of panics. Panics come at or near business cycle peaks. The interpretation is not that panics caused downturns. . . . Rather the idea is that depositors received in-formation forecasting a recession and withdrew in an anticipation of the recession, a time when bank failures were more likely."

19. Friedman and Schwartz (1963), p. 799, report that banks were rela-tively highly levered in 1907 compared to previous years. The ratio of deposits to bank reserves reached 8.87 in June 1907, compared to a ratio of 6.8 in June 1900 and 5.54 in June 1897.

20. Bordo and Meissner (2005), p. 1, report that "more foreign currency debt leads to a higher chance of having a debt crisis or a banking crisis."

21. The mechanics of this economic inflection are described in Keynes (1936), pp. 30-31.

22. Schumpeter (1976), p. 82–84.

23. See, e.g., Christensen, Clayton. 2003. *The Innovator's Dilemma*. New York: Collins.

24. Schumpeter (2004), pp. 228-229, wrote: "Why do entrepreneurs ap-pear, not continuously, that is, singly in every appropriately chosen interval, but in clusters? *Exclusively because the appearance of one or a few entrepreneurs facilitates the appearance of others, and those the appearance of more in ever-increasing numbers* [his italics]. . . . Hence the first leaders are

effective beyond their immediate sphere of action and so the group of entrepreneurs increases still further and the economic system is drawn more rapidly and more completely than would otherwise be the case into the process of technological and commercial reorganisation which constitutes the meaning of periods of boom."

25. See Lamoreaux (1988), p. 158. Naomi Lamoreaux illustrated creative destruction in her study of the merger wave of 1894–1904. During that period, more than 1,800 firms disappeared into the formation of 93 consolidated firms with an important, if not dominant, share of market in their respective industries. She found that the bulk of the M&A activity occurred within selected industries—those characterized by capital-intensive and mass-production manufacturing processes in which new firms had recently entered with new and more devastating technology. With high fixed costs, these industries faced high operating leverage, and the resulting impulse to cut prices in an effort to maintain market share and, more importantly, volume. This triggered severe price competition during the depression of the mid-1890s. Entrepreneurs entered this turbulent environment to remove older and less efficient excess capacity from the industry through a new form of organization, the Trust. J. P. Morgan is a preeminent example of this entrepreneur. He personally led the reorganization of numerous industries, including U.S. Steel and various regional railroads. Though the newly structured firms successfully removed excess capacity, in the longer run they proved to be no more efficient than their nontrust rivals, and therefore proved unable to maintain their dominance unless they erected entry barriers. Lamoreaux notes that federal antitrust policy should have been focused on minimizing the erection of barriers, in lieu of offering the "hodge-podge of policies that, as the example of the steel industry indicates, sometimes hindered the combines' efforts, sometimes helped them."

26. Heilbroner, Robert. 1986. *The Worldly Philosophers.* Gloucester, Mass.: Peter Smith Publisher, p. 291.

27. The problems of adverse selection and moral hazard are discussed in Mishkin (1990), p. 2: "If Market interest rates are driven up sufficiently because of increased demand for credit or because of a decline in the money supply, the adverse selection problem might dramatically increase and there will be a substantial decline in lending, which in turn,

leads to a substantial decline in investment and aggregate economic activity. ... These mechanisms suggest than in important manifestation of a financial crisis would be a large rise in interest rates to borrowers for which there is substantial difficulty in obtaining reliable information about their characteristics, that is, for which there is a serious asymmetric information problems." Reprinted from Chapter 3, "Asymmetric Information and Financial Crises: A Historical Perspective," by Frederic S. Mishkin, in *Financial Markets and Financial Crisis*, R. Glenn Hubbard, ed. Published by The University of Chicago Press, © 1991 by the National Bureau of Economic Research. All rights reserved.

28. Mishkin (1991), p. 4, stated: "The importance of collateral for reducing the adverse selection problem in debt markets provides another mechanism whereby financial disruption adversely affects aggregate economic activity ... A sharp decrease in the valuation of firms' assets in a stock market crash lowers the value of collateral and thereby makes adverse selection a more important problem for lenders since the losses from loan defaults are now higher." Reprinted from the *Journal of Evolutionary Economics*, Volume 2, Number 2, June 1992, pp. 115–130, "Anatomy of a Financial Crisis," by Frederic S. Mishkin: with kind permission of Springer Science and Business Media.

29. Gorton and Huang (2001) argue that banks are not individually unstable. Rather, the source of instability begins from the structure of the industry. A banking industry populated with many small and undiversified banks will be more prone to panic than will an industry with a few large and well-diversified banks. They point out that states with branch banking laws have featured many fewer bank failures than those states with unit-banking laws (laws that prohibit branching). Gorton and Huang (2002), pp. 19073, 6. Also Calomiris and Gorton (1991), p. 118, argue that branch banking systems tended to be less prone to the effects of panics. States that allowed branching weathered crisis better than unit-banking states.

30. Donaldson (1993, page 5) stated: "That the large banks were able to profit from the sale of cash to the trusts during the panic of 1907 is no doubt due in part to the fact that the trust companies did not belong to the New York clearing house and were therefore not entitled to the cheap-cash-in-times-of-crisis 'insurance' that seems to have been

extended by the clearinghouse to its own illiquid members. Furthermore, while the trusts were forced to sell securities to obtain the funds
necessary to extinguish debts, members of the cash-supplying syndicate
were able to meet many of their obligations by issuing 'clearinghouse
certificates' that were generally accepted in lieu of cash during times of
crisis. This ability to economize on the internal use of cash meant that
the clearinghouse banks could protect themselves from being driven
to bankruptcy during the panic of 1907 and still supply at least limited funds to the rest of the economy." Also, Calomiris and Gorton
(1991), p. 119, stated that clearing houses started in 1853 in New
York City and provided mutual regulation: audited banks, set capital
requirements, and penalized violations. Clearing houses created a market for the illiquid assets of member banks by accepting such assets as
collateral in exchange for clearing house loan certificates, which were
liabilities of the association of banks. Member banks then exchanged
the loan certificates for depositors' demand deposits. Clearing house
loan certificates were printed in small denominations and functioned
as a hand-to-hand currency. Moreover, since these securities were the
liability of the association of banks rather than any of individual bank,
depositors were insured against the failure of the individual bank. Initially, clearing house loan certificates traded at a discount against gold.

31. Calomiris (2000), p. 110, stated that neither the nature of debt con-
    tracts nor the presence of exogenous shocks which reduce the value of
    bank asset portfolios provide "sufficient conditions" for banking pan-
    ics. Banking panics are not inherent in banking contracts—institutional
    structure matters. As examples of such structures he cited branch bank
    laws, bank co-op agreements, and formal clearing houses.

32. Hunter, Kaufman, and Pomerleano (2003), p. xxvi.

33. Horwitz (1990), p. 625, noted, "The difficulty facing the system then
    (and facing unregulated banks) is how to prevent localized runs from
    spreading to the whole system. One way banks tried to prevent con-
    tagion in 1907 was through advertising and use of their brand name
    capital. In addition to advertising the acceptability of the currency
    substitutes, banks advertised the soundness and trustworthiness of their
    institutions. Advertising trust and confidence was common practice in
    an era before federal deposit insurance programs. During the panic,
    banks immediately resorted to stronger and more innovative ways of

advertising, especially through the use of their brand names. After the panic first began in New York, there was a marked increase in general advertising by banks. There were also changes in the kind of ads they ran. It became more common for banks to list their directors and owners in their advertising. They also offered such standard information as length of time in business and volume of business. In normal times, a bank might only rarely advertise its balance sheet. During the panic, however, various issues of the *New York Times* indicate that advertisements frequently included abbreviated balance sheets. In the October 25, 1907, issue at the height of the panic, there was a full page of bank ads (compared to the usual quarter or half page.). The ads included short versions of balance sheets and long, detailed lists of bank personnel, including specific information on other business connections of the board members and management. The banks, like the public, were sensitive to concerns about interlocking directorates, and any connection with anyone questionable was bad for business."

34. Noyes (1909a), p. 188, found that, "In 1907 NYC banks issued $101,060,000 clearing house loan certificates (vs. $41,490,000 in 1893). All US banks issued $238,053,175 in clearing house certificates versus $69,111,000 in 1893." This article was published in the *Journal of Monetary Economics*, Vol. 31, Issue 1, R. Glenn Donaldson, "Financing Banking Crises: Lessons from the Panic of 1907," pp. 69–95. Copyright Elsevier Science B. V. © 1993. All rights reserved.

35. Kaminsky and Schmukler, (1999), p. 1, said that some people claim the currency crises are a new breed never before seen, as liberalization and innovation have become more prevalent. This paper examines stock market cycles in 28 countries and concludes that, overall, financial markets have not become more unstable.

36. *Commercial and Financial Chronicle*, September 7, 1907, p. 554.

37. Harvey, George. 1907. "Exeunt Roosevelt and Bryan." *Harper's Weekly*, (November 9): 51 (2655) 1640–1642.

38. Quoted in, Ibid.

39. Friedman and Schwartz (1963), p. 418.

40. *Commercial and Financial Chronicle*, March 30, 1907, p. 714: "The Sub-Treasury is beyond a doubt the agency which is working the discomfiture of our money market. The vaults of that attachment to our

Treasury arrangements hold today 20 million dollars more cash than was so held on the first of January 1907. . . . Suppose the banks had continued to have that money through these three months."

41. Tallman and Moen (1990), p. 3, discussed the economic foundations of the panic. They highlighted these factors: (1) seasonal liquidity fluctuations; (2) export of gold to Europe and to the interior; and (3) absence of finance bills. However, Calomiris and Gorton (1991), pp. 133–137) offer evidence that changes in system liquidity were not significantly different in 1907 from 1906. They argue that the panic of 1907 had more to do with problems of asymmetric information than with system liquidity.

42. Calomiris and Gorton (1991), p. 115, argue that the Great Depression tells one less about the inherent instability of the banking system than about the extent to which unwise government policies can destroy banks.

43. Donaldson (1992), p. 279. This article was published in the *Journal of Monetary Economics*, Vol. 30, Issue 2, R. Glenn Donaldson, "Sources of Panics: Evidence from the Weekly Data," pp. 277–305. Copyright Elsevier Science B.V. © 1992. All rights reserved.

44. Calomiris and Gorton (1991), Friedman and Schwartz (1963), and Sprague (1910) contend that "real disturbances" cause erosion of trust in the banking system and are the precursors to panics.

45. Sornette (2003), p. 321, attempted to identify telltale inflection points in security prices that might predict market crashes, but he concluded that such identification was exceptionally hard and not to be trusted.

46. Selden, G. C. 2005. *The Psychology of the Stock Market*. New York: Cosimo Inc., p. 69 (originally published in 1912).

47. Lefevre, Edwin L. 1994. *Reminiscences of a Stock Operator*. New York: John Wiley & Sons, p. 286.

48. Harris (2003), p. 556, said: "Bubbles occur when prices rise to levels that are substantially above fundamental values. (Fundamental values, of course, are not common knowledge. If they were, crashes and bubbles would not occur.) Some bubbles occur very quickly. Others occur over long periods. Many bubbles end with a crash. Traders say that such bubbles pop. Crashes occur when prices fall very quickly. Crashes often follow bubbles, but they also occur in other circumstances. Crashes

sometimes are called market breaks because the price path breaks when prices fall very quickly. They are also called market meltdowns when they overload the order handling capacity of a market. . . . Bubbles start when buyers become overly optimistic about fundamental values. The potential of new technologies and the potential growth of new markets can greatly excite some traders. Unfortunately, many of these traders cannot recognize when prices already reflect information about these potential. They also may not adequately appreciate the risks associated with holding the securities that interest them. If enough of these enthusiastic traders try to buy at the same time, they may push prices up substantially. The resulting price increases may encourage momentum traders to buy, in the hope that past gains will continue. . . . Order anticipators may buy in anticipation of new uninformed buyers. They will profit it they can get out before prices fall. The combined trading of these traders can cause a bubble in which prices exceed fundamental values. " . . . Value traders and arbitrageurs may recognize that prices exceed values, but they may be unable or unwilling to sell in sufficient volume to prevent the bubble from forming."

49. The theory of rational choice (or "rationality" for short) presumes that individuals are self-interested, prefer more wealth as opposed to less, and generally that their preferences are transitive (if you like A better than B, and B better than C, you will like A better than C.) The rational decision maker is guided by outcomes and chooses the best. Researchers in behavioral finance point to disorderly patterns in markets that are not consistent with rationality:

- Herding and excessive volatility. Investors crowd together and follow trends.
- Market anomalies documented by research include the January effect, existence of "momentum" and autocorrelation in stock prices; delays in the response to news; impact of trading hours on price volatility; post-earnings announcement drift; Siamese twin securities that have identical cash flows but trade at different prices; underpricing of closed-end funds.
- Winner's curse. The winner's curse is a phenomenon first identified by Capen, Clapp, and Campbell (1971) in their analysis of bidding for oil leases. Oil companies that win auctions of

lease rights on oil lands tend to overpay—whether or not they actually lose money on the bidding, the winners will usually be disappointed that the asset is worth less than they thought. The winner's curse is also important in mergers and acquisitions, and has been offered as a possible explanation for the poor returns to buyers [see, e.g., Roll (1986), and Varaiya and Ferris (1987)].

- Loss aversion. People view value asymmetrically: the utility of gaining a dollar is less than the disutility of giving one up. This is the outgrowth of path breaking research by Nobel Laureate Amos Tversky and others.

50. Sprague (1908), p. 361.

51. See, particularly Wicker (2000). Tallman and Moen (1990), p. 1, wrote "The Panic of 1907, the last and most severe of the National Banking Era panics in the United States, provides an example of how private market participants, in the absence of government institutions, react to a crisis in their industry."

52. See Wicker (2000).

53. The prisoner's dilemma was first discussed in Anatol Rapoport and A. M. Chammah, *Prisoner's Dilemma* (Ann Arbor: University of Michigan Press, 1965). To illustrate the problem, consider this hypothetical case: Two robbers are arrested by the police in the belief that they acted together in committing a crime. The prisoners are separated in different cells and interrogated independently. The prosecutor encourages each to confess and implicate the colleague. If neither prisoner confesses, the prosecutor believes the court can be convinced to send the suspects to jail for five years. If both prisoners confess *and* implicate each other, the court will send the suspect to jail for 10 years. If one prisoner confesses and implicates the other, and the other neither confesses nor implicates, the one who confesses will get three years (time off for assisting the prosecution), and the other will get eight years. The "prisoner's dilemma" is whether to confess or not, and offers four possible outcomes. Plainly, the incentives are structured in a way to encourage each prisoner to rat on the other. The "corner solutions" are the best outcomes for the two prisoners individually, since these result in lower jail terms for each. However, if *both* prisoners take the incentive offered, they will wind up with the longest sentences, 10 years each. The safest course of action is for neither to confess, since

it results in a jail term materially shorter than eight or 10 years, and not much longer than three years. Unfortunately, with the prisoners separated and unable to communicate, the collaboration and mutual assurances necessary to achieve quadrant I are unlikely.

54. Excerpted from Greenspan's famous speech, "Redundancy of Funding Sources" (also known as the "spare tire speech"). Downloaded from www.federalreserve.gov/boarddocs/speeches/ 1999/199909272.htm.

55. Mishkin and White (2003), p. 55. Their identification of 15 major crashes is the result of judgment rather than a fixed rule.

56. Noyes (1909a), p. 186.

57. Calomiris and Gorton (1991) define a panic as "an event in which bank debt holders (depositors) at many or even all banks in the banking system suddenly demand that their banks convert their debt claims into cash (at par) to such an extent that banks cannot jointly honor these demands and suspend convertibility" [Gorton and Huang (2002), p. 5].

58. Mishkin (1990), pp. 26-27: "[I]t is worth asking what do [these crises] have in common and what does this tell us bout the nature of financial crises. The following facts emerge from our study of episodes in the last half of the nineteenth century and the first half of the twentieth.

1. With one exception in 1873, financial panics always occurred after the onset of a recession.

2. With the same exception in 1873, stock prices decline and the spread between interest rates on low and high-quality bonds rises before the onset of the panic.

3. Many panics seem to have features of a liquidity crisis in which there are substantial increases in interest rates before the panic.

4. The onset of many panics follows a major failure of a financial institution, not necessarily a bank. Furthermore this failure is often the result of financial difficulties experienced by a nonfinancial corporation.

5. The rise in the interest rate spread associated with a panic is typically soon followed by a decline. However, in several cases, most notably after the 1873 panic, the 1907 panic, and the Great Depression, the interest rate spread rises again when there is a deflation and a severe recession.

6. The most severe financial crises are associated with severe economic contractions.

7. Although stock market crashes often appear to be a major factor in creating a financial crisis, this is not always the case. Both the stock market crash in October 1929 and in May 1940 did not have appreciable effects on the interest rate spread." Reprinted from Chapter 3, "Asymmetric Information and Financial Crises: A Historical Perspective," by Frederic S. Mishkin, in *Financial Markets and Financial Crisis*, R. Glenn Hubbard, ed. Published by The University of Chicago Press, © 1991 by the National Bureau of Economic Research. All rights reserved.

59. "Locus Pocus." *The Economist*, May 5, 2005. Downloaded from www.economist.com/displaystory.cfm?story_id=3935994.

60. Chan, Nicholas, Mila Getmansky, Shane Haas, and Andrew Lo. 2005. "Systemic Risk and Hedge Funds." Manuscript prepared for NBER Conference on Risks of Financial Institutions, dated August 1, 2005. Downloaded from http://web.mit.edu/alo/www/Papers/systemic2.pdf.

61. "The Committee on the Global Financial System (CGFS), chaired by Donald Kohn, monitors developments in global financial markets for the central bank governors of the G10 countries. The Committee has a mandate to identify and assess potential sources of stress in global financial markets, to further the understanding of the structural underpinnings of financial markets, and to promote improvements to the functioning and stability of these markets. It fulfills this mandate by way of quarterly monitoring discussions among CGFS members, through coordinated longer-term efforts, including working groups involving central bank staff, and throughthevarious reportsthat the CGFSpublishes." Downloaded from the BIS web site, www.bis.org/cgfs/index.htm.

Appendix A: Key Figures after 1907

1. De Long (1991) quotes Davison, 1913, p. 17.

2. Manuscript of "The Life of F. Augustus Heinze," by Otto Heinze (1943), found among the papers of Sarah McNelis, Heinze's biographer, p. 62.

3. Fettig, David (ed.). 1989. *F. Augustus Heinze of Montana and the Panic of 1907*. Federal Reserve of Minneapolis; also, *New York Times*, May 15, 1909, and November 5, 1914.

4. Forbes (1981), p. x.

5. U.S. Government. 1913. *Money Trust Investigation: Hearings*, I, p. 1084.

6. Quotation of Morgan's illness given in Forbes (1981), p. 72.

7. Quotation of Thomas Lamont given in Forbes (1981), p. 74. Source of quotation is a letter from T. W. Lamont to H. S. Commager, March 17, 1938, Partners file, J. P. Morgan Jr. Papers.

8. Zuckoff, Mitchell. 2005. *Ponzi's Scheme*. New York: Random House, p. 49.

9. Details about Morse are drawn from Zuckoff (2005), pp. 49, 50.

10. Details about Morse after his return from Europe are drawn from Pringle (1939). Downloaded from www.doctorzebra.com/prez/z_x27morse_g.htm#zree16.

11. *New York Tribune*, June 19, 1920, p. 4.

12. Quotation from George W. Perkins Collection, General File, Obituaries 1920. Box 18, Rare Books and Manuscripts, Butler Library, Columbia University.

13. Letter to Douglas Robinson, November 16, 1907. excerpted in Hart and Ferleger (1941), p. 410.

14. Letter to Hamlin Garland, November 23, 1907, excerpted in Hart and Ferleger (1941), p. 411.

15. Quoted in Hart and Ferleger (1941), p. 607.

16. Brands (1997), p. 812.

17. Burr biography of Stillman.

18. Quotation of Stillman from Huertas (1985), pp. 147–148. Originally drawn from James Stillman, letter to Frank A. Vanderlip, February 12, 1907, Vanderlip MSS, Columbia University.

19. Friedman and Schwartz (1963), p. 411.

20. Roberts (2000), p. 13: "Strong's 'easy money' policies designed to assist Britain's return to the gold standard produced a speculative rise in stock prices on the New York Stock Exchange. . . . But this picture hardly fits the Benjamin Strong who, in his support of the fateful decision in 1928 to raise interest rates and force a monetary contraction to bring down stock prices, was an economic nationalist. High interest rates in the United States pulled capital out of Europe and forced monetary

deflation there and elsewhere. The international gold standard that Strong had labored so hard to create became an engine of worldwide deflation."

21. Friedman and Schwartz (1963), p. 411.

22. Quotation of *Wall Street Journal* on Benjamin Strong given in *Time* magazine article, October 29, 1928. Downloaded from www.time.com/time/magazine/article/0,9171,928986,00.html.

23. Vanderlip's leadership in the design of the Federal Reserve System is discussed in chapter 2 of James Neal Primm's *A Foregone Conclusion: The Founding of the Federal Reserve Bank of St. Louis*, at http://stlouisfed.org/publications/foregone/chapter_two.htm.

24. Details of Vanderlip's relations with Stillman are drawn from Huertas (1985).

Appendix B: Key Definitions

1. The attributes of a good definition are drawn from Copi, Irving M., and Carl Cohen. 1998. *Introduction to Logic*, 10th ed. New York: Prentice-Hall. Their five attributes are:
   a. Focus on essential features.
   b. Avoid circularity.
   c. Capture the correct extension.
   d. Avoid circularity.
   e. Be affirmative rather than negative.

2. Kindleberger, Charles, and Robert Aliber. 2005. *Manias, Panics, and Crashes: A History of Financial Crises*, 5th ed. New York: John Wiley and Sons, p. 94.

3. Mishkin, Frederick S., and Eugene N. White. 2003. "U.S. Stock Market Crashes and Their Aftermath: Implications for Monetary Policy," chapter 6 in W. C. Hunter, G. G. Kaufman, and M. Pomerleano (eds.), *Asset Price Bubbles: The Implications for Monetary, Regulatory, and International Policies*. Cambridge: MIT Press, p. 55.

4. Kindleberger and Aliber (2005), p. 94.

5. Calomiris (2000), p. 112.

6. Noyes (1909a), p. 186.

7. Mishkin (1991), p. 1.

8. Kindleberger and Aliber (2005), p. 9.

9. Ibid., p. 10.

10. Ibid., p. 25.

11. Ibid., p. 33.

12. Ibid., p. 11.

13. Ibid., p. 25.

14. Dash, Mike. 1999. *Tulipomania*. New York: Three Rivers Press, p. 219.

15. Shiller, Robert. 2000. *Irrational Exuberance*. Princeton: Princeton University Press, p. xii.

16. Shiller (2003), "Diverse Views on Asset Bubbles," chapter 4, p. 35.

17. Palgrave, R. H. 1926. *Dictionary of Political Economy*. London: Macmillan, quoted in Garber, Peter M. 2001. *Famous First Bubbles: The Fundamentals of Early Manias*. Cambridge: The MIT Press, p. 7.

18. Garber (2001), p. 4.

19. Meltzer, Allan H. 2003. "Rational and Nonrational Bubbles," chapter 3, in W. C. Hunter, G. G. Kaufman, and M. Pomerleano (eds.), *Asset Price Bubbles: The Implications for Monetary, Regulatory, and International Policies*, Cambridge: MIT Press.

20. See, e.g., Blanchard, Olivier. 1979. "Speculative Bubbles, Crashes and Rational Expectations," *Economic Letters* 3, 387–389; and Blanchard, O. J., and M. W. Watson. 1982. "Bubbles, Rational Expectations and Speculative Markets," in P. Wachtel (ed.), *Crisis in Economic and Financial Structure: Bubbles, Bursts, and Shocks*. Lexington, Mass.: Lexington Books).

21. Meltzer (2003), p. 24.

22. Derived from the authors' analysis, synthesizing field observation and insights from Shiller (2000); Kindleberger and Aliber (2005); Lowenstein (2004); Hunter, Kaufman, and Pomerleano (2003); and Caverley (2004). Caverley (p. 13) offers his own abbreviated list.

23. Alan Greenspan's speech is worth reading in full, and may be found at www.federalreserve.gov/BoardDocs/speeches/1996/ 19961205.htm.

24. Shiller (2000), p. xii.

25. Ibid., p. 63.

26. Meltzer (2003), pp. 23, 27.

About the Authors

Robert F. Bruner is the dean of the Darden Graduate School of Business Administration at the University of Virginia. He has published research in various areas, including corporate finance, mergers and acquisitions, and investing in emerging markets. His books, *Applied Mergers and Acquisitions* (2004) and *Deals from Hell* (2005), were published by John Wiley & Sons. He has been recognized for his teaching and development of teaching materials. *BusinessWeek* magazine cited him as one of the "masters of the MBA classroom." He is the author or coauthor of over 400 case studies and notes, and of *Case Studies in Finance: Managing for Corporate Value Creation* published by McGraw-Hill and now in its fifth edition. He has been on the faculty of the Darden School since 1982. He holds a BA degree from Yale University and MBA and DBA degrees from Harvard University. Copies of his papers and essays may be obtained from his web site, http://faculty.darden.edu/brunerb/. He may be reached via e-mail at brunerr@virginia.edu.

Sean D. Carr is the director of corporate innovation programs at the Batten Institute, an endowed foundation committed to fostering thought leadership in business innovation and entrepreneurship at the Darden

Graduate School of Business Administration, University of Virginia. His applied research in new ventures and corporate finance has contributed to the development of award-winning case studies, digital media, and other teaching materials. Previously, he spent nearly 10 years as a journalist, having served as a producer for both CNN and for ABC's *World News Tonight with Peter Jennings*. As a writer and researcher he contributed to numerous business-related books. He holds an MBA degree from the University of Virginia, an MS in journalism from Columbia University, and a BA from Northwestern University. He may be reached via e-mail at carrs@virginia.edu.

Index